NEGOTIABLE INSTRUMENTS & PAYMENT SYSTEMS

(formerly entitled *Commercial Paper*)

By

CLAYTON P. GILLETTE

Perre Bowen Professor of Law
University of Virginia School of Law

SMITH'S REVIEW

Published by

 **emanuel**®

Negotiable Instruments & Payment Systems, 2nd Edition (1995)
Emanuel Law Outlines, Inc. • 1865 Palmer Avenue • Larchmont, NY 10538

ISBN 1-56542-113-2

Preface

This outline is intended to supplement a course in Commercial Paper, Payments Systems, or Negotiable Instruments that concentrates on Articles 3 and 4 of the Uniform Commercial Code. The Uniform Commercial Code is best understood by comparison to a jigsaw puzzle. In order to appreciate the meaning and relevance of an individual section of the Code, the student must see how it interacts with other sections in a particular context. Only when the picture is complete can the student truly understand the function of individual parts. Study of each section in isolation will not provide either comprehension of the Code as a cohesive document or recognition of how the drafters attempted (and sometimes failed) to create an orderly body of law from which individuals who deal with commercial paper can predict outcomes with certainty. Thus, this outline is organized by subject matter rather than by sequential attention to the provisions of Articles 3 and 4.

I wish to thank Jonah E. Gillette, who spent a summer performing the hazardous task of assisting his father with legal research.

TABLE OF CONTENTS

CHAPTER 1

INTRODUCTION:
THE CONCEPT OF NEGOTIABILITY

THE CONCEPT OF
HOLDING IN DUE COURSE

CHAPTER 4

LIABILITIES OF PARTIES: CONTRACT LIABILITY, WARRANTY LIABILITY, AND CONVERSION

CHAPTER 5

LIABILITIES ON FORGED AND ALTERED INSTRUMENTS

CHAPTER 6

CHECKS AND CHECK COLLECTION

CHAPTER 7

BANK'S RELATIONSHIP WITH ITS CUSTOMER

CHAPTER 8

ELECTRONIC FUNDS TRANSFERS AND CREDIT CARDS

CHAPTER 9

DOCUMENTARY DRAFTS AND LETTERS OF CREDIT

CHAPTER 1

INTRODUCTION:
THE CONCEPT OF NEGOTIABILITY

I. SCOPE OF ARTICLES 3 AND 4

    A. Payment systems: The law of payment systems involves common mechanisms that are used to pay for goods or services in an exchange economy. The seller of goods or services may ultimately desire to receive currency, i.e., a widely accepted (and often governmentally endorsed) medium of exchange. For purposes of the Uniform Commercial Code, a medium of exchange that has been authorized or adopted by a government constitutes "money." See U.C.C. § 1-201(24). Currency allows exchange to occur freely, because the seller knows that he or she will be able to exchange it for other goods or services. Thus, currency allows a more efficient exchange than a *barter system*. In the absence of a common medium of exchange, one who wished to obtain a good owned by another would have to find some other good or service that the potential seller desired as much as the potential buyer desired the first good or service. In such a barter economy, substantial time and effort would be spent identifying goods that could be exchanged.

        1. Money substitutes: Although money can play the role of a medium of exchange, there are risks attached to transactions in money. First, in order to flow freely through the economy, the ownership of money must not be open to question on transfer. Unlike the case of goods (where the purchaser from a thief does not take valid title to the goods), the thief of money can *pass good title* to a person who takes the money in good faith. Thus, there is significant risk that the true owner of money will lose rights to it through loss, destruction, or theft and will be unable to get it back from someone who accepted the stolen money in good faith. Second, money may be *inconvenient* to exchange in transactions for expensive goods and services. Thus, exchange economies have developed money substitutes. These substitutes may have many, but not all, the characteristics of money. The law of payment systems involves definition of these attributes and the governing law applicable to many of these money substitutes. The primary form of these substitutes is the *negotiable instrument*.

        2. Collection: Payment systems also require a mechanism for converting money substitutes to money and for allowing the debits and credits that instruments typically authorize in the monetary assets of buyers and sellers. This collection mechanism is usually performed through the banking system, most frequently in the collection of checks.

B. Negotiable instruments: Negotiable instruments are the subject of Article 3 of the Uniform Commercial Code ("U.C.C."). While the definition of negotiable instruments permits inclusion of a wide range of writings that evidence promises or orders to pay, the U.C.C. explicitly excludes money, electronic fund transfers, and securities from coverage in Article 3. U.C.C. § 3-102(a). The process by which instruments are collected by banks is the subject of *Article 4* of the U.C.C.

C. Mercantile sources: The law of commercial paper has evolved from mercantile practices that seek to facilitate commercial transactions by reducing the risk to buyers and sellers that payment for goods and services will not be forthcoming. These practices originated during a period when payment for goods was frequently made through *bills of exchange* or drafts drawn on private banks or money lenders. Use of these drafts made transportation of large sums of money unnecessary. The practice, however, was only as valid as the willingness of sellers to accept these instruments as forms of payment. The willingness of sellers, in turn, was contingent on their belief that payment in currency would be forthcoming when due and that they would not face claims and defenses from the payor arising from transactions to which the seller was not a party.

> **Example:** Smith, a medieval retailer of goods in London, desired to purchase supplies from Brown, who lived in Paris. Smith received the goods in return for his note, in which Smith promised to make payment to the order of Brown at a forthcoming fair of merchants in Milan. As Smith's name was known throughout mercantile markets in Europe, Brown was able to purchase additional supplies from Black by negotiating to Black the note made by Smith. When Black presented Smith with the note in Milan, Smith complained that he did not want to pay as the goods he had received from Brown were substandard. If Black had been subject to the defense that Smith had against Brown, Black's willingness to accept the note as payment would have been substantially reduced. Thus, the law of commercial paper evolved to cut off defenses against certain holders of these payment devices.

II. SIGNIFICANCE OF NEGOTIABILITY

A. Negotiable instrument: The most important concept within the law of commercial paper is that of *negotiability*. The rights of one in possession of a writing that satisfies the requirements of a negotiable instrument, termed an ***instrument*** in the U.C.C., U.C.C. § 3-104(b), differ in substantial ways from the rights of the obligee of a simple contract.

1. **Transferee's rights to the instrument:** One to whom a writing or a good has been transferred typically has no greater rights than one's transferor. If the writing satisfies the requirements of a negotiable instrument, however, the possessor may (on satisfying the criteria of becoming a ***holder in due course***) have even greater rights than the transferor. For the requirements of being a holder in due course, see pages 19-54, *infra*.

   Example 1: Smith owned $100 worth of law books. Jones stole the law books and sold them to Brown for $95. Smith found the law books in Brown's hands and demanded their return. Smith is entitled to recover the law books from Brown because Brown traces his title through a thief. See U.C.C. § 2-403.

   Example 2: Smith owned a negotiable instrument payable to bearer on demand in the amount of $100. Jones stole the instrument and sold it to Brown, a holder in due course, for $95. Smith found the instrument in Brown's hands and demanded its return. Brown may keep the instrument, even though Brown traces his title through a thief. See U.C.C. § 3-305(a).

   Example 3: In an early application of the doctrine of negotiability, *Miller v. Race*, 1 Burr. 452, 97 Eng. Rep. 398 (K.B. 1758), Lord Mansfield considered whether a bank note that had been stolen was the property of the true owner or of a subsequent purchaser. Lord Mansfield held that bank notes were treated in commerce like "money itself" and that where transfer was made for valuable consideration and without knowledge of the theft, it was necessary "for the purposes of commerce" that they be transferable without question of ownership. Thus, the possessor of the stolen bank note was entitled to retain it and to obtain payment on it.

2. **Transferee's freedom from defenses:** An assignee of the obligations under a contract is subject to the same defenses that the obligor could have asserted against the obligee/assignor. A holder in due course of a negotiable instrument, however, takes free of most defenses that could have been asserted against the obligee/assignor.

   Example 1: Smith agreed to sell her automobile to Jones for $1,000, payable in 30 days. Smith warranted that the car was in good working condition. Immediately after the sale, Smith assigned her right to payment under the contract to Brown. At the end of 30 days, Jones refused to pay Brown on the grounds that the car was not in good working condition. Brown is subject to the defense of breach of warranty that Jones could have asserted against Smith.

Example 2: Smith agreed to sell his automobile to Jones for $1,000, payable in 30 days. Jones gave Smith a negotiable instrument evidencing her promise to pay. Immediately after the sale, Smith negotiated the instrument to Brown in a manner that made him a holder in due course. At the end of 30 days, Jones refused to pay Brown on the grounds that the car was not in good working condition. Jones must pay Brown, even if Jones has a valid breach of warranty claim against Smith. U.C.C. § 3-305(a).

3. **Merger of obligation and instrument:** The obligation for which the instrument has been given is *"merged"* into the instrument so that any performance on the underlying obligation is suspended until the instrument is payable. Conversely, *discharge* on the instrument constitutes a discharge on the underlying obligation. U.C.C. §§ 3-310, 3-602.

   Example 1: Smith purchased an automobile from Jones. In return, he entered into a contract with Jones promising to pay her $1,000 in 30 days. Unknown to Smith, Jones assigned her right to payment to Brown. Thirty days later, Smith paid Jones $1,000. If Brown seeks payment from Smith, Smith may establish his payment to the assignor as a defense.

   Example 2: Smith purchased an automobile from Jones and in return gave Jones a negotiable note promising to pay $1,000 to the order of Jones 30 days after the date of the note. Unknown to Smith, Jones negotiated the note to Brown. Thirty days later, Smith paid Jones $1,000 and failed to obtain return of the note. If Brown seeks payment from Smith, Smith must still pay $1,000 to Brown since the obligation to pay was merged into and travelled with the instrument. If Smith had paid Brown $1,000, he would owe nothing to Jones.

4. **Procedural advantages:** Unlike the obligee of a simple contract, one in possession of an instrument is entitled to certain procedural presumptions that facilitate the right to payment. For instance, all signatures on an instrument are deemed admitted unless specifically denied in legal pleadings. U.C.C. § 3-308.

B. **Critique of negotiability:** The above examples suggest that negotiability may lead to questionable results in particular cases, *e.g.,* where an obligor with a valid defense against an obligee is nevertheless required to make payment to a third party to whom an instrument has been negotiated. Whether the concept should continue depends on whether its benefits outweigh these occasional adverse effects.

1. **Historical justification:** Negotiability developed as a concept when there was little in the way of established currencies and merchants needed other reliable forms of payment. As long as merchants could use personal notes and drafts as a medium of exchange, markets could function efficiently. But before sellers would accept these writings, they needed to be certain that efforts to obtain payment would not be derailed by competing claims and defenses to payment. Given the subsequent development of international markets and currencies, it is useful to inquire whether the concept of negotiability remains viable.

2. **Modern justification:** One potential explanation for maintaining the doctrine is that it allocates losses from fraud or theft to the party who is in the best position to avoid those losses in the first instance or to spread the costs of those losses that remain. As you examine the law of commercial paper, it is useful to consider whether the current law satisfies that objective.

III. LAW APPLICABLE TO PAYMENTS SYSTEMS

A. **Non-paper payment systems:** Not all contemporary payment systems involve obligations that have been reduced to written promises or orders to pay. ***Electronic fund transfers*** through automatic teller machines, point of sale terminals, or wire, and sales through credit cards, do not fall easily within the U.C.C. requirement of writings. Currently, legal doctrines concerning these payment mechanisms are governed by federal regulations and developing case law rather than by the U.C.C. In addition, transfers of large sums of money, particularly in international sales transactions, are often effected through electronic funds transfers. The law applicable to these transfers can be found in Article 4A of the U.C.C. Discussion of this law, however, is typically outside the scope of a course on negotiable instruments and payments law, and only casual reference to Article 4A will be found in this volume. Finally, promises to pay for goods in long-distance transactions are often guaranteed through a mechanism known as a letter of credit. The law relating to letters of credit can be found in Article 5 of the U.C.C. Many contracts that require a letter of credit, however, incorporate the Uniform Customs and Practice for Documentary Credits, which are promulgated by the International Chamber of Commerce. Where applicable, these provisions may displace provisions of the U.C.C.

B. Revision of U.C.C.: The American Law Institute has adopted ***substantial revisions*** to Article 3 of the Uniform Commercial Code and has amended Article 4. As of this writing, these revisions and amendments have been adopted by approximately 30 states. Other states are currently considering their adoption. Throughout this volume, references to provisions of Articles 3 and 4 will be to the Revision promulgated in 1990. There will, however, be discussion of the most substantial changes made by the Revision and comparison to prior law. References to pre-Revision provisions of Article 3 will be indicated by the designation "PR," e.g., ***U.C.C. PR § 3-419.***

CHAPTER 2

FORMS AND REQUIREMENTS
OF NEGOTIABLE INSTRUMENTS

I.   SUMMARY OF REQUISITES OF NEGOTIABILITY

A. Criteria: Section 3-104 of the U.C.C. establishes the criteria for a negotiable instrument. A negotiable instrument must

1. Contain an ***unconditional promise or order*** to pay;

2. Require payment of a ***fixed amount of money,*** with or without interest;

3. Be ***payable to bearer or to order*** at the time it is issued or first comes into the possession of a holder;

4. Be ***payable on demand or at a definite time;*** and

5. Not state ***any other undertaking*** or instruction.

B. Forms of instruments: Although U.C.C. § 3-104 does not explicitly require instruments to be in written form (as did U.C.C. PR § 3-104), both an "order" and a "promise," as those terms are used in Article 3, must take the ***form of a writing***. See U.C.C. § 3-103(a)(6), (9). Since a negotiable instrument must contain a promise or order to pay money, a negotiable instrument itself must take the form of a writing. While any reduction to tangible form of the terms necessary to constitute a negotiable instrument will suffice for a writing, U.C.C. § 3-104 defines some particular types of writings that fall within the classification of negotiable instruments.

1. **Note:**   The most basic form of instrument is a two-party instrument in which the maker promises to make payment to the order of the payee, or promisee, in accordance with the requirements of U.C.C. § 3-104. Any such writing constitutes a note. U.C.C. § 3-104(e).

PROMISSORY NOTE

$ _____2,000.00_____   _____December 5__, 19 _95_

____90 DAYS____   *AFTER DATE* __I__ *PROMISE TO PAY TO*

THE ORDER OF _____Law Student's National Bank_____

____Two Thousand and 00/100____ *DOLLARS*

_____/s/ Joe Student_____

a. **Interest and location for payment:** The above note assumes a zero percent interest rate per annum and does not specify a location for payment of the note. Most notes will include these provisions.

b. **Certificate of deposit:** If the promisor is a bank and the promise to repay acknowledges receipt of money that is the source of the repayment, the writing constitutes a certificate of deposit. U.C.C. § 3-104(j).

2. **Draft:** A *"draft,"* unlike a note, is always a three-party instrument. One party, the *drawer*, has placed funds in the hands of (or has credit with) a second party, the *drawee*. Through use of the draft, the drawer instructs the drawee to pay some or all of the funds held on behalf of the drawer to the order of the third party, the *payee*. The draft used to be known under the name "bill of exchange." The most common draft is the *check*, defined as a draft that is drawn on a bank and that is payable on demand, U.C.C. § 3-104(f). An instrument that meets all the other requirements of negotiability, but that is not made payable to bearer or to order, and that otherwise satisfies the definition of a check will still be considered a negotiable instrument and a check. U.C.C. § 3-104(c). In this way, transferees of instruments that appear to be checks, but that are made payable to an identified party rather than to the order of that party, are still able to attain the status of holders. Presumably, these parties would be surprised unfairly if they discovered that the writing in their possession was not a check.

David Drawer **1313 Mockingbird La.** **Brookline, MA**	November 20 19 95
Pay to the Order of _____ Pamela Payee _____	$ 75.00
_____ Seventy-five and 00/100 _____ Dollars	
Drawee National Bank Brookline, MA	/s/ David Drawer

3. **Special forms of instruments:**

a. A *"teller's check"* is a draft drawn by a savings bank or savings and loan association on or payable at a commercial bank with which the drawer maintains a checking account. It may also be referred to as an "official check." U.C.C. § 3-104(h).

b. A *"cashier's check"* is a draft drawn by a bank on its own funds. U.C.C. § 3-104(g). Since banks are generally solvent, cashier's checks are often treated as *"cash equivalents"* and will be accepted in lieu of cash.

c. A *"money order"* or *"personal money order"* is an instrument drawn on either the issuer or on another drawee with which the issuer maintains an account. Thus, a money order is typically used in place of a personal check. The money order is purchased by a "remitter", who gives the issuer an amount of money on which the order is to be drawn, plus a handling fee. U.C.C. § 3-103(a)(11). For instance, if Jones purchases a cashier's check, issued by First Bank and payable to the order of the Telephone Company, First Bank may request Jones to sign the cashier's check as purchaser. Jones would then be the remitter of the check.

PERSONAL MONEY ORDER   No. 1671

FIRST BANK
SPRINGFIELD, IOWA

Date _____ October 7, 1995 _____

Pay to
the order of ____ Pamela Payee _____

* * * **$500.00** * * *

/s/ Ron Remitter
_____
Remitter

Memo ____ Rent _____

_____
Address

---

d. A *"share draft"* is drawn on the drawer's account at a credit union the same way that a check is drawn on the drawer's account at a bank. Similarly, a *"negotiable order of withdrawal"* is drawn on the drawer's account at a savings institution.

e. A *"traveler's check"* is an instrument that is payable on demand, is drawn payable at or through a bank, is designated by the term "traveler's check" or some similar designation, and requires before payment that a person whose specimen signature appears on the instrument also provides a countersignature. U.C.C. § 3-104(i).

II. FORMAL REQUISITES OF NEGOTIABLE INSTRUMENTS

A. **Fixed amount of money:** In order to be a negotiable instrument, the writing must include a promise or order to pay a fixed amount of money "with or without interest." U.C.C. § 3-104(a). As a general matter, the amount payable will be considered fixed if it can be determined from the instrument *without reference to any external source*. Under the Revision, however, the requirement of a "fixed amount" *applies only to principal*. Interest may be expressed as a fixed or variable amount or rate and may require reference to information outside the instrument. U.C.C. § 3-112(b).

1. **Effect on interest:** This is a change from pre-Revision law, which required a negotiable instrument to be payable for a "sum certain." That phrase was defined under U.C.C. PR § 3-106 to preclude reference to any external information for determination of the principal or interest due.

   > **Example 1:** Smith, as maker, signed a writing promising to pay $100 plus 6% interest to Brown's order on or before July 1, 1996. Since any holder can compute the amount payable from the note itself, the note states both a fixed amount under U.C.C. § 3-104 and a sum certain under U.C.C. PR § 3-106.

   > **Example 2:** Smith, as maker, signed a writing promising to pay $100 plus interest at the rate of 2% over the First Bank prime rate to Brown's order on or before July 1, 1996. The note states a fixed amount under U.C.C. § 3-104, because the principal amount due at maturity can be determined from the face of the instrument. The note does not state a sum certain under U.C.C. PR § 3-106 because a holder can calculate the amount payable at maturity only by referring to First Bank's prime rate.

   > **Example 3:** Smith, as maker, signed a writing promising to pay $100 plus interest to Brown's order on or before July 1, 1996. Even though no specific interest rate is stated, this provision does not destroy negotiability. If an instrument provides for interest, but the amount of the interest payable cannot be ascertained from the instrument, the applicable interest rate is the judgment rate in effect at the place of payment and at the time interest first accrues. U.C.C. § 3-112(b). No interest is payable, however, unless provided for in the instrument. U.C.C. § 3-112(a).

2. Money: *Money* is defined as "a medium of exchange authorized or adopted by a domestic or foreign government" and thus may constitute more than legal tender. See U.C.C. § 1-201(24).

> **Example:** Smith was a wholesaler of kitchen cabinets. Jones was a carpenter. In return for a loan made by Smith, Jones executed a note by which she promised to make monthly payments to the order of Smith of $100 each "to be paid in cabinets figured at the prevailing builder's price." The note is not a negotiable instrument because cabinets are not a recognized form of exchange and so the obligation is not payable in money.

> **a. Foreign currency:** A promise to pay made payable in a foreign currency may satisfy the "money" requirement. Notwithstanding specification of the foreign currency, such an obligation may be satisfied by payment in dollars at the bank-offered rate for that currency at the place of payment on the date the instrument is paid. U.C.C. § 3-107. Although this conversion requires reference to a source outside the document, a promise to pay made payable in a foreign currency does not, by that fact alone, violate the sum certain requirement.

B. Unconditional promise or order: In order to ensure that payment of the instrument is not defeated by additional conditions over which the holder has no control, a negotiable instrument generally cannot contain a promise other than the one to make payment, and that payment must be unconditional. Nevertheless, the Revision has limited the range of situations in which a promise will be found to be conditional. Instead of declaring that instruments issued with certain conditions cannot be negotiable at all, the drafters of the Revision have allowed holders of instruments to accept the risk that instruments will not be paid as a result of the non-materialization of those conditions.

1. Terms of instrument: Whether or not an instrument is taken for an unconditional promise will depend on the terms of the instrument itself. Conditions not stated in the instrument will not defeat the unconditional requirement. Thus, conditions implied or construed by courts to decipher the parties' intent will not destroy negotiability. Every promise to pay, for instance, is subject to the implied condition that the obligor has the funds to make payment.

2. Impermissible conditions: A promise or order will not be unconditional, and thus will not be negotiable, if it states an express condition to payment, states that the promise or order is subject to or governed by another writing, or states that rights or obligations with respect to the promise or order are stated in another writing. U.C.C. § 3-106(a).

Example: Smith gave Jones a note in return for goods. The note recited, "I, Smith, promise to pay on June 30, 1996 to the order of Jones, $1,000, in accordance with the contract executed between us on this day." If this language is interpreted as requiring performance in accordance with conditions stated in the underlying contract before payment is made, then the note is non-negotiable. U.C.C. § 3-106(a)(iii). If, however, the language is interpreted only as a reference to the agreement that gave rise to the note, then the note is negotiable, because a reference to another writing does not of itself make the promise or order conditional. U.C.C. § 3-106(a). Notice the effect of this ambiguity on the justification for formal requirements of negotiability. Those requirements are generally considered necessary to ensure that any holder can readily determine from the face of the instrument whether it is negotiable. But if, as here, satisfaction of those requirements is uncertain, their function of providing certainty is defeated.

3. **Statement of payment obligations:** A promise or order may still be negotiable even though it contains certain terms that might be construed as conditions. These include a reference to another writing for a statement of rights with respect to collateral, prepayment, or acceleration of payment.

4. **Particular fund:** The fact that the source of the expected payment is limited to a particular fund does not make a promise or order conditional. U.C.C. § 3-106(b). The willingness of a potential purchaser of the instrument to accept the risk that the fund will be insufficient to pay the debt on maturity is considered to be an issue of pricing the note in the market rather than a condition that destroys negotiability. This constitutes a change from the law prior to the Revision. Under U.C.C. PR § 3-105(2)(b), limitation on the source of payment to a particular fund was a condition that rendered the instrument non-negotiable.

Example: Smith gave Jones a note in return for goods. The note recited, "I, Smith, promise to pay on June 30, 1995, to the order of Jones $1,000, such sum to be paid from my bank account at First Bank." Prior to the Revision, this language could have been interpreted as language of limitation on the sources available for payment, and thus the note would have been non-negotiable. Pre-Revision law, however, also permitted an interpretation of the reference to First Bank as language of expectation, in which case the reference to First Bank would not defeat negotiability. U.C.C. PR § 3-105(1)(f), (2)(b). Under the Revision, the note would be negotiable regardless of whether the reference was interpreted as a limitation or expectation.

C. Payable on demand or at a definite time: Negotiability requires that the holder be able to determine *from the instrument* the precise time at which payment is due. U.C.C. § 3-108.

1. **Demand:**   If there is no time for payment stated on the written promise, then it is *payable on demand*. The most obvious example of such an instrument is the typical check. Instruments payable at sight or on presentation also fall within the classification of demand instruments. See U.C.C. § 3-108. An instrument may also state explicitly that it is payable on demand, or at sight, in which case it is payable on demand.

2. **Definite time:**   An instrument is *payable at a definite time* if it is payable at any of the following times:

   a. On or before a *stated date* or at a definite period after a stated date;

   b. At a fixed period *after sight or acceptance*; or

   c. At a time readily ascertainable at the time the promise or order is issued.

3. **Alteration of time of payment:** The definiteness of the time for payment is not destroyed by the fact that the time of payment is subject to certain events that alter the time of payment from the original maturity date. These events include prepayment, acceleration, extension at the option of the holder, or extension to a further definite time at the option of the maker or acceptor or automatically on or after a specified act or event. U.C.C. § 3-108(b).

4. **Uncertain event:**   A writing that is payable only on the occurrence of an act that may not occur or that will occur at an uncertain time is not payable at a definite time.

   Example 1: Jones, as maker, signed a writing that recited, "I, Jones, promise to pay to the order of Brown, $1,000." Brown transferred the writing to Smith who attempted to enforce it against Jones. Jones refused payment, arguing that she had not received any consideration for the promise and that Smith was not a holder of an instrument because the writing was not payable on demand or at a definite time. Jones loses. The absence of any payment date means that the note is payable on demand.

   Example 2: Jones, as maker, signed a writing that recited, "I, Jones, promise to pay to the order of Brown $1,000 on or after July 1, 1996." Brown transferred the writing to Smith who attempted to enforce it against Jones. Jones refused payment, arguing that she had not received any consideration for the promise and that Smith was not a holder of an instrument because the writing was not payable on demand or at a definite time. Jones wins. The writing permits Jones to pay at any time after July 1, 1996 within her discretion. Thus, the writing is not payable at a definite time. If the promise to pay matured at a specific period of time, e.g., 30 days after July 1, 1996, the instrument would have been payable at a definite time.

Example 3: Jones, as maker, signed a writing that recited, "I, Jones, promise to pay to the order of Brown $1,000 on or before July 1, 2010." Brown transferred the writing to Smith who attempted to enforce it against Jones. Jones refused payment, arguing that she had not received any consideration for the promise and that Smith was not a holder of an instrument because the writing was not payable on demand or at a definite time. Jones loses. Although she has substantial discretion about the time of payment, there is a stated date by which she must pay.

Example 4: Jones, as maker, signed a writing that recited, "I, Jones, promise to pay to the order of Brown $1,000 within ten days after he completes installation of a swimming pool in my backyard." Brown transferred the writing to Smith who attempted to enforce it against Jones. Jones refused payment, arguing that she had not received any consideration for the promise and that Smith was not a holder of an instrument because the writing was not payable on demand or at a definite time. Jones wins. The writing fails to state a definite time that can be discerned at the time the promise or order is issued; the writing thus frustrates the policy of negotiability that requires instruments to be certain in their essential terms without additional inquiry.

Example 5: In *Calfo v. D. C. Stewart Co.*, 717 P.2d 697 (Utah 1986), a holder of a note brought an action for recovery against the maker and the holder's transferor. The maker of the note contended that it represented a promise to pay a real estate commission that would be due only if the maker exercised an option to purchase. The option was allowed to lapse. The holder of the note, of course, would not be subject to the maker's defense if the note was negotiable. The note recited that it would be due "upon final closing between...seller and...buyers, which shall be on or before May 1, 1980, when buyers exercise their option to purchase...." The court held that the stated date referred only to the time of exercise of the option and not to the maturity date of the note. Thus, the note was both conditional and indefinite. The claim of negotiability therefore failed.

D. Payable to order or to bearer: U.C.C. § 3-109.

1. **Payable to order:** An instrument is payable to order when it recites that it is payable to the order of *an identified person* or to that person *"or his order."* An instrument may be payable to the order of two or more persons, either together or in the alternative.

> **Example:** Jones purchased goods from Smith on credit and gave Smith a writing in which she promised "to pay Smith $100, 30 days from the date hereof." Smith transferred the note to Brown, who presented it to Jones on the date of maturity. Jones refused to pay because the goods were defective. Brown contends that he took the note as a holder of an instrument and free from any such defense. Brown loses. The note was payable only to Smith and not to his order or to bearer. Thus, it was not a negotiable instrument and no one can assert against Jones any rights greater than those of Smith. Prior to the Revision, Article 3 would still have governed the rights of parties to the instrument, except that no one could become a holder in due course of it. U.C.C. PR § 3-805. Under the Revision, however, Article 3 has no applicability to non-negotiable writings. See U.C.C. § 3-104, Comment 2. An exception to this rule would apply in the case of a check. An instrument that is made payable to an identified person rather than to the order of that person or to bearer but that otherwise satisfies the criteria for a check is still a check and a negotiable instrument. U.C.C. § 3-104(c).

   a. **Conjunctive or alternative:** An instrument may be made payable to the order of more than one person. If multiple payees are named in conjunction, *both must indorse* to negotiate the instrument. If they are named in the alternative, either may indorse to negotiate the instrument. Any ambiguity is resolved in favor of the instrument being payable to the persons alternatively. U.C.C. § 3-110(d).

   b. **Estate, trust, or fund:** Unlike pre-Code law, which deemed an instrument payable to a nonlegal entity as being payable to the entity itself, the U.C.C. considers an instrument payable to the order of an estate, trust, or fund as being payable to the order of the *trustee or representative* of that entity. An instrument payable to a partnership or unincorporated association may be indorsed by any person authorized to do so for the partnership or association. U.C.C. § 3-110(c)(2).

    c. Officer: An instrument payable to the order of an office or a person described as holding an office payable to the named person, the incumbent, or a successor to the incumbent. U.C.C. § 3-110(c)(2)(iv). The fact that such a person can deal with the instrument as a holder does not determine ownership of the instrument or entitlement to its proceeds.

2. Payable to bearer: A promise or order is payable to bearer when it states that it is payable to bearer, or to the order of bearer, or otherwise indicates that the person in possession is entitled to payment. Alternatively, a promise or order is payable to bearer if it does not state a payee or states that it is payable to or to the order of cash or otherwise indicates that it is not payable to an identified person. U.C.C. § 3-109(a).

> **Example 1:** Jones drew a check to the order of "Cash" and signed her name as drawer. On her way to the bank, Jones lost the check. Smith found the check on the street. Smith is the holder of a bearer negotiable instrument since the check does not purport to designate a specific payee.

> **Example 2:** Jones drew a check in the amount of $100 and sent it to her nephew for his high school graduation. Jones neglected to insert the name of her nephew as payee. The instrument is an incomplete instrument, but is enforceable as a bearer instrument because it does not state a payee. If the nephew were to complete the check by adding his name, the check would become an instrument payable to the order of the nephew. U.C.C. §§ 3-109(a)(2), 3-115.

3. Order and bearer: An instrument made payable both to order and to bearer is *payable to bearer.* See U.C.C. § 3-109, Comment 2. An order instrument is, by definition, one that is not made payable to bearer. One who obtains such an instrument is entitled to rely on the language of bearer and therefore to enforce or negotiate the instrument without obtaining the indorsement of a prior party.

E. Opting out of negotiability: Parties to a writing that would otherwise constitute a negotiable instrument may render the writing non-negotiable by the addition of a conspicuous statement to that effect. Parties, however, may not render an instrument that constitutes a *check* non-negotiable because of the commercial value of checks and the expectations of parties who accept them as payment. U.C.C. § 3-104(d).

III. "NEGOTIABILITY" FOR NON-INSTRUMENTS

A. **Negotiability by contract:** Writings that do not satisfy the requirements of negotiability do not constitute negotiable instruments that can convey the rights of a holder in due course. Nevertheless, pre-U.C.C. case law recognized that parties to such writings may agree that their contract bears many of the indicia of negotiability. If the parties attempt to transform an otherwise non-negotiable instrument into a negotiable one by adding a statement to that effect, a court is likely to ignore the statement. Nevertheless, some pre-U.C.C. cases suggest that, in certain circumstances, those in possession of writings which promise or order the payment of money may have rights similar to those conferred by negotiability.

B. **Negotiability by custom:** Some courts have recognized that a writing that does not otherwise satisfy the requirements of a negotiable instrument may attain that status if it has been treated as negotiable for a substantial period. Other pre-U.C.C. courts, however, rejected the notion of negotiability by custom.

> **Example:** In *Ashford v. Thos. Cook & Son (Bankers) Ltd.*, 471 P.2d 530 (Haw. 1970), the plaintiff, a subsequent purchaser of blank travelers' checks, sought to recover from the issuer of the checks after they had been dishonored. The court recognized that there was a split of opinion over whether blank travelers' checks that had been stolen constituted negotiable instruments when completed by a subsequent purchaser or by the thief. The court concluded, however, that it should "take a more realistic approach," and recognized that travelers' checks have "acquired negotiable characteristics by established custom" even if not by conformity with statutory law. Thus, the court held that travelers' checks were negotiable on printing and risk of theft was with the issuer in any action brought by a bona fide purchaser.

C. **Negotiability by estoppel:** Both pre-U.C.C. law and the Official Comments to the U.C.C. recognize that a court may treat a writing as having characteristics similar to those of negotiability by finding that the obligor on a writing is estopped from asserting a defense against a bona fide purchaser. U.C.C. § 3-104, Official Comment 2. That finding, however, does not transform the writing into a negotiable instrument.

> **Example:** In *Manhattan Co. v. Morgan*, 242 N.Y. 38, 150 N.E. 594 (1926), Judge Cardozo considered the various ways in which a non-negotiable instrument could attain the indicia of negotiability. The plaintiff bank had purchased stolen certificates in good faith and for value. The issuer refused to honor the terms of the certificates and the bank sued, arguing that it was the

holder of negotiable instruments. Judge Cardozo found that the certificates were not instruments because payment of them was conditional and was not to be made in money. The court concluded, however, that merchants have the capacity "to create new forms of negotiability by contract or estoppel." Nevertheless, the merchants involved in this case had failed to create any new form. Judge Cardozo expressed additional doubt about whether merchants could avoid the statutory requirements of negotiability by pointing to a custom that conferred the same rights that would be available to a holder of a negotiable instrument. Ultimately, Cardozo determined that no custom had been established with respect to the certificates involved in the case.

D. Effect of non-negotiability: Article 3 no longer applies to a writing, other than a check, that is not payable to order or to bearer but that otherwise satisfies the requirements of negotiability. Prior to the Revision, Article 3 did apply to such an instrument, but there could be no holder in due course of such an instrument. U.C.C. PR § 3-805.

> **Example:** Jones purchased an automobile from Brown and gave Brown a note in which she agreed "to pay Brown $5,000 on June 30, 1996." Brown transferred the note to Green, who took it in good faith, for value, and without notice of any defenses that Jones might have against payment. Jones subsequently sought to rescind the sale on the ground that the automobile was defective. When Green presents the note for payment, he will have no greater rights than Brown, as Green is not a holder in due course of the note. The note was not payable to order or to bearer and thus was not a negotiable instrument. If Jones has no valid defense against payment, Green's pre-Revision rights against Jones would include Green's Article 3 rights against Jones based on her contract as a maker of the note, as that right is not dependent on holder in due course status. Green would not have Article 3 rights under the Revision and would have to rely on contract law to recover against Jones.

CHAPTER 3

THE CONCEPT OF HOLDING IN DUE COURSE

I. INTRODUCTION

One who is a holder of an instrument generally has no greater rights than does an assignee of a simple contract. In order to attain greater rights than the transferor or to receive the full benefits of negotiability, a holder must also qualify as a "holder in due course" ("HDC").

A. Requirements: In order to be a HDC, one must

1. be a *"holder"* of an instrument,

2. take the instrument for *value*,

3. take the instrument in *good faith*,

4. take the instrument *without notice* of defenses that might be available to the obligor on the instrument or that there are defects in the instrument, and

5. the instrument when issued or negotiated to the holder must *not bear apparent evidence of forgery or alteration* or otherwise appear so irregular or incomplete as to call into question its authenticity. U.C.C. § 3-302(a).

B. Preclusion of HDC status: Notice of the following defenses or defects at the time when the instrument is taken by the holder will preclude HDC status:

1. the instrument is *overdue* or has been dishonored or is part of a series with respect to which there has been an uncured default in payment;

2. the instrument contains an *unauthorized signature* or has been *altered*;

3. a third party has made a *property or possessory* claim to the instrument or its proceeds;

4. a party to the instrument has a *defense* or *claim in recoupment* against payment of the instrument.

II. A HDC MUST BE A "HOLDER"

A. Definition of "holder": In order to qualify as a HDC, a person must first be a holder. U.C.C. § 3-302(a). In the case of a bearer instrument, the holder is the person in possession of the instrument. In the case of an order instrument, the holder is the person identified as the party to whom the instrument is payable, if that person is in possession of the instrument. U.C.C. § 1-201(20).

> **Example:** Smith drew a check to the order of Jones and mailed it to Jones. At the time that Smith drew the check and prior to the time that it was received by Jones, there was no holder of the check. Smith could not be the holder of the check even when he possessed it, because he was not the person identified as the person to whom the instrument was payable. Although Jones was the person to whom the check was payable, she was not the holder of the check until she received it, because it was only at that point that she was in possession of it.

B. Possession: Although the concept of possession is not defined in the Uniform Commercial Code, it has posed few interpretive difficulties.

    1. Lost or stolen instruments: There are some situations in which a party without actual possession of an instrument is ***entitled to enforce the instrument*** under Article 3, as if he or she were a holder of the instrument. For instance, the owner of an instrument that has been lost or stolen may recover from any party liable on it by proving (i) that he or she had possession of the instrument and the right to enforce it when the loss of possession occurred, (ii) that loss of possession was not the result of a transfer by him or her or a lawful seizure, and (iii) that he or she cannot reasonably obtain possession of the instrument because of destruction, loss, or theft. U.C.C. § 3-309.

C. Issuance and delivery: The concept of becoming a holder should not be confused with issuance or delivery of an instrument. Although one may become a holder through issuance or delivery, these concepts are not synonymous.

    1. Issuance: An instrument is issued when it is ***first delivered*** by the maker or drawer for the purpose of giving rights on the instrument to any person. The person to whom the instrument is issued need not be a holder. U.C.C. § 3-105(a).

    2. Delivery: Delivery consists of a ***voluntary transfer of possession***. U.C.C. § 1-201(14). Thus, transfer of an instrument to a thief will not constitute a delivery.

> **Example 1:** Smith requested First Bank to issue a cashier's check in the amount of $1,000 to the order of Jones. First Bank completed a cashier's check form as requested and gave it to Smith, who signed as remitter. A remitter is one who purchases

an instrument to be completed by the purchaser by making it payable to the order of another party. The remitter is not a holder, even though in possession of an instrument issued to him or her because the instrument is not made payable to his or her order. U.C.C. § 3-103(a)(11). When First Bank delivers the cashier's check to Smith, it has issued the check, even though Smith is not a holder of it.

Example 2: Smith made a check payable to the order of Jones and placed it in his desk drawer. Brown stole the check from Smith's desk drawer. The check has never been issued because it was never delivered by the drawer. Nonissuance is a defense against payment of the check, but the defense will not be valid against a holder in due course. U.C.C. § 3-105(b).

D. **Becoming a holder:** One may become a holder of an instrument either through *initial issuance or by negotiation*. In the case of an order instrument, the person to whose order the instrument is originally made payable becomes a holder when he or she comes into possession of the instrument. In the case of a bearer instrument, the person to whom the instrument is issued is a holder when he or she comes into possession of it.

1. **Negotiation:** Negotiation of an instrument consists of its *transfer*, whether voluntary or involuntary, by a person other than the issuer to a person who *thereby becomes its holder*. U.C.C. § 3-201. Thus, the person to whom the instrument is initially issued may become a holder, but that person is not one to whom the instrument is negotiated. Instead, the person to whom the instrument is initially issued may negotiate the instrument to a third party and, by the act of negotiation, makes that third party a holder.

2. **Order instruments:** In the case of an instrument payable to an identified person, negotiation requires *transfer of possession* of the instrument along with *indorsement* by the holder. U.C.C. § 3-201(b).

3. **Bearer instruments:** In the case of an instrument payable to bearer, negotiation requires transfer of possession alone. No indorsement is necessary to make the transferee of the instrument a holder. U.C.C. § 3-201(b).

4. **Means of indorsement:** In the case of an order instrument, where an indorsement is necessary for a negotiation, only a holder may make the indorsement and therefore make the transferee of the instrument a holder. U.C.C. § 3-201(b). The indorsement must be written on the instrument or on a paper, called an allonge, that is so firmly affixed to the instrument as to become a part of it.

Example 1: Smith drew two checks, one to the order of Jones in the amount of $100 and one to bearer in the amount of $150. Smith delivered both checks to Jones in return for an antique desk that Jones owned. Jones then delivered the order check to Brown, who had loaned Jones $100 and the bearer check to Green, as a down payment on an automobile. Jones neglected to sign either check before she delivered them. Brown is not a holder of the $100 check and may not become a holder in due course because an order instrument may be negotiated only with the indorsement of a holder. Green is a holder of the $150 check and may become a holder in due course because a bearer instrument may be negotiated by delivery alone.

Example 2: Smith issued a note for $1,000 to the order of Brown. Brown wished to borrow $500 from Jones. Brown offered to negotiate Smith's note to Jones as collateral. Although there was room on the back of Smith's note for Brown's indorsement, Brown did not sign there. Instead, Brown stapled to Smith's note a piece of paper that read "payable to the order of Jones." Some courts have held that a person in the position of Jones is not a holder in due course because an allonge is permissible only where there is insufficient space for an indorsement on the instrument itself and because stapling is an insufficient form of attachment. In *Crossland Savings Bank FSB v. Constant*, 737 S.W.2d 19 (Ct. App. Tex. 1987), the court denied holder status on both these grounds.

The Revision rejects this result. § 3-204 states that a paper affixed to the instrument on which a signature is made is part of the instrument. Comment 1 to that section states that an indorsement on an allonge is valid even if there was sufficient room on the instrument for the indorsement.

5. **Theft:** These rules of indorsement and negotiation are particularly important in theft situations. Because one must be a holder to indorse, and a person can only be a holder if in possession of an instrument that is payable to that person, or that is a bearer instrument, ***a thief of an order instrument cannot be a holder***. The thief will not be a person to whom the instrument is made payable. Nor can anyone taking the instrument subsequent to the thief be a holder, as the thief cannot indorse the instrument to any subsequent party. (Remember that only a holder can indorse.) But because no indorsement is necessary to negotiate a bearer instrument, ***a thief can negotiate a bearer instrument***, and a person taking the instrument subsequently from the thief can be a holder.

Example 1: Brown owned a negotiable note made by Jones that recited her promise "to pay to bearer, on demand, $1,000." Smith stole the note from Brown and sold it to Green for $995. Brown found the note in Green's hands and brought an action for its return. Green may keep the note. U.C.C. § 3-305 provides that a holder in due course takes the instrument free from competing claims, such as the claim of Brown. Green is in possession of an instrument that was issued to bearer. The transfer of the bearer instrument to Green by Smith constitutes a negotiation and confers holder status on Green. Thus, Green is a holder and can be a holder in due course. This doctrine can be traced to Lord Mansfield's opinion in the famous case of *Miller v. Race*, 1 Burr. 452, 97 Eng. Rep. 398 (King's Bench 1758). Note, however, that the original theft made Smith a holder because Smith obtained the bearer instrument through a transfer of possession. A bearer instrument is negotiated when there is a transfer of possession, whether voluntary or involuntary. U.C.C. § 3-201(a). The theft would constitute an involuntary transfer of possession and thus would constitute a negotiation. The thief, of course, cannot be a holder in due course and thus remains subject to the defense that the instrument was acquired by theft. However, since the thief is a holder, the thief can negotiate the instrument to someone else in a manner that makes that transferee a holder in due course.

Example 2: Brown owned a negotiable note made by Jones that recited her promise "to pay to the order of Brown, on demand, $1,000." Smith stole the note from Brown and signed Brown's name on the back. Smith then sold the note to Green for $995. Brown found the note in Green's hands and brought an action for its return. Brown may recover the note. Smith was not himself a holder of the note, as he was not the identified person to whom it had been made payable and it was not a bearer instrument. Because the note was payable to an identified person, the indorsement of a holder was necessary for a negotiation. Since Smith was not a holder, his signing of the note does not constitute an indorsement, as only a holder can indorse. The delivery of the note to Green, therefore, does not constitute a negotiation and does not confer on Green the status of holder. Green cannot be a holder in due course and must surrender the note to Brown's superior claim.

6. **Incorrect name:** If an instrument has been made payable to a person under a misspelled or incorrect name, he or she may indorse it in either the correct or incorrect name or in both. A person paying

or giving value for the instrument may require indorsement in both names. U.C.C. § 3-204(d).

7. **Special and blank indorsements:**   An indorsement that identifies the person to whom or to whose order it makes the instrument payable is a ***special indorsement***. Such an instrument becomes payable only to the order of the special indorsee, even if the instrument was originally a bearer instrument. The Revision establishes principles by which to determine the identity of the special indorsee. In general, ***the intent of the person*** who makes the special indorsement will govern the question of who constitutes the special indorsee. U.C.C. § 3-110. An indorsement that specifies no particular indorsee or that consists only of a signature is a ***blank indorsement***. Any such instrument becomes a bearer instrument, even if the instrument was originally made payable to the payee's order. U.C.C. § 3-205.

> **Example 1:** Brown owned a negotiable note made by Jones that recited her promise "to pay to the order of Brown, on demand, $1,000." Brown indorsed the note by signing his name on the back. Smith stole the note from Brown. Smith then sold the note to Green for $995. Brown found the note in Green's hands and brought an action for its return. Green may keep the note. Although the note was originally an order instrument, Brown has indorsed it in blank and has transformed it into a bearer instrument. Thus, Green gets the same benefits as if the instrument had originally been a bearer instrument.

> **Example 2:** Brown owned a negotiable note made by Jones that recited her promise "to pay to the order of Brown, on demand, $1,000." Brown indorsed the note by signing on the back, "pay to the order of Black, [signed] Brown." Smith stole the note from Brown. Smith then sold the note to Green for $995. Brown found the note in Green's hands and brought an action for its return. Brown may recover the note. The indorsement written by Brown was a special indorsement, so the instrument can only be further negotiated by Black's signature. The transfer of the note to Green, therefore, does not constitute a negotiation and does not confer on Green the status of holder. Green cannot be a holder in due course and must surrender the note to Brown's superior claim.

> **Example 3:** Brown issued a check in the amount of $100 to his neighbor Smith. Smith owed Black $100 and indorsed the check to Black, but misspelled her name as "Block." Black is a special indorsee of the check. She was the person to whom the indorser,

Smith, intended the check to be payable. U.C.C. §§ 3-110(a), 3-205(a).

8. **Restrictive indorsement:** An indorsement may also be ***restrictive***. A restrictive indorsement is one that purports to restrict a transferee's use of the instrument. The effectiveness of these restrictions varies. U.C.C. § 3-206.

   a. An indorsement that purports to limit payment to a particular person or to prohibit further transfer or negotiation of the instrument is ineffective to prevent further transfer or negotiation.

   b. An indorsement that states a condition to payment does not affect the right of the indorsee to enforce the instrument. A person who pays the instrument or takes it for value or for collection may disregard the condition.

   c. An instrument indorsed as "pay any bank" or indorsed with the words "for deposit" or otherwise indicating that the instrument is to be collected by a bank for an indorser gives the indorser the right to have a depositary or collecting bank act consistently with the indorsement.

      Example: Smith drew a check to the order of Brown. Brown indorsed the check "Pay Green only, [signed] Brown." Green may indorse the check and negotiate it to Jones, and thereby make Jones a holder, notwithstanding the restrictive indorsement.

E. **Shelter principle:** Under certain circumstances, one may have the rights of a holder, and the rights of a HDC, even though one is not a holder or HDC in his or her own right. This occurs when one is ***sheltered*** by the holder status of a prior transferee of the instrument. A person who is sheltered to the rights of a holder is a ***person entitled to enforce the instrument***, just as if the person were a holder. U.C.C. § 3-301(a).

   1. **Rights of the transferor:** Any transferee of an instrument obtains whatever rights the transferor had in the instrument. U.C.C. § 3-203(b). These rights may include the ***right to enforce the instrument***, and any rights the transferor may have had as a HDC.

      a. For purposes of the shelter principle, transfer of the instrument occurs when the instrument is delivered by a person other than its issuer for the purpose of giving the transferee the right to enforce the instrument. U.C.C. § 3-203(a). Recall that a negotiation requires only a transfer of possession, whether voluntary or involuntary. U.C.C. § 3-201(a). A transfer that vests the transferee with the rights of the transferor, however, requires a transfer of the instrument. A transfer of the instrument that triggers the shelter principle consists of a *delivery*, which is defined to require a voluntary transfer of possession. U.C.C. § 1-201(14). Thus, an involuntary transfer of possession, such as where a finder or thief comes into possession of the instrument, does not shelter the possessor with the rights of prior possessor.

b. **Exception:**   The important exception to this shelter principle is that a transferee who has been a *party to a fraud or illegality* affecting the instrument cannot acquire rights of a HDC by a transfer. U.C.C. § 3-203(b). Prior to the Revision, this limitation also applied to a transferee who, as a prior holder, had notice of a defense or competing claim. U.C.C. PR § 3-201.

Example 1: Smith fraudulently induced Jones to make a note payable to his order in return for Smith's promise to perform work on Jones' house. Smith sold the note to Brown for value. Brown, who had no notice of Smith's fraud, gave the note to Green as a gift. Green, who also had no notice of the fraud, attempted to enforce the note against Jones. Green wins. Even though Green gave no value for the instrument, and thus is not a holder in due course, Brown was a holder in due course. Green, as Brown's transferee, succeeds to Brown's rights as a holder in due course under the shelter principle.

Example 2: Smith fraudulently induced Jones to make a note payable to Smith's order in return for his promise to perform work on Jones' house. Smith sold the note for value to Brown, who had no notice of the fraud. Smith later repurchased the note from Brown for value. Smith cannot succeed to Brown's rights as a HDC and remains subject to the defense of fraud because he was a party to the original fraud affecting the instrument.

Example 3: Jones made a note payable on June 15 to the order of Smith. Smith indorsed the note to the order of Brown on May 15. On July 1, Brown sold the note to Green. Green can have the rights of a holder in due course even though the note is overdue (and, thus, Green cannot be a holder in due course in her own right) because Green succeeds to Brown's rights as a HDC.

Example 4: Brown fraudulently induced Jones to issue him a note payable on March 31. Brown negotiated the note to Smith who knew of the fraud, but did not participate in the transaction between Brown and Jones. Smith negotiated the instrument to Green for value. Green neither knew of Brown's fraud nor participated in the transaction between Brown and Jones. Subsequently, Smith repurchased the note from Green. Smith presented the note to Jones for payment on March 31. If the jurisdiction that governs the transaction has adopted the Revision, Smith is sheltered to Green's rights as a HDC, even though Smith knew of Brown's fraud. If the jurisdiction has adopted the pre-Revision U.C.C., Smith will not be sheltered to Green's rights as a HDC because Smith had knowledge of Brown's fraud.

2. **Right to indorsement:** Any transferee for value who accepts an instrument is entitled to have the unqualified indorsement of the transferor. U.C.C. § 3-203(c). Thus, a depositary bank that accepts a check is entitled to the indorsement of its customer.

   a. **Depositary bank and indorsements:** If a depositary bank receives an item for collection and the customer was a holder of the item at the time of delivery to the depositary bank, the depositary bank itself automatically becomes a holder. No indorsement of the item by the customer is necessary. The depositary bank may therefore become a HDC even in the absence of its customer's indorsement. U.C.C. § 4-205(1).

   b. **Bank becomes a holder:** Note that, under U.C.C. § 4-205, the bank not only attains the rights of a holder under the shelter principle, but it also ***becomes a holder***. This distinction may be important because, in order to attain the status of a HDC, one must be a holder, not just have the rights of one. This important distinction was ignored in the early case of *Bowling Green, Inc. v. State Street Bank & Trust Co.*, 425 F.2d 81 (1st Cir. 1970). There the court conferred both the rights and status of a holder in due course on a depositary bank that—under pre-Revision law— could, but did not, supply a customer's signature. The plaintiff in the case had negotiated a check to the bank's customer, who had deposited the check with the bank but had failed to indorse it. Nor did the bank supply the missing signature under U.C.C. PR § 4-205. The plaintiff never received the merchandise for which the check had been given and brought an action to recover its payment from the bank. The bank claimed that it was a HDC of the check and held it free from the plaintiff's claim. The First Circuit correctly determined that the bank succeeded to the rights of its transferor under the shelter principle. Since the bank's transferor had no rights to the check without performing its contract with the plaintiff, the bank should have received no more. But the First Circuit went further and held that since the bank's customer was a holder, it also transferred that status to the bank, and that once the bank took the check in good faith and for value it could become a holder in due course. The shelter provision, however, did not confer that status. U.C.C. § 4-205 now makes the placement of the customer's indorsement on the check unnecessary.

> **Example:** Jones issued a check to the order of Brown, who deposited it in her account at First Bank, but failed to indorse it. First Bank did not supply the missing indorsement. Jones never received the merchandise for which he had given the check to Brown, and stopped payment on the check. When First Bank could not obtain payment of the check from the drawee bank, it sought to recover the amount of the check from Jones. Jones claimed that he could assert against First Bank the defense he had against Brown, because First Bank was not a holder since the check had never been negotiated to First Bank. First Bank wins under the Revision. First Bank became a holder of the check when Brown deposited it for collection, and, hence, could become a HDC if it otherwise satisfies the requirements for that status. Alternatively, if First Bank's customer had been a HDC, First Bank would have the rights of a HDC under the shelter principle, even if First Bank did not have the status of a holder or a HDC in its own right.

3. **Rationale of the shelter principle:** The shelter principle makes sense insofar as it *expands the market* for commercial paper without placing obligors on the instrument in a worse position than they would have occupied had the transferor retained it.

> **Example:** Brown gave Smith a note for $1,000 in return for Smith's promise to perform work on Brown's house. Smith negotiated the note to Jones, who took it as a HDC. Subsequently, Brown widely advertised the fact that Smith's work was substandard and that he (Brown) would not make any payment to Smith. Jones wants to negotiate the note to Green, who has heard of Brown's complaints. Since Green has notice of Brown's defense, Green cannot be a HDC and, thus, may be unwilling to purchase the note. But since Green can be sheltered by the rights of Jones as a HDC, Green will be more willing to purchase the note. Brown is no worse off than he otherwise would have been, since he would not have had a valid defense against Jones, if Jones had attempted to enforce the note against him.

4. **Enforcement of the instrument:** Obligations of a drawer or indorser run to a *"person entitled to enforce the instrument."* U.C.C. § 3-301. Such a person includes (i) a holder of the instrument, (ii) a nonholder in possession of the instrument with the rights of a holder, and (iii) a person not in possession who is entitled

to enforce an instrument that has been lost or stolen. The second category includes primarily a person who takes the instrument under the shelter principle. Such a person is not necessarily a holder in his or her own right, but has the rights of the transferor, including the rights of a holder if the transferor was a holder.

III. A HDC MUST TAKE THE INSTRUMENT FOR VALUE [U.C.C. § 3-302(a)(2)(i)]

A. **General meaning:** Outside of Article 3, *"value"* consists of any *consideration that will support a simple contract*, including an executory promise. U.C.C. § 1-201(44). The definition of "value" for Article 3 is narrower; a holder takes an instrument for value only to the extent that:

1. The instrument has been issued or transferred for a promise of performance and the *promise has been performed* (thus, partial performance will constitute value only in an amount proportionate that the performance bears to the promise);

2. The transferee acquires a *security interest* or other lien in the instrument, other than a lien obtained by a judicial proceeding;

3. The instrument is issued or transferred as payment of or as security for an *antecedent claim*; or

4. The instrument is issued or transferred *in exchange for another instrument*; or

5. The instrument is issued or transferred in exchange for the incurring of an *irrevocable obligation* to a third party by the person taking the instrument. U.C.C. § 3-303(a).

B. **Value vs. consideration:** Although the giving of value is necessary to confer holder in due course status, consideration may still play an important role in the law of negotiable instruments. The fact that a maker or drawer has given a note for consideration may confer the right of enforcement on the holder of the note, and the absence of consideration may provide a defense to enforcement. U.C.C. § 3-303(b). All value will constitute consideration for purposes of Article 3, but not all consideration will constitute value.

> **Example:** Jones was the maker of a negotiable demand note in the amount of $1,000, payable to the order of Smith. Smith agreed that, in return for this note, he would drive Jones' automobile to California next July. In June, Smith demanded payment from Jones. Jones must pay since she issued the note for consideration. If Smith attempted to enforce the payment in

August and had not yet begun to drive the automobile to California, Jones would have a defense against payment, because the promised performance was due and had not been performed. Value has not been given because no part of the promise for which the instrument was given has been performed.

C. **Executory promise:**   In contract law, consideration is a concept that includes executory promises to perform. Thus, even a promise that has not been fulfilled will support enforcement of a common law contract. In contrast, a holder who has agreed to pay consideration in return for receiving an instrument is only a holder in due course to the extent that the payment has been made.

> **Example:** Jones was the maker of a negotiable demand note in the amount of $1,000, payable to the order of Smith, for the purchase of Smith's automobile. Smith negotiated the note to Brown in return for Brown's promise to pay Smith $1,000 in 30 days. Ten days later, Brown demanded payment on the note from Jones. Jones refused on the grounds that the automobile was not in the condition warranted by Smith at the time of sale. If Brown has not yet paid the $1,000 to Smith, Brown is not a HDC. Even though Brown promised to make the payment, he cannot enforce the note against Jones.

1. **Rationale:**   The rationale for this rule is that the holder who has not yet parted with value *may rescind the transaction* with his transferor on a breach of warranty theory and may not need to enforce the instrument against the innocent drawer or maker.

2. **Partial performance:**   A holder who has only partially performed the promise made in exchange for the instrument is a holder in due course only to the extent the promise has been performed. The doctrine of partial performance, however, may also affect a holder who has fully performed. In order to attain HDC status, one must satisfy all the requirements necessary to that status. Thus, a holder who learns of the maker's or drawer's defenses to payment after the holder has partially performed his or her promise cannot subsequently give additional value without failing the requirement that a HDC not have notice of a defense or claim in recoupment. As a result, the holder can only be a HDC to the extent that he or she performed the promise prior to learning of the defense.

> **Example 1:** Jones was the maker of a negotiable demand note in the amount of $1,000, payable to the order of Smith, for the purchase of Smith's automobile. Smith negotiated the note to Brown in return for Brown's promise to pay Smith $1,000 in two installments, $500 in 30 days and $500 in 60 days. Forty-five

days later, after Brown had paid Smith $500, Brown attempted to enforce the note against Jones. Jones had been having difficulty with the automobile and refused to pay the note, claiming that she was entitled to a claim in recoupment for the lesser value of the automobile. Brown is only a HDC for $500 because he has only given value in that amount at the time he is attempting to enforce the note.

Example 2: Jones was the maker of a negotiable demand note in the amount of $1,000, payable to the order of Smith, for the purchase of Smith's automobile. Smith negotiated the note to Brown in return for Brown's promise to pay Smith $1,000 in two installments, $500 in 30 days and $500 in 60 days. Forty-five days later, after Brown has paid Smith $500, Jones informs Brown that she will not make any further payments on the note because the automobile was not in the condition warranted by Smith at the time of sale. Brown subsequently pays Smith the additional $500 and seeks to enforce the entire $1,000 note against Jones. Brown is a HDC only in the amount of $500. He had partially performed the promise at the time he learned of a defense to payment, and, thus, is a HDC to the extent of his partial performance at that time.

3. **Exceptions to the executory promise rule:** Under U.C.C. § 3-303, if the holder takes the instrument either for another instrument or in return for an irrevocable commitment to a third person, the holder has taken the instrument for value, even though the other instrument or the irrevocable commitment is executory.

Example: In return for Smith's promise to deliver furniture to her office, Jones negotiated to Smith a note made payable by Green to the order of Jones. Smith entered into an irrevocable commitment with Black to purchase the furniture ordered by Jones. Subsequently, Smith learns that Green has a valid defense to payment of the note. Smith's commitment to Black constitutes value and Smith may enforce the note against Green even though he has knowledge of a defense prior to payment.

D. **Discounted notes and partial performance:** Difficulties arise where the payee negotiates the note at a discount. Prior to the Revision, it was unclear whether the holder should be deemed to have given value in the amount of her actual payment or in proportion to all payments she agreed to make. The Revision adopts the ***proportionality rule*** and provides that the holder of the discounted note may assert HDC rights to the fraction of the amount payable under the instrument that is equivalent to the value of the partial performance divided by the value of the promised performance. U.C.C. § 3-302(d). Hence, to determine the amount to which the holder of a discounted note has given value, apply the formula:

$$\frac{\text{Amount performed}}{\text{Discounted price}} \text{ x face value of instrument}$$

Example: Smith, the payee of a note made by Jones with a face amount of $3,000, negotiated the note to Brown in return for Brown's promise to pay Smith $2,800. After Brown paid Smith $1,000, Jones informed Brown that he had valid defenses against Smith. Should Brown be considered a HDC in the amount of $1,000, or 1000/2800 of $3,000 ($1,071.43)? The Revision adopts the latter result. This is consistent with the pre-Revision decision in *O.P. Ganjo, Inc. v. Tri-Urban Realty Co.*, 108 N.J. Super. 517, 261 A.2d 722 (1970), where the court held that the holder who purchased a note at a discount and had made partial payment had given value for a pro rata share of its discount as well as the amount of actual payment. The result allows the holder to retain a pro rata portion of its bargained-for profit in purchasing the instrument.

E. **Security interests and value in banking channels:** § 3-303(a)(2) provides that a transferee gives value for an instrument by acquiring a *security interest* in it. The transferee may acquire a security interest by taking direct possession of it under Article 9 of the U.C.C. See U.C.C. § 9-305. More commonly, however, this provision is relevant for depositary and drawee banks that seek *HDC status on checks* that they have received or accepted. If those checks are subsequently dishonored, a bank that has permitted its customer to withdraw funds may wish to proceed against the drawer to recover the funds the bank has made available to its customer. This will especially be the case if the bank's customer cannot be found or has exhausted the withdrawn funds. U.C.C. Section 4-211, provides that a bank has given value for an *item* (defined as an instrument handled by a bank for payment or collection, such as a check, U.C.C. § 4-104(a)(9)) "to the extent it has a security interest" in the item and has otherwise complied with the requirements of being a HDC. Any security interest that the bank asserts under these conditions will typically be created by Article 4 of the U.C.C. rather than by Article 9. The circumstances under which a bank has a security interest in an item are set forth in U.C.C. § 4-210.

1. **Discretionary withdrawal:** A bank has a security interest in an item that it has received for deposit to the extent to which *credit given for the item has been withdrawn or applied*. U.C.C. § 4-210(a)(1). It is irrelevant whether the bank has collected the funds represented by the check prior to the time that the withdrawal

occurred. In *Citizens Nat'l Bank of Englewood v. Fort Lee Savings and Loan Ass'n*, 89 N.J. Super. 43, 213 A.2d 315 (1965), the court held that a bank that permitted a depositor to withdraw funds before deposited checks cleared had given value, even though the bank was under no obligation to permit the withdrawals. The court determined that it "would hinder commercial transactions if depositary banks refused to permit withdrawal prior to clearance of checks."

> **Example 1:** Jones had a zero balance in her checking account. She deposited into her account at Local Bank a check drawn by Smith and made payable to her order in the amount of $100. Local Bank gave Jones a provisional credit for the amount of the check. Nevertheless, Local Bank is not a HDC of the check as she has not made a withdrawal against the credit.

> **Example 2:** Jones had a zero balance in her checking account. She deposited into her account at Local Bank a check drawn by Smith and made payable to her order in the amount of $100. Local Bank gave Jones a provisional credit for the amount of the check. The next day, before Local Bank finalized the credit, it permitted Jones to withdraw $75 from her account. Local Bank has a security interest in $75 of the Smith check and is a HDC of the check to the extent of $75.

> **Critique of the rule:** The depositary bank is under no legal obligation to permit withdrawals against provisional credits. Sometimes banks will permit such withdrawals to accommodate their customers. When they do so, arguably they should not be transformed into HDCs, as such status permits them to take free of defenses of the drawer to which the customer would be subject. Assume in the above examples that Jones received the check from Smith in return for a chair that was fraudulently misrepresented by Jones to be a valuable antique. Even if Smith discovered the fraud shortly after the purchase, Local Bank may enforce the instrument against Smith if it has permitted withdrawal against a provisional credit.

2. **Withdrawal as of right:** A bank has a security interest in an item that it has received for deposit to the extent that it has given credit *available for withdrawal as of right*. U.C.C. § 4-210(a)(2). It is irrelevant that the bank has a right of charge-back against its customer in the event that it cannot collect the amount of the check from the drawee bank.

> **Example:** Jones had a zero balance in her checking account. She deposited into her account at Local Bank a check drawn by

Smith and made payable to her order in the amount of $100. Local Bank gave Jones a provisional credit for the amount of the check. The next day, Local Bank received payment on the check from the drawee bank, so that the funds represented by the check are available for withdrawal by Jones as of right. Local Bank has a security interest in the check, even if Jones has not withdrawn the funds.

3. **FIFO system:**   For purposes of calculating which checks are subject to the bank's security interest, the Code adopts a "first in, first out" system, so credits first given are deemed first withdrawn. U.C.C. § 4-210(b).

> **Example 1:** On February 1, Jones deposited into her account at First Bank a check drawn by Smith and made payable to Jones' order in the amount of $100. At that time, there were no other funds in the account. On February 2, Jones deposited another check, also in the amount of $100, drawn to her order by Brown. In each case, First Bank gave Jones provisional credit for the check. On February 3, First Bank permitted Jones to withdraw $150 from her account. First Bank has a security interest in the entire Smith check and $50 of the Brown check.

> **Example 2:** On February 1, Jones deposited $200 in cash into her account at First Bank. At that time, there were no other funds in the account. On February 5, Jones deposited a check drawn to her order by Smith in the amount of $100. On February 8, Jones deposited another check, drawn to her order by Green in the amount of $100. On February 10, First Bank paid a properly payable check from the account in the amount of $300. On February 11, First Bank received notification that Smith's check was dishonored. First Bank could charge back the $100 amount against the balance remaining in Jones's account from Green's check. But First Bank has given value for the Smith check under the "first in, first out rule," so it may also qualify as a holder in due course and enforce the check against Smith.

4. **Simultaneous items:**   Where credits for several items are given simultaneously and a ***withdrawal is made in part***, the security interest remains on all the items.

> **Example:** On February 1, Jones deposited into her account at First Bank a check drawn by Smith and made payable to Jones' order in the amount of $100 and a check drawn by Brown and made payable to her order in the amount of $100. At that time, there were no other funds in the account. On February 3, First Bank permitted Jones to withdraw $150 from her account. First

Bank retains a security interest in both checks. But the U.C.C. does not make clear whether the security interest is for the full amount of each check ($100 each) or only a pro rata share of each check ($75 each).

5. **Bank credits as value:** In *Marine Midland Bank – New York v. Graybar Electric Co.*, 363 N.E.2d 1139 (N.Y. 1977), a bank set off a check received by one of its customers and deposited in the bank against an indebtedness owed to the bank by the customer. The drawer of the check had issued a stop payment order against it and the depositary bank was unable to collect from the drawee. Since it could not recover the amount of the check from the drawee, the depositary bank reversed the credit that it had applied against its customer's indebtedness in respect of the check. The depositary bank then brought an action against the drawer of the check, claiming that it (the depositary bank) had given value by setting off the amount of the check against its customer's outstanding indebtedness, and thus was a HDC of the check. The New York Court of Appeals determined that the provisional nature of the credit given by the depositary bank to its customer prevented that credit from constituting value. Nor could the use of the setoff constitute value. The bank was using the setoff only to protect itself rather than to provide any benefit to its customer. To the court, the creation of a benefit for the customer was the standard that underlies the giving of value. In the absence of such a benefit, there was no reason to allow the bank to profit from the credit by conferring on the bank the status of a HDC.

F. **Antecedent debt:** A holder who takes an instrument as payment or security for an antecedent debt has taken it for value.

> **Example:** On January 1, Jones borrowed $1,000 from Smith payable June 1. On May 1, Smith hears that Jones is having financial difficulties and demands that she provide some collateral for the loan. Jones negotiates to Smith a note made by Brown, payable to Jones in the amount of $1,500 due June 15. Smith has taken the note for value and may be a HDC of it.

IV. A HDC MUST TAKE THE INSTRUMENT IN GOOD FAITH [U.C.C. § 3-302(a)(2)(ii)]

A. **Subjective vs. objective tests:** Good faith is an elusive concept about which numerous legal battles have been fought. Historically, a major issue has been whether the holder's good faith should be determined by a subjective standard (what did the holder actually believe?)

or an objective standard (what would a reasonable person in the holder's circumstances have believed?). The Revision adopts the latter standard by including in Article 3 a ***special definition of good faith*** that requires "honesty in fact and the observance of reasonable commercial standards of fair dealing." U.C.C. § 3-103(a)(4). This is a ***change from prior law***, which applied a subjective test to good faith in the law of negotiable instruments. The new definition becomes objective by virtue of the reference to commercial standards. The same definition of good faith is incorporated into the revised version of Article 4. See U.C.C. § 4-104(c). Thus, for purposes of negotiable instruments, the Code now adopts the early English case of *Gill v. Cubitt*, 3 B. & C. 466, 107 Eng. Rep. 806 (K.B. 1824), which required that, in order to take commercial paper in "good faith," one must exercise "a proper and reasonable degree of caution necessary to preserve the interest of trade."

1. **Honesty in fact:** Prior to the Revision, Article 3 incorporated the general U.C.C. definition of good faith in U.C.C. § 1-201(19). This definition adopted a subjective standard by defining "good faith" as "honesty in fact in the conduct or transaction concerned." This definition has been called the test of the "pure heart and the empty head."

2. **Fair dealing vs. ordinary care:** Fair dealing, as required by Article 3, is not the same as exercising ordinary care or being ***nonnegligent***. The Comment to U.C.C. § 3-103 specifies that fair dealing "is concerned with the fairness of conduct rather than the care with which an act is performed. Failure to exercise ordinary care in conducting a transaction is an entirely different concept than failure to deal fairly in conducting the transaction."

B. **Objective element of prior test:** Even where good faith was defined subjectively, the concept necessarily incorporated an objective element in practice. Juries will often resolve the issue of what the holder actually knew or believed by asking what a reasonable person in the circumstances would have known or believed. Thus, the objective test may creep in through the back door. For instance, in *Funding Consultants v. Aetna Casualty & Surety Co.*, 187 Conn. 637, 447 A.2d 1163 (1982), the payee of a $68,000 note payable over four years negotiated it for $5,000 and a $35,000 note payable within a year. The Supreme Court of Connecticut directed the trial court to admit expert testimony to show what a reasonable commercial party would have paid for the note. The court concluded: "The price actually paid, the present value of the instrument actually bought, are elements which may be considered in determining a holder's good faith."

> **Example 1:** A woman representing herself to be Jones entered Brown's antique shop and offered to purchase a rare table for

$10,000. The woman offered to pay for the table by indorsing over to Brown a check drawn by Smith to the order of bearer in the amount of $10,000. Brown accepted the check without requesting any identification and released the table to the woman's possession without waiting for the check to clear. Brown now seeks to enforce the check against Smith, who alleges that the check was stolen and that the person purporting to be Jones was likely the thief. Even if Brown truly believed that the woman representing herself to be Jones was not misrepresenting her identity, Brown was under a duty of inquiry and cannot hold the check in good faith if reasonable commercial standards of the trade required him to investigate her identity before accepting the check.

Example 2: Jones owns an automobile dealership and finances purchases made by customers. Jones then discounts the promissory notes made by customers to First Bank. First Bank is aware that a large number of Jones' customers seek to avoid payment on their notes because of poor service they receive from Jones on their automobiles. Smith purchased an automobile from Jones with a small cash payment and a note, payable to the order of Jones, in the amount of $10,000. Jones immediately discounted the note with First Bank. Shortly thereafter, Smith's automobile broke down and Jones was unable to fix it properly. Smith seeks to avoid payment on the note. First Bank may still claim that it is a holder in due course as it took the note without any knowledge of defects in the particular auto. Smith may contend that First Bank knew that a large percentage of Jones' transactions ended in complaint. Whether or not First Bank took the note in good faith will depend on whether financers who are aware that their debtors engage in misconduct observe reasonable commercial standards by continuing to accept instruments from their debtors without determining that the debtor has properly performed under the contract giving rise to the instrument.

C. *Unico v. Owen:* Some courts, however, have expanded the concept of good faith in consumer transactions where there was a pre-existing relationship between the payee of a note and the holder to whom the note had been transferred. In *Unico v. Owen*, 50 N.J. 101, 232 A.2d 405 (1967), the maker of a note agreed to purchase 140 records for $698, payable in installments. The payee transferred the note to a company that had been organized to finance the transferor, that set policies and standards for the transferor, and that had agreed to accept a substantial quantity of the negotiable paper backed by such standards. The maker of the note ceased making payments because records that had been ordered did not arrive. The New Jersey Supreme Court refused to accord HDC status to the transferee under these circumstances on the grounds that it was so closely connected with the payee of the note that the payee's misconduct could be attributed to it.

V. REQUIREMENT THAT HDC TAKE WITHOUT NOTICE OF CERTAIN CIRCUMSTANCES [U.C.C. § 3-302(a)(2)(iii-vi)]

A. **Notice:**   In order to qualify as a HDC, a transferee cannot, at the time he or she takes the instrument, have notice of certain circumstances. These circumstances include that the instrument is overdue, that is, it has not been paid at maturity; that the instrument has been dishonored or that there is an uncured default with respect to payment of another instrument issued as part of the same series; that the instrument contains an unauthorized signature or alteration; that some other person is making a claim of a property or possessory right to the instrument or its proceeds; or that the obligor on the instrument has a defense or claim in recoupment against payment.

1. **Subjective or objective:** Notice involves a mixture of subjective and objective elements. Thus, the U.C.C. provides that a person has *notice of a fact* if he or she has *actual knowledge* of the fact, or has *received notification* of it, or from all the facts actually known at the time in question, *has reason to know* of the fact. U.C.C. § 1-201(25).

2. **When notice received:** A notice is effective to deny HDC status only if it is received at such time and in such manner as to permit the holder a *reasonable opportunity to act* on it. U.C.C. § 3-302(f).

3. **Taking the instrument:**   The relevant time at which to measure whether a holder has notice is at the time the holder "takes" the instrument. U.C.C. § 3-302(a)(2). Thus, one who takes an instrument and subsequently learns of a defense to it can still qualify as a HDC.

   Example: In return for Smith's promise to deliver furniture to her office, Jones negotiated to Smith a note made payable by Green to the order of Jones. After Smith delivered the furniture, but before the note was due, Smith read in the newspaper that Green had won a lawsuit against Jones in the transaction that gave rise to the issuance of the note. Smith may still enforce the note against Green, because Smith took the note without notice of Green's defense.

B. Notice that the instrument is overdue: The time when an instrument becomes overdue depends on whether it is a demand instrument or one payable at a definite time.

1. **Demand instrument:** A demand instrument becomes overdue at the earliest of the following:

   a. The day after the day demand for payment is duly made;

   b. In the case of a check, 90 days after its date; or

   c. In the case of a demand instrument other than a check, when the instrument has been outstanding for a period of time after its date which is unreasonably long under the circumstances of the particular case in light of the nature of the instrument and usage of trade. U.C.C. § 3-304(a).

   Example: On July 1, Smith issued a check in the amount of $250 and drawn on First Bank to Brown's order in return for some books. Brown negotiated the check to Black on September 28. Five days later, Black deposited the check in his account at Second Bank. First Bank received the check on October 5. First Bank paid the check over a stop payment order. The bank, however, can still charge Smith's account if it is a HDC. Smith may claim that First Bank cannot be a HDC because it paid a stale check when it took the check more than 90 days after its date. First Bank may respond that it acted immediately on receipt of the check. Nevertheless, it will not be able to assert the rights of a HDC because the instrument was overdue when it was negotiated to First Bank.

2. **Time instrument:** An instrument payable at a definite time becomes overdue in accordance with the following rules:

   a. If the principal is payable in installments and a due date has not been accelerated, the instrument becomes overdue on default for nonpayment of an installment;

   b. If the principal is not payable in installments and the due date has not been accelerated, the instrument becomes overdue on the day after the due date;

   c. If a due date with respect to principal has been accelerated, the instrument becomes overdue on the day after the accelerated due date. U.C.C. § 3-304(b).

C. Notice of claims and defenses: One cannot be a HDC if he or she takes the instrument with notice of competing claims to the instrument or defenses available against payment. Defenses for these purposes include both "real" defenses, such as infancy, duress, illegality, or fraud (U.C.C. § 3-305(a)(2)) and "personal" defenses such as nonissuance or a defense of the obligor that would be available if the person entitled to enforce the instrument were enforcing a right to payment under a simple contract. Claims for these purposes include possessory claims to the instrument or its proceeds and claims in recoupment under U.C.C. § 3-305(a)(3), in which the obligor claims that it is entitled to reduce the amount owed on the obligation. For further consequences of claims and defenses against one who does qualify as a HDC, see pp. 43-44, *infra*.

D. What does not constitute notice: Prior to the Revision of Article 3, the U.C.C. listed certain facts which were insufficient by themselves to provide the purchaser with notice of a defense or claim. U.C.C. PR § 3-304(4). Although the U.C.C. no longer contains a similar listing, there does not appear to be any intent to change the result that knowledge of these facts does not constitute notice of a defense. These facts include the following:

1. Knowledge that the instrument is *antedated* or *postdated*.

2. Knowledge that the instrument was issued or negotiated for an executory promise or agreement so long as the purchaser has no knowledge of an existing claim or defense.

3. Knowledge that the instrument was initially incomplete, unless the purchaser knows it has been improperly completed.

4. Knowledge that there has been default in the payment of interest on the instrument or in payment of another instrument that is not in the same series as the instrument in question.

5. In addition, purchasing an instrument at a substantial discount does not, of itself, constitute the absence of good faith or notice of suspicious circumstances that places the purchaser on a duty of inquiry. In *Northwestern National Insurance Co. v. Maggio*, 976 F.2d 320 (7th Cir. 1992), the court found that the purchase, in 1988, of a note due in 1990 at a discount of 50% did not deprive the purchaser of good faith or indicate that the purchaser was deliberately avoiding an inquiry, the results of which might indicate the existence of a defense by the note's maker. The court indicated that the discount might reflect a lack of the maker's creditworthiness or a fear by the purchaser that the maker would raise specious defenses to payment. Placing an obligation on the purchaser to investigate, the court concluded, would unjustifiably raise transaction costs in financial markets.

E. Irregular or incomplete instrument: A holder of an instrument cannot be a HDC if, at the time the instrument was issued or negotiated to the holder, the instrument bore such evidence of forgery or alteration or other irregularity or incompleteness as to call into question its authenticity.

1. **Authenticity:** Authenticity relates to the fact that the irregularity or incompleteness may indicate that the instrument is not what it purports to be.

2. **Irregular or incomplete instrument:** A person who takes an obviously irregular or incomplete instrument will not receive protection against defenses of the obligor or claims of third parties beyond what would be available to an obligee on a simple contract. Not every variation or marking on an instrument, however, renders it irregular.

> **Example 1:** Smith makes a note payable "90 days after the date hereof" to the order of Jones. The note bears the date January 3, 1996. There is an obvious erasure indicating that "1995" was changed to "1996." Jones sells the note to Brown. Brown does not have notice of a claim or defense as it is common to make such mistakes early in the year and the erasure would not arouse suspicion about the terms of the instrument.

> **Example 2:** *United States v. Hibernia Nat'l Bank*, 841 F.2d 592 (5th Cir. 1988) involved a check that contained the figure "24844 DOLLARS/50 CENTS" in the center of the check where words are typically used and the figure "$244844.50" on the right side of the check where figures are used. The court concluded that the former amount controlled, so that the check was valid for the smaller amount. The court further determined that if the amount of the check was ambiguous, the check was non-negotiable for failure to state a sum certain. In either event, a bank that paid the larger sum to the payee of the check was liable for the overpayment. The inconsistency of the words and figures was not an irregularity that would preclude a transferee from becoming a HDC because U.C.C. § 3-114 provides that, in the case of contradictory terms, words prevail over figures.

F. **Discharge:** Notice that a party has been discharged of its obligation on the instrument, other than a discharge in an insolvency proceeding, is not notice of a defense for purposes of barring a holder from becoming a HDC. Nevertheless, discharge is effective against a HDC who took the instrument with notice of the discharge. U.C.C. § 3-302(b).

> **Example:** Jones issued a check to Brown in connection with a sale of Brown's house to Jones. Jones obtained certification of the check before its delivery, an act that serves to discharge Jones from liability on the check. See U.C.C. § 3-414(c). Brown

negotiated the check to Smith. Smith would be aware that a party to the instrument, Jones, has been discharged. Smith could still be a HDC of the check, notwithstanding this knowledge. However, Smith's status as a HDC would not permit him to bring an action against Jones, free from the defense of discharge.

VI.   SPECIFIC TRANSACTIONS THAT AFFECT HDC STATUS

A. **Transactions outside the ordinary course of business:** Some holders who take an instrument for value, in good faith, and without notice, will still fail to become holders in due course. This is because they become holders under unusual circumstances in which the *law implies that they seek only to become successors to whatever interest their transferors had.* Typically, these involve situations in which it would be difficult to investigate the underlying transaction or the knowledge of all prior parties. These include purchase of an instrument through legal process, acquisition of the instrument through bankruptcy or other insolvency proceedings, or purchase of the instrument as part of a bulk transaction not in the transferor's ordinary course of business. U.C.C. § 3-302(c). If the transferor of the instrument was a HDC, however, the purchaser succeeds to the rights of a HDC through the shelter principle.

B. **The payee as a HDC:** Prior to enactment of the U.C.C., there was some debate as to whether a payee could be a HDC. The Code allows the payee to become a HDC, although a payee will rarely obtain substantial advantage from achieving that status because some of the major benefits of being a HDC apply only to claims or defenses that are raised "against a person other than the holder." U.C.C. § 3-302(b).

1. **"Other than the holder":** U.C.C. § 3-305(b) provides that the right of a HDC to enforce the obligation of a party to pay the instrument is not subject to the personal defenses stated in U.C.C. § 3-302(a)(2) or to claims in recoupment stated in U.C.C. § 3-302(a)(3). The HDC, however, takes the instrument free of those defenses and claims only where they arise from a transaction with a person "other than the holder." Thus, this provision permits an obligor to assert any defenses or claims against the person whose conduct gave rise to the defense or claim, even if that person qualifies as a HDC. Typically, this will include a payee on a draft. The payee may qualify as a HDC, but does not take free of personal defenses or claims in recoupment if the obligor's defense or claim arises out of the payee's conduct. Prior to the Revision, the U.C.C. attempted to

reach the same result by allowing a HDC to take free of defenses only when the defense arose from the conduct of a person *"with whom the holder has not dealt."* See U.C.C. PR § 3-305(2).

> **Example 1:** In *Eldon's Super Fresh Stores v. Merrill Lynch, Pierce, Fenner & Smith*, 296 Minn. 130, 207 N.W.2d 282 (1973), a drawer drew a check to the order of a stock broker for the purchase of stock for the drawer's account. The drawer gave the check to his agent for delivery to the stock broker. The agent gave the check to the broker, but stated that it was to pay for stock for the agent's own account. The brokerage used the check to purchase stock for the agent's account. The court held that the brokerage was a HDC who could take free of the drawer's defense. It had not dealt with the drawer and, thus, was not subject to the defense of wrongful delivery. The same result would be reached under Revised Article 3, because the defense arose out of conduct of someone "other than the holder."

> **Example 2:** Jones sells goods to Smith, but insists on a bank check in payment. Smith gives his personal check to First Bank in return for a cashier's check on which First Bank is the drawer, Smith is the remitter, and Jones is the payee. If, therefore, Smith's check to First Bank turns out to be no good, First Bank will not be able to resist payment on its cashier's check by asserting against Jones that it received no consideration. That personal defense did not arise from any conduct by Jones; thus, as long as she took the check for value, in good faith, and without notice of defenses, she is a HDC and can take free of defenses, even though she is a payee of the instrument.

VII. RIGHTS OF A HDC

A. **Introduction:** A HDC takes an instrument free from all claims to the instrument, claims in recoupment, and numerous defenses that can be asserted by other parties to the instrument. This will be the case even if the HDC's transferor was subject to claims or defenses. Thus, the HDC doctrine provides one of the few instances in which the law permits a transferee to obtain greater rights than those possessed by the transferor.

B. **Free from claims:** A HDC takes free of all claims of all property or possessory rights in the instrument or its proceeds. These include claims to rescind a negotiation or to recover the instrument or its proceeds. U.C.C. § 3-306.

> **Example:** Brown issued to Jones a note payable to "bearer" in the amount of $1,000 in return for Jones' rare book collection. Jones lost the note and it was found by Smith. Smith sold the note to Black who took it for value, in good faith, and without notice that it had been lost by Jones. Black is a HDC of the note and can resist any claim made by Jones for its return. In addition, any payment made by Brown to Jones will not be effective to discharge Brown of his maker's liability to Black. U.C.C. § 3-602.

C. **Free from personal defenses:** A HDC takes free of a variety of defenses asserted against parties other than the holder. U.C.C. § 3-305(b). These "personal" defenses of which a HDC takes free include defenses that arise from Article 3, such as nonissuance or breach of warranty when a draft is accepted, and defenses that would be available to the obligor if the HDC were enforcing a right to payment under a simple contract, such as lack of consideration, nondelivery, or conditional delivery of the goods for which the instrument was given. As a consequence of the doctrine, the HDC has no obligation and little incentive to investigate the transaction that gave rise to the instrument.

> **Example:** Jones purchased an automobile from Smith and issued a promissory note to Smith's order for $5,000, payable in 30 days. Smith was to deliver the automobile the nexst day after removing personal effects from it. Smith immediately gave the note to First Bank in satisfaction of Smith's debt to the bank in the amount of $5,500. Smith, however, never delivered the automobile to Jones. When First Bank presents the note for payment at maturity, Jones refuses to pay because she never received the agreed consideration. This defense is a personal one that is not effective against a HDC. Assuming that First Bank satisfies the requirements of U.C.C. § 3-302, First Bank may enforce the note against Jones.

D. **Free from claims in recoupment:** The Revision reclassifies some of the defenses that had been previously classified as personal defenses. These defenses are now termed "claims in recoupment." U.C.C. § 3-305(a)(3). The legal effect of these defenses, however, remains the same. A claim in recoupment exists where the underlying performance was defective, but still provided some value to the obligor. The claim in recoupment is stated in an amount equal to the ***difference in value between the promised performance and the actual performance.*** A HDC takes free of claims in recoupment that are stated against a person other than the holder.

Example 1: Jones purchased an automobile from Smith and issued a promissory note to Smith's order for $5,000, payable in 30 days. Smith had informed Jones that the automobile had 20,000 miles on it, as shown by the odometer. In fact, Smith had rolled back the odometer, and the car actually had been driven 50,000 miles. Thus, the car was only worth $3,000. Jones discovered the fraudulent misrepresentation and breach of express warranty when the car broke down three weeks after she purchased it. When Smith seeks to enforce the note against Jones, Jones may state a claim in recoupment to avoid payment of more than $5,000. Smith's misrepresentation prevents him from attaining the status of HDC. Even if he were a HDC (perhaps he had rolled back the odometer several years before and had forgotten), he would not take free of the claim in recoupment because he was the person whose conduct gave rise to the claim; thus, the claim would not be stated against a person "other than the holder."

Example 2: Jones purchased an automobile from Smith and issued a promissory note to Smith's order for $5,000, payable in 30 days. Smith immediately gave the note to First Bank in satisfaction of Smith's debt to the bank in the amount of $5,500. Smith had informed Jones that the automobile had 20,000 miles on it, as shown by the odometer. In fact, Smith had rolled back the odometer, and the car actually had been driven 50,000 miles. Thus, the car was only worth $3,000. Jones discovered the fraudulent misrepresentation and breach of express warranty when the car broke down three weeks after she purchased it. First Bank, which had no notice of the fraud, is a HDC and may recover the full $5,000 from Jones because the claim in recoupment is stated against Smith, a person other than the holder.

Example 3: Jones purchased 1,000 pounds of Grade A widgets from Green at $10 per pound and gave Green a check, payable to Green's order, for $10,000. On subsequent examination of the widgets, Jones realized that she had been given Grade B widgets, worth only $8,000. Jones stopped payment of the check and Green subsequently brought an action against her to recover on the instrument. Jones can assert a claim in recoupment against Green in the amount of $2,000. She can do so even though Green is a HDC of the check, since he is also the person against whom the underlying claim is stated. If Green had negotiated a check to First Bank in a manner that made First Bank a HDC, Jones would not be able to assert a successful claim in recoupment against First Bank, since it was not a party to the transaction that gave rise to the claim in recoupment.

E. Subject to real defenses: The HDC remains subject to a few defenses that have become known as "real" defenses. U.C.C. § 3-305(b). These defenses include the following:

1. *Infancy*, where it is a defense to a simple contract;

2. *Incapacity, duress, or illegality*, under circumstances that nullify the obligation of the obligor;

3. *Fraud in the factum*, where the obligor has been induced to sign the instrument with neither knowledge nor reasonable opportunity to learn of its character or its essential terms;

4. *Discharge* in insolvency proceedings.

> **Example 1:** Jones was not well versed in English and had previously asked Brown to help her with business transactions without adverse incident. Brown asked Jones to sign a paper that Brown represented was a receipt for certain goods that Jones had ordered and received. Jones signed the paper which was, in fact, a note payable to the order of Brown. Brown sold the note to Smith who took it for value, in good faith, and without notice of the underlying fraud. Smith attempts to enforce the note against Jones. Jones may defend on the grounds that she did not intend to sign such an instrument at all, even though Smith is a HDC. See *Schaeffer v. United Bank & Trust Co. of Maryland,* 360 A.2d 461 (Md. Ct. App.), *aff'd,* 370 A.2d 1138 (Md. 1977).

> **Example 2:** On similar facts, the court in *First National Bank v. Fazzari,* 10 N.Y.2d 394, 223 N.Y.S.2d 483, 179 N.E.2d 493 (1961), found that fraud in the factum existed. But the court also noted that the real defense would bar the HDC from recovery only if the maker of the note was not negligent. The court upheld a finding by the court below that the maker, who was unable to read or write English, was negligent in failing to ask his wife to read the instrument before he signed it.

5. **Burden of establishing:** If a defense exists, a person claiming to take free of the defense has the burden of establishing his status as a HDC or his rights under the shelter principle as the successor to a HDC. U.C.C. § 3-308(b).

6. **Effect of other law:** The effect of a defense on the rights of the HDC may depend on the underlying state law with respect to the facts that give rise to the defense. Where the party against whom the instrument is to be enforced asserts a defense of incapacity,

duress, or illegality, and state law renders an obligation *void* under these circumstances, a HDC who takes an instrument will be subject to the defense. If state law renders the obligation merely *voidable*, however, these defenses cannot be successfully asserted against a HDC.

> **Example 1:** In order to start his new business, Brown took out two loans. He borrowed $10,000 from Jones and issued to her order his promissory note, which provided that its terms were governed by the laws of state A. He borrowed $10,000 from Smith and issued to his order a promissory note, which provided that its terms were governed by the laws of state B. Both Jones and Smith discounted their notes with First Bank. Both notes provided for usurious interest rates. The law of state A declares obligations with usurious interest rates to be nullities. The law of state B declares that obligees on such notes may recover the principal, but no interest. First Bank may be a HDC of both notes, but is subject to the real defense of illegality with respect to the note issued to Jones and governed by the law of state A.

> **Example 2:** Jones lost a bet with Brown and issued Brown her note in lieu of immediate payment. Brown sold the note to Smith, who took it for value, in good faith, and without notice that it had arisen from a gambling contract. The law of the state in which these transactions occurred declare obligations arising from gambling contracts to be null and void. When Smith seeks to enforce the note against Jones, she can defend on the grounds of illegality since state law renders the underlying transaction a nullity and not simply voidable.

7. **Justifications for real defenses:** There exist a variety of rationales for requiring a HDC to take subject to the real defenses, even though the HDC takes free of other defenses and claims. One rationale is simply *paternalism*, i.e., the desire to protect certain classes of parties, such as infants and incompetents, from their own misconduct, even though the effect is to reduce the certainty of negotiable instrument transactions. A second rationale is that in some of these transactions, there is a substantial likelihood that the person attempting to enforce the contract has *notice of the underlying defect*, but actual proof of that notice is difficult, and it saves judicial time and expense to make the investigation unnecessary. Third, it may be that enforcement of the obligation by a HDC *creates costs that offset the benefits* of the HDC doctrine. For instance, we may desire to deter illegal transactions by making instruments that arise from them unenforceable, even though doing so reduces the certainty of negotiable instrument transactions.

VIII.RIGHTS OF A HOLDER WHO IS NOT A HDC

A. **General limitation:** Generally a holder who does not qualify as a HDC takes no greater rights than his transferor had. Recall that under the *shelter principle* of U.C.C. § 3-203, however, the transferee of a HDC can obtain the rights (though not the status) of a HDC. (Of course, a transferee who satisfies the requirements of U.C.C. § 3-302 becomes a HDC in his or her own right.) There is some limit to this principle. A transferee may improve his or her position as a prior holder, as long as the transferee did not actually engage in fraud or illegality. The fact that the transferee, as a prior holder, had notice of such activity will not preclude the transferee from taking the right of a HDC under the shelter principle. This was not the case prior to the Revision. See U.C.C. PR § 3-201(1).

> **Example 1:** Jones issued a note payable to the order of Brown as consideration for a car sold by Brown to Jones. Brown sold the note to Black, who took it for value, in good faith, and without notice of any claim or defense. Black gave the note to his daughter as a gift. Jones sought to avoid payment to the daughter on the grounds that the car failed to perform as warranted. Although the daughter is not a HDC in her own right, because she gave no value for the note, she can enforce the note free of the breach of warranty claim, as she takes Black's rights and those include his rights as a HDC.

> **Example 2:** Same as above, but Brown knew at the time he sold the car that it would not operate as warranted. Brown subsequently purchased the note from Black, to whom he had negotiated it. Brown cannot improve his position by virtue of Black's status as a HDC because he was a party to the fraud that gave rise to the defense that Jones will assert against him. This doctrine prevents collusion between Black and Brown to increase a wrongdoer's rights against an obligor.

B. **Claims and defenses:**　One who is not a HDC, of course, has no greater rights than a HDC, and therefore takes an instrument subject to the real defenses that would apply to a HDC. In addition, one who does not have the rights of a HDC, either in his or her own capacity or under the shelter principle, takes the instrument subject to the following:

1. *Valid claims* to it and claims in recoupment on the part of others;

2. Any *defense* that would be available in an action on a *simple contract*;

3. The defenses of *failure or want of* consideration, failure of delivery or of a condition precedent;

4. The defense that the *chain of title was broken* by a thief; or

5. Defenses that *arise from Article 3*, such as nonissuance or conditional issuance.

C. Valid claims by another person: Any person who takes an instrument is subject both to valid claims of the true owner to the instrument (whether in the nature of a property or possessory right) and the proceeds of the instrument. Such claims may include a claim to rescind a negotiation and to recover the instrument and its proceeds. U.C.C. § 3-306.

1. **Elimination of claim by payment to holder:** Recall, however, that even a true owner may not have a valid claim for the return of bearer paper. A claim may be effectively nullified if the payor pays the holder rather than the true owner, for the payor will then be discharged on the obligation and will have no further liability to the true owner. The possessor of bearer paper will be a holder, U.C.C. § 1-201(20), and the holder will be a person entitled to enforce the instrument, U.C.C. § 3-301.

2. *Jus tertii* -- **Asserting the rights of a third party:** As a general matter, an obligor may not assert against a person entitled to enforce the instrument a defense, claim, or claim in recoupment of another person. The U.C.C., however, provides a remedy to the claimant who acts expeditiously. If one who claims the instrument *joins an action* to enforce the instrument and *personally asserts the claim* against the person entitled to enforce the instrument, the obligor may use the claimant's assertion to resist payment to the party entitled to enforce. U.C.C. § 3-305(c). Note, however, that the language of U.C.C. § 3-305(c) purports to cover *only property or possessory claims* to the instrument, not defenses or claims in recoupment.

> **Example 1:** Jones purchased an automobile from Brown and indorsed to Brown a cashier's check made payable to Jones and issued by First Bank. Jones learned that the automobile was defective before Brown cashed the check. Brown is a holder of the check, but if he knew of the defect at the time he sold the automobile, he cannot be a HDC. Brown can enforce the cashier's check against First Bank, even if Jones has a right to rescind her negotiation of the check to Brown, since First Bank may not assert Jones' claim against Brown. If Jones joins the action brought by Brown against First Bank, however, First Bank may pay the amount of the check into court and permit the

court to determine whether Brown or Jones is entitled to the proceeds.

> **Example 2:** In *Fulton National Bank v. Delco Corp.*, 128 Ga. App. 16, 195 S.E.2d 455 (1973), a remitter gave plaintiff a bank check in payment of a franchise fee. The remitter subsequently requested the bank to stop payment on the check, which it did. The remitter undertook to defend for the bank and claimed that the franchise agreement was never consummated. The court held that the remitter could intervene only if he had a valid claim to the instrument and not if he had a mere defense to its payment. The court interpreted the U.C.C. to include as a "claim" both rescission of a prior negotiation and a claim to either an uncashed check or the fund represented by a check that arose from the negotiation.

D. Indemnity or injunction: U.C.C. § 3-602(b)(1)(i) permits the adverse claimant to obtain an injunction to prevent the obligor from obtaining a discharge by making payment to the holder.

   1. Lost or stolen instrument: An obligor is not required to pay an instrument to one who does not have the rights of a HDC if the obligor proves that the instrument is a lost or stolen instrument. U.C.C. § 3-305(c). Thus, although the finder of a bearer instrument will be a holder of that instrument, he or she will not be a HDC of the instrument and cannot require the obligor to pay. That finder, however, may be able to negotiate the instrument to a HDC, who will be able to enforce it against the obligor.

E. Bad faith payment: Even though payment to a person entitled to enforce the instrument generally results in a discharge of the obligor, see p. 42, *supra,* the payor will not be discharged if he or she makes payment knowing that payment is prohibited by a judicial injunction or similar process arising out of a competing claim to the instrument; or, in the case of a check other than a cashier's check, teller's check, or bank check, the payor accepted indemnity against loss resulting from refusal to pay the person entitled to enforce the instrument; or, the person making payment knows that the instrument has been stolen and pays a person known to be in wrongful possession of the instrument. U.C.C. § 3-602(b).

F. Burden of establishing: Even where the holder is not a HDC, the obligor has the burden of establishing the defenses that would permit nonpayment. U.C.C. §§ 3-305, Official Comment 4; 3-308(b).

G. Conditions precedent: A holder other than a HDC takes the instrument subject to any condition precedent to payment. Where enforcement is sought against a drawer or indorser, the relevant conditions precedent to payment include dishonor and notice of dishonor. A holder who has satisfied these conditions should make a specific pleading to that effect.

H. Alteration: One who is not a holder in due course also takes an instrument subject to the defense that it has been *altered* in a manner that discharges a party to the instrument.

1. **Scope of alteration:** An alteration is *any unauthorized change* in an instrument that purports to modify in any respect the obligation of a party, or an unauthorized addition of words or numbers or other change to an incomplete instrument that affects the obligation of a party. U.C.C. § 3-407(a). Unlike the prior version of the Code, the Revision does not require a change to an instrument to be "material" to qualify as an alteration. In addition, the effect of an alteration is the same regardless of who makes the alteration. Prior to the Revision, a material alteration made by someone other than the holder had consequences different from those that resulted from alteration by the holder.

2. **Discharge:** An alteration that is *fraudulently made* will discharge a party whose obligation is affected by the alteration. Discharge does not occur, however, if that party either assented to the alteration or is precluded from asserting it. U.C.C. § 3-407(b). Discharge is a personal defense, and, therefore, will only be effective against a person entitled to enforce the instrument who does not have the rights of a HDC.

   Example 1: Jones purchased a computer from Brown for an agreed price of $1,000. Jones gave Brown her personal check, filled out to include the numbers $1000.00 on the right hand side of the check. Jones forgot, however, to write the words "One thousand" in the center of the check. Brown noticed the omission, and wrote the words "One thousand." This addition could be construed not to be an alteration by Brown, since one may infer that it was an authorized addition and it did not purport to modify the obligation of a party. Arguably, Jones was already liable on the instrument as a result of the numbers. In any event, any alteration was not made with intent to defraud. Thus, the addition of the words by Brown does not discharge Jones of her obligation on the instrument.

   Example 2: Smith issued Jones a note payable to the order of Jones in the amount of $1,000. Smith neglected to complete that part of the instrument that called for an interest rate. Jones subsequently filled in that part of the instrument with an interest rate of 8%, which was the interest rate on which Jones and

Smith had agreed. Brown stole the note from Jones and fraudulently raised the amount to $10,000. Brown then negotiated the note to Jones, who took it for value, in good faith, and without notice of the alteration. Smith has not been discharged from his original $1,000 obligation. The completion of the note with the interest rate was not fraudulent. The alteration of the amount, although fraudulent, does not discharge Smith with respect to his obligation on the original terms of the instrument as against one who took the instrument for value, in good faith, and without notice of the alteration. U.C.C. § 3-407(c).

IX. ABROGATION OF HOLDER IN DUE COURSE DOCTRINE

A. **Motive for rule:** Consumers who purchase on credit are unlikely to be aware of their inability to assert defenses against a holder in due course when the goods that were received for the instrument turn out to be defective. In addition, consumers, who will likely purchase goods only occasionally from the same seller, typically are ***not in as good a position to monitor*** the performance of a seller as a financer who maintains a continuing relationship with the seller. Both these reasons suggest that financers who systematically purchase instruments from a seller should not be able to utilize the HDC doctrine to avoid valid defenses that consumers would otherwise have against sellers.

B. **FTC Rule:** The Federal Trade Commission has adopted a regulation, 16 C.F.R. § 433, that eliminates the holder in due course doctrine in ***consumer transactions*** where the holder of a note is a creditor who is affiliated with the seller by common control, contract, or business arrangement, or to whom the consumer is referred by the seller.

1. **Notice:** The regulation requires any seller who takes or receives a credit contract arising out of a consumer transaction to provide notice to the buyer that any holder of the contract is ***subject to all claims and defenses*** that the buyer could assert against the seller.

   Example: Smith purchases an automobile from Jones's auto dealership for $10,000. Smith intends to use the automobile only for personal purposes. In return for the automobile, Smith pays Jones $2,000 in cash and gives Jones a promissory note payable to the order of Jones in the amount of $8,000. Jones negotiates the note to First Bank. First Bank has a long-standing arrangement with Jones by which it finances her purchases of automobiles from the manufacturer and accepts all notes made payable to her from customers. The note taken by Jones must comply with the FTC regulation, as Jones is affiliated with First Bank through a business arrangement.

2. **Close-connectedness doctrine:** The FTC Rule is an application of a doctrine that some courts applied under common law reasoning to find exceptions to the HDC doctrine. Under these decisions, the benefits of the doctrine were denied to holders who were "closely connected" with the payee of the instrument, typically by serving as the financing arm of the payee. Most of the decisions that adopted the "closely connected" doctrine involved consumer transactions. See, e.g., *Unico v. Owen*, 50 N.J. 101, 232 A.2d 405 (1967). Although "close connectedness" has been raised in some commercial cases, it is usually rejected in that context. See *Leasing Service Corp. v. River City Construction, Inc.*, 743 F.2d 871 (11th Cir. 1984).

X.   THE FEDERAL GOVERNMENT AS A HOLDER IN DUE COURSE

A. **Federal agencies and bank failures:** In recent years, the large number of failures of financial institutions has required federal agencies, primarily the Federal Deposit Insurance Corporation and the Resolution Trust Corporation, to seize these institutions. The federal agency has a series of options with respect to failed institutions. It can become the receiver of the institution and sell its assets; it can arrange a purchase of the institution by a more solvent one, with the acquiring bank assuming the liabilities of the failed institution; it can infuse funds into the insolvent institution. Regardless of its choice, the agency may want to enforce the instruments that serve as part of the assets of the failed institution or include them in a purchase and assumption transaction. Those instruments will have greater value if the federal agency can enforce those instruments as, and pass on the rights of, a holder in due course. Federal agencies cannot attain the status of a HDC, however, since they assume the obligations of the failed institution as part of a bulk transaction not in the ordinary course of business of the transferor. U.C.C. § 3-302(c)(ii). Nevertheless, both court decisions and legislation essentially grant the federal agencies many of the same rights that apply to a HDC under the U.C.C.

1. **Federal holder in due course doctrine:** The federal agency may take advantage of a judicially created federal holder in due course doctrine that permits it a complete defense to state and common law fraud claims acquired by the agency in the execution of a purchase and assumption transaction. The doctrine applies if the agency takes the instrument for value, in good faith, and without actual knowledge of the alleged fraud at the time it enters into the

purchase and assumption transaction. See *First City, Texas – Beaumont v. Treece,* 848 F. Supp. 727 (E.D. Tex. 1994). Some courts have held, however, that the doctrine is only available when the federal agency acts in its corporate capacity to effect a purchase and assumption transaction, and not when it acts as a receiver to liquidate the assets of the failed institution.

> The use of "federal common law" has been limited by the recent Supreme Court decision *O'Melveny & Myers v. FDIC,* 114 S. Ct. 2048 (1994). That case held that courts should apply federal common law only where state law causes "significant conflict with an identifiable federal policy or interest." The Court disapproved the use of federal common law to augment a "comprehensive and detailed" statutory scheme. In *Resolution Trust Corp. v. A. W. Assocs., Inc.,* 869 F. Supp. 1503 (D. Kan. 1994), the court concluded that *O'Melveny* precluded application of a federal holder in due course doctrine to the FDIC.

2. **The *D'Oench, Duhme* doctrine:** A federal agency may also take advantage of a doctrine articulated by the Supreme Court in *D'Oench, Duhme & Co. v. FDIC,* 315 U.S. 447 (1942). In that case, the Court fashioned a rule that prohibits an obligor on an instrument held by a failed institution from asserting against the FDIC any secret or unwritten agreement as a defense to enforcement of the obligation. Thus, an agreement between the failed bank and an obligor that a note would not be called will not be enforceable once the note has been taken by the federal agency.

> Because the doctrine elaborates the statutory powers of the FDIC, its vitality is also called into question by the Supreme Court's decision in *O'Melveny & Myers, supra.* In *Murphy v. FDIC,* ___ F. 3d ___ (D.C. Cir. 1995), the court held that, under the guidelines of *O'Melveny,* the statute granting rights to the FDIC was sufficiently comprehensive and detailed to preclude overlapping federal common law defenses, such as the *D'Oench, Duhme* doctrine.

3. **Section 1823(e):** Congress has codified the primary principles of the *D'Oench, Duhme* doctrine in 12 U.S.C. § 1823(e). That provision requires agreements which "tend to diminish or defeat . . . interests" of the FDIC to be in writing, executed contemporaneously with the acquisition of the asset by the bank, approved by the bank's board of directors, and maintained as an official record of the bank. If there is any deviation from these standards, the agreement will not be enforceable as against the federal agency.

CHAPTER 4

LIABILITIES OF PARTIES: CONTRACT LIABILITY, WARRANTY LIABILITY, AND CONVERSION

I. THE NATURE OF CONTRACT LIABILITY

A. Promise to pay: Each party to an instrument agrees to pay the holder of the instrument under specific conditions and in accordance with the *capacity in which that party* has signed the instrument, *e.g.*, as drawer, maker, or indorser. As the contract made by each of these parties varies, it is essential to determine the capacity in which each party has signed.

    1. Signature requirement: No contract liability applies, however, unless the signature of the person against whom enforcement is sought *appears on the instrument* or the person is represented by an agent or representative and the agent or representative has made a signature on the instrument that is binding on the person. U.C.C. § 3-401(a).

B. Valid signature: A person signs an instrument by making any symbol intending to *authenticate the writing* to which the symbol is attached. U.C.C. § 1-201(39). A *signature*, therefore, need not consist of the signer's actual name. U.C.C. § 3-401(b). The signature may be made manually or through a device or machine and by any name or mark that the signer chooses to use. All that is necessary is that there be a *present intention on the part of the person that the writing be authenticated*.

    Example 1: Smith, as maker, typed a promise to pay $100 to Brown's order on July 1, 1990, on a piece of Smith's personal stationery. Smith did not sign the writings but intended it to constitute his binding promise to pay. The letterhead on Smith's stationery may serve as his signature and the writing may constitute a negotiable instrument.

    Example 2: Smith, as maker, typed a promise to pay $100 to Brown's order on July 1, 1990, on a blank piece of paper. Smith typed his name at the bottom of the writing and did not otherwise sign it, but intended it to constitute his binding promise to pay. The typing of his name may serve as his signature and the writing may constitute a negotiable instrument.

1. **Signature of another:** An unauthorized signature in another's name is ***wholly ineffective*** as that of the person whose name is signed unless he ratifies it or is precluded from denying it. U.C.C. § 3-403(a).

2. **Effect of unauthorized signature on signer:** A signature in another's name, however, does operate as the ***valid signature of the unauthorized signer*** in favor of any person who pays the instrument or takes it for value. U.C.C. § 3-403(a).

   Example: Jones made a promissory note to the order of Smith in return for Smith's law books. Brown stole the note from Smith prior to the time Smith indorsed it. Brown forged Smith's indorsement on the back of the note and transferred it to Green in return for Green's promise to mow Brown's lawn. After Green mowed Brown's lawn, she attempted to enforce the note against Smith on the forged indorsement of his name. Smith is not liable on the note as the forgery of his name is wholly inoperative as his signature. Thus, his signature does not appear on the note. Green may, however, enforce the note against Brown, as his forgery of Smith's signature constitutes Brown's own signature, even though his actual name appears nowhere on the note. Keep in mind that if Green had attempted to enforce the note against Brown prior to mowing his lawn, Brown would be able to claim that Green's promise to mow the lawn was only executory and that she had given no value for it.

3. **Presumption:** A signature on an instrument is ***deemed admitted*** unless specifically denied in the pleadings. If the validity of a signature is denied in the pleadings, the person claiming validity has the burden of establishing validity. The signature is presumed to be authentic and authorized, except in a case where the action is to enforce the liability of a purported signer who is dead or incompetent at the time of trial of the issue of validity. U.C.C. § 3-308(a).

C. **Signature by representative:** Once it is established that an agency relationship exists, two issues remain. The first is whether the representative or agent is ***personally liable***, notwithstanding his or her agency status. The second is whether the ***principal is bound*** by the agent's signature.

1. **Power to sign:** A signature may be made by an agent or other representative of the party whose name appears on the instrument. The power to sign may be express, implied, or apparent, and may be established in accordance with agency law.

2. **Liability of principal:** If the representative signs an instrument by signing either the name of the represented party (the principal)

or the representative's own name, the represented party is bound by the signature to the same extent as he or she would be on a simple contract under general *principles of agency law*. U.C.C. § 3-402(a). This result applies even where the agent has not disclosed the name of the principal. Prior to the Revision, however, an undisclosed principal did not have liability on an instrument.

> **Example:** Jones was in need of money, but did not want her creditors to know of her situation. She authorized Smith to borrow $1,000 from Brown and to sign an instrument evidencing the indebtedness. Brown loaned the money to Smith, who signed only his name to the instrument and did not indicate his agency status. Smith turned the money over to Jones. Before the note became due, Smith became insolvent and Brown discovered that Smith had served as agent for Jones. Brown can enforce the note against Jones, since Smith's signature was an authorized signature of Jones.

3. **Liability of representative:** An agent or representative may also become personally liable on the instrument. An agent avoids liability by signing in a manner that shows *unambiguously* that the signature is made on behalf of the represented person identified in the instrument. The agent is personally liable, however, if either the signature does not unambiguously show representative capacity, or if the represented person is not identified in the instrument.

   a. **Scope of liability:** In both cases (failure to show representative capacity and failure to identify the represented person), the representative is liable to a HDC who took the instrument without notice that the representative was not intended to be liable. The representative may, where the person seeking to enforce the instrument is not a HDC, prove that the original parties to the instrument did not intend the representative to be liable on it. The liability of the representative occurs even though the representative was authorized to act for the representative person.

   b. **Parol evidence:** Presumably, parol evidence is admissible for the purpose of showing the intent of the original parties to the instrument.

   > **Example 1:** Jones employed Smith to serve as her agent for purposes of indorsing checks and depositing them in Jones's checking account. Jones received a check from Brown and gave it to Smith for deposit. Smith indorsed the check by signing "Smith" on the back and depositing the check in Jones's account. Smith may be personally obligated as an indorser on the instrument.

Example 2: Jones employed Smith to serve as her agent for purposes of indorsing checks and depositing them in Jones' checking account. Jones received a check from Brown and gave it to Smith for deposit. Smith indorsed the check by signing "Jones by Smith, Agent" and deposited the check in Jones' account. Smith is not personally obligated on the instrument. Jones is obligated on the instrument even though she never personally affixed her signature to it.

Example 3: Jones employed Smith to serve as her agent for purposes of indorsing checks and depositing them in Jones' checking account. Jones received two checks from Brown and gave them to Smith for deposit. Smith indorsed one as "Smith, Agent," the second as "Jones, Smith." In each case, Smith is liable to a HDC who had no notice of the arrangement between Jones and Smith. In the first case, Smith has not identified the represented person in the instrument. In the second case, there is no unambiguous statement of representative capacity. If a person who does not qualify as a HDC is attempting to enforce the instrument, however, Smith can prove that the original parties to the instrument did not intend for him to be liable.

c. **Business Expectations Rule:** In *Valley National Bank, Sunnymead v. Cook*, 136 Ariz. 232, 665 P.2d 576 (1983), a company treasurer signed and issued checks that were negotiated to Bank. When Bank could not collect the checks, it sought recovery against the treasurer. The checks failed to indicate the office held by the treasurer. The court, however, looked to the entire instrument for evidence of the signer's capacity. The checks were imprinted with the corporate name at the top and above the signature line. The court concluded that the business expectations of the transferee of such a check would be that only the corporation was liable. Therefore, the court determined that the treasurer was not personally liable. The ***Revision adopts this rule*** in the case of a check. If a representative signs his or her name as drawer, but does not indicate representative capacity, the signer still will not be personally liable if (i) the signature was authorized, (ii) the check is payable from the account of the represented person, and (iii) the represented person is identified on the check. U.C.C. § 3-402(c). These conditions will typically be satisfied where a ***corporate officer*** signs a corporate check as drawer, even though the officer does not indicate representative capacity.

D. Ambiguous capacity: If the capacity in which a party has signed the instrument is unclear, the signature is construed as an indorsement. U.C.C. § 3-204(a).

II. CONTRACT LIABILITY OF ISSUER OR ACCEPTOR

A. Issuer liability: The issuer of a note or of a cashier's check (or other draft drawn on the drawer) is the person primarily liable on the instrument. Thus, an issuer agrees to pay the note according to its terms at the time it was issued or first came into possession of a holder or, in the case of an incomplete instrument, at the time it was effectively completed in accordance with Article 3. The issuer owes this obligation to a person entitled to enforce the instrument or to an indorser who properly pays the instrument. U.C.C. § 3-412.

1. **Person entitled to enforce:** A person entitled to enforce the instrument includes the holder of the instrument; a nonholder who is in possession of the instrument and who has the rights of a holder, such as under the shelter principle; and a person who is not in possession of the instrument but who can demonstrate that the instrument was lost or stolen. U.C.C. § 3-301.

2. **Incomplete instrument:** If the instrument is not completed in accordance with the maker's authorization, the completion is treated as an alteration. U.C.C. § 3-407. The burden of establishing that words or numbers were added to an incomplete instrument without authority is on the person who asserts the absence of authority. U.C.C. § 3-115(d).

3. **Joint and several liability:** Where there are numerous makers or acceptors on an instrument, they are jointly and severally liable for the full amount, unless the instrument provides otherwise. U.C.C. § 3-116(a). Any jointly and severally liable party who pays the instrument is entitled to receive from any other such party contribution for pro rata shares of the payment. *Discharge* of one jointly and severally liable party does not effect the right of contribution. U.C.C. § 3-116(c).

4. **Cashier's checks:** The liability of an issuer of a cashier's check, or other draft drawn on the drawer, is the same as the liability of the issuer of a note. U.C.C. § 3-412.

B. Acceptor's liability: An acceptor of a draft is obliged to pay the draft in accordance with its terms at the time it was accepted; or, if the acceptance varies the terms of the draft, according to its terms as varied; or, if the acceptance was of an incomplete draft, as it was completed in accordance with Article 3. The acceptor owes this obligation to a person entitled to enforce the instrument or to a drawer or indorser who properly pays the instrument. U.C.C. § 3-413.

C. **What constitutes acceptance:** A draft is accepted when the drawee signs it, intending to honor it as presented. In order to be effective, the acceptance must be ***written on the draft*** and must be accompanied by delivery or notification that acceptance has occurred. U.C.C. § 3-419(a).

1. **Check not an assignment:** Because a drawee is not obligated on an instrument until acceptance, it is not required to pay out any funds prior to that time. Thus, the holder of an unaccepted check is not entitled to funds maintained by the drawee on behalf of the drawer. The U.C.C. codifies this principle by stating that a check does not of itself operate as an assignment of any funds in the hands of the drawee. U.C.C. § 3-408. A contrary rule would subject the drawee to liability if the drawer issued drafts in excess of the amount on deposit.

2. **"Of itself":** Admission of other facts: Nevertheless, other facts may indicate an agreement to hold funds for, or assign funds to, a particular holder of a draft.

    Example 1: Smith drew a check on his account in First Bank to the order of Jones for $1,000. Jones took the check to First Bank and attempted to cash it. First Bank determined that Smith only had $500 in his account and refused to honor the check, even for $500. First Bank has no liability on the instrument to Jones as it has not accepted the check.

    Example 2: Smith drew a check on his account in First Bank to the order of Jones for $1,000. Prior to taking the check to First Bank, Jones called the Bank to inquire whether Smith had sufficient funds in his account to cover the $1,000 check. An authorized representative of First Bank correctly told Jones that Smith's balance was sufficient to cover the check. The representative also told Jones that the Bank would not allow any other checks to be debited against Smith's account until she arrived with the $1,000 check. Between the time of the conversation and the time Jones arrived at the Bank, however, another check drawn by Smith was presented at and paid by the Bank with the result that Smith's account balance fell below $1,000. Jones may contend that the conversation with the Bank representative constituted an assignment of the funds in Smith's account to her, and that the Bank is therefore liable, even though the Bank had not accepted the check.

3. **Certification:** One way that a drawee can accept a check is to certify it. A certified check is one accepted by the bank on which it is drawn. U.C.C. § 3-409(b). Certification indicates that the funds are available for its payment on proper presentment. Thus, the certifying drawee typically will freeze funds in the drawer's account in the amount of the certified check.

   a. **Primary liability:** Even if the customer subsequently withdraws funds, leaving an insufficient amount to pay the check on presentment, the drawee remains primarily liable as an acceptor. Thus, where a draft is accepted by a bank, the drawer is discharged. U.C.C. § 3-414(c). Under the revision, this result applies regardless of by whom the acceptance was obtained. Prior to the Revision, discharge occurred only if a holder obtained the acceptance. Under the Revision, a drawer who obtains certification can discharge herself from her contract as drawer of the instrument (see *infra*).

   b. **No obligation:** The drawee, however, has no obligation to certify a check. Refusal to certify does not constitute dishonor of a check. U.C.C. § 3-409(d).

4. **Personal money orders and acceptance:** A personal money order may be viewed as a single deposit checking account. The purchaser, or remitter, deposits with the bank a sum of money and receives in return the money order in the amount of the deposit (less a small fee). Thus, the bank has the opportunity to obtain and set aside sufficient funds to ensure that the personal money order will be paid when presented to the bank, as the bank would do when it certifies a check. The bank will typically imprint the amount of the money order on the face of the instrument. The bank's name may also be pre-printed on the form. The remitter typically will sign the personal money order, but bank officials typically do not. This raises the issue of whether a personal money order is accepted by the bank on issuance, as its "signature" arguably does not appear on the instrument. Given the broad definition of "signed" in U.C.C. § 1-201(39), however, it would appear appropriate to hold that the bank's "signature" consists of imprinting the amount of the check, or that issuing it (an act that involves voluntary delivery) with the bank's name on it involves an intent to authenticate the writing.

   a. ***Sequoyah State Bank* case:** The court in *Sequoyah State Bank v. Union National Bank*, 274 Ark. 1, 621 S.W.2d 683 (1981) went even further. It held that a personal money order was authenticated from the time of issuance because the bank's printed name evidenced an intent to be bound thereby. The problem with that rationale is that, taken at face value, it would provide that even blank money order forms that contain the pre-printed name of the issuing bank have been "signed." Courts finding a "signature" in the pre-printed check alone seem to be motivated by a belief that the public treats personal money orders like cashier's checks or other cash equivalents. These courts are reluctant to permit the bank issuing a personal money order to avoid payment on the instrument. This same result could be achieved, however, by holding that the money order is accepted, and the bank's authenticating signature is affixed, when the money order is issued.

    b. No acceptance: Other courts, however, have refused to find that the issuing bank has signed a personal money order or otherwise accepted it until there has been some act in addition to issuance. The leading case in this line is *Garden Check Cashing Service, Inc. v. First National City Bank*, 25 A.D.2d 137, 267 N.Y.S.2d 698 (1966), aff'd 18 N.Y.2d 941, 223 N.E.2d 566, 277 N.Y.S.2d 141 (1966).

  5. Acceptance varying draft: If the drawee's acceptance varies in any manner the draft as presented, the holder may ***refuse the acceptance*** and treat the draft as dishonored. U.C.C. § 3-410(a).

    a. Cancellation: If, after being notified that drawee's acceptance varied from the terms of the draft, the holder elects to consider the draft dishonored, the drawee may cancel its acceptance.

    b. Discharge: If the holder assents to an acceptance that varies the terms of the draft, any drawer or indorser who does not also assent to the variation is ***discharged***.

III. CONTRACT LIABILITY OF DRAWER AND INDORSER

A. Secondary parties: Prior to the Revision, a drawer or indorser was known as a "secondary party" to the instrument. While this phrase does not appear in the Revision, its effect remains. Basically, secondary liability means that these parties are not the primary sources to which the holder looks for payment. Instead, they are ***required to pay the instrument only if it is dishonored*** by the party who is primarily liable. U.C.C. PR § 3-102(1)(d).

B. Contract of drawer: The drawer of a draft agrees that if the drawee ***dishonors*** the draft, the drawer will pay it according to its terms at the time it was issued; when it first came into the possession of a holder; or in the case of an incomplete instrument, according to its terms as completed in accordance with Article 3. The obligation is owed to a person entitled to enforce the draft or to an indorser who properly pays it. U.C.C. § 3-414(b).

> **Example:** Smith drew a check on his account at First Bank to the order of Jones in the amount of $100 in return for some law books. Jones indorsed the check and deposited it in her account at Second Bank. Second Bank permitted Jones to withdraw the funds shortly after the deposit, thus giving value for the check. Second Bank presented the check to First Bank for payment, and was informed that Smith had insufficient funds in his account to pay the check. Second Bank sued Smith on the instrument. Smith defended by claiming that the books were missing important chapters. Second Bank, having given value for the check, is a HDC and is entitled to the amount of the check on Smith's contract as drawer.

1. **Notice of dishonor:** As a general matter, a notice of dishonor is ***not a prerequisite*** to enforcement of an instrument against a drawer. Under the Revision, notice of dishonor must be given ***only to indorsers*** on whom the holder seeks to impose liability and to drawers whose draft has been accepted by a party other than a bank. Recall that if the draft is accepted by a bank, the drawer is discharged.

2. **Disclaimer:** A drawer may disclaim its contract liability by drawing ***"without recourse."*** No disclaimer is permitted, however, in the case of a ***check***. U.C.C. § 3-414(e). Allowing a disclaimer could leave no one liable on such an instrument, since the drawee is not liable until acceptance, and such an instrument would have no commercial purpose.

C. **Contract of indorser:** The indorser of an instrument agrees that if the drawee ***dishonors*** the draft, the indorser will pay it according to its terms at the time it was issued; when it first came into the possession of a holder; or, in the case of an incomplete instrument, according to its terms as completed in accordance with Article 3. The obligation is owed to a person entitled to enforce the draft or to a subsequent indorser who properly pays it. U.C.C. § 3-415(a).

> **Example:** Smith drew a check on his account at First Bank to the order of Jones in the amount of $100 in return for some law books. Jones indorsed the check and negotiated it to Brown. Brown deposited it in his account at Second Bank. Second Bank permitted Brown to withdraw the funds shortly after the deposit, thus giving value for the check. Second Bank presented the check to First Bank for payment, and was informed that Smith had insufficient funds in his account to pay the check.

Second Bank gave due notice of dishonor to Jones and sued her on her indorsement. Jones defended by claiming that she received no consideration from Brown for the check. Second Bank, having given value for the check, is a HDC and is entitled to the amount of the check on Jones's indorser's contract, notwithstanding her defense. Jones may then sue Smith on his drawer's contract.

1. **Disclaimer:** An indorser may disclaim liability by indorsing *"without recourse."*

2. **Liability among indorsers:** Unless they otherwise agree, indorsers are liable to one another *in the order in which they indorse*. Of course, a subsequent indorser has no liability to a prior indorser. There is a rebuttable presumption that the parties indorsed in the order in which their signatures appear on the instrument.

3. **Notice of dishonor and discharge:** Notice of dishonor is necessary to impose liability on an indorser. U.C.C. § 3-503(a). Failure to give the required notice serves to discharge the indorser. U.C.C. § 3-415(c).

IV. PRESENTMENT AND NOTICE OF DISHONOR

A. **Need for presentment and notice:** Prior to the Revision, Article 3 contained numerous technical requirements for the presentment of instruments and the giving of notice of dishonor. Failure to comply with these requirements could preclude a holder from imposing liability on a party to the instrument. The Revision has substantially relaxed or eliminated these technical requirements. In addition, failure to comply with those requirements that remain does not necessary release parties from liability.

B. **Presentment:** Presentment consists of a *demand* made by, or on behalf of, a person entitled to enforce the instrument either *to pay the instrument or to accept a draft.* Thus, presentment for payment must be made to the party obliged to pay it, or, in the case of presentment of a draft for acceptance, to the drawee of the draft. U.C.C. § 3-501(a). For instance, presentment of a check occurs when the payee takes the instrument to the drawee bank and attempts to "cash" it. Article 4 permits "truncation" of this process by providing for transmission of information about an instrument, rather than presentment of the physical item. The deposit of a check by the payee at the depositary bank, which is not also the drawee bank, is not a presentment.

1. **Where and how made:** Presentment may be made by any commercially reasonable means, including an oral, written, or electronic communication. U.C.C. § 3-501(b)(1). Thus, ***telephonic requests*** for payment qualify as a presentment. It may be made at the place of payment specified in the instrument, and must be made at that place if the instrument is payable at a bank in the United States. Presentment is effective when the ***demand is received*** by the party to whom presentment is made. The person to whom presentment is made may require exhibition of the instrument, identification of the presenter, and a signed receipt on the instrument.

2. **Presentment by notice:** A collecting bank may present an item by sending to the party who is to pay or accept a written notice that states that the bank holds the item for payment or acceptance. U.C.C. § 4-212. This form of presentment may not be used, however, if the item is payable by, through, or at a bank, and is, therefore, primarily used with respect to trade acceptances and documentary draft drawn on nonbank drawees.

3. **Multiple payors:** If there is more than one maker, acceptor, drawee, or other payor of the instrument, presentment made to only one of them is effective as to all. U.C.C. § 3-501(b)(1).

4. **When presentment necessary:** Prior to the Revision, presentment for acceptance was necessary to charge the drawers on a draft where the draft required or where the draft was payable at a place other than the residence or place of business of the drawee. Presentment for payment was always necessary before the holder could charge an indorser. Presentment for payment was also necessary to charge a drawer or certain acceptors and makers. U.C.C. PR § 3-501. Under the Revision, presentment is required for acceptance of a draft. U.C.C. § 3-409. As a practical matter, presentment will still have to be made for payment in order to determine whether there has been a dishonor. But the ***technical requirements*** of presentment have been eliminated.

5. **Time of presentment:** Prior to the Revision, the Code contained technical time limits for presentment, which varied with the type of instrument involved and the time of payment. U.C.C. PR § 3-503. The Revision establishes fewer rules, but makes the issues of dishonor and liability for dishonor dependent on the time when the instrument has been presented. The only timing requirement that remains relates to checks. With respect to the liability of a drawer, a check must be presented for payment or deposited with a depositary bank for collection within 30 days after its date. U.C.C. § 3-414(f). With respect to the liability of an indorser, a check must be presented within 30 days after the indorsement was made. U.C.C. § 3-

415(e). Nevertheless, the consequences of late presentment do not necessarily involve discharging the party who is otherwise liable. See the discussion of consequences of late presentment, *infra*.

> **Example 1:** On January 1, Smith delivered a check to the order of Jones for $1,000, dated on that date. On February 15, Jones indorsed the check and negotiated it to Brown. Brown deposited the check in his account on February 23. On February 25, Brown discovered that Smith's check had been dishonored. He now seeks to recover against Smith on the latter's drawer's contract by presenting the check to him, or against Jones on her indorser's contract by presenting the check to her. Smith may claim that the presentment to him is late, since it is more than 30 days after the date of issue. Jones may not claim that the presentment to her is late, since it occurred within 30 days of her indorsement.

> **Example 2:** On January 1, Smith delivered a check to the order of Jones for $1,000, dated on that date. On January 3, Jones indorsed the check and negotiated it to Brown. On January 19, Brown indorsed the check and negotiated it to Green. On February 6, Green negotiated the check to First Bank. First Bank put the check through the collection process and learned on February 10 that Smith drew the check against insufficient funds. First Bank may proceed directly against Green on his indorser's contract under U.C.C. § 3-415(a). Green may proceed against Brown on the same theory. But when Brown attempts to recover from Jones, she will claim that presentment to her is late, as no presentment for payment was made for more than 30 days after her indorsement was made.

6. **Consequences of late presentment:** In the case of a check, if a presentment is not made when due, and there is no excuse for the delay, any ***indorser is discharged***. U.C.C. § 3-415(a). The liability of a drawer is discharged if there has been a late presentment, only if the drawee suspends payments after expiration of the permissible 30-day period for presentment without paying the check, and only if the drawer is deprived of funds maintained with the drawee to cover payment of the check. Even in that case, the drawer who seeks discharge must assign to the person entitled to enforce the check the drawer's rights against the drawee. U.C.C. § 3-414(f).

> **Example:** On January 1, Smith delivers a check to the order of Jones for $150,000, dated on that date. On February 15, Jones indorses the check and negotiates it to Brown. On February 10, the drawee bank declares insolvency. The Federal Deposit

Insurance Corporation provides insurance to all depositors up to $100,000, but Smith has no other means for covering the check. Brown deposits the check in his account on March 23. On March 25, Brown learns that Smith's check has been dishonored. He now seeks to recover against Smith on his drawer's contract by presenting the check to him or against Jones on her indorser's contract by presenting the check to her. Unless Brown can show some excuse or rebut the presumption of a reasonable time for presentment, Jones is entirely discharged as the presentment to her comes more than 30 days after her indorsement. Smith may claim that the presentment to him is late, as it is more than 30 days after the date of issue. Nevertheless, he is discharged only in the amount of $50,000, as that was the amount of which he was deprived by the insolvency of the drawee bank. In order to obtain discharge, Smith must assign his claim for the additional $50,000 to Brown.

7. **Rationale for the distinction between discharge of drawers and of indorsers:** An indorser has presumably given value in the amount of the check to obtain it and has received value in the amount of the check when negotiating it to another person. Thus, the indorser's gains and losses cancel each other out and the indorser receives no windfall if discharged as a result of the holder's delay. A drawer, however, has presumably received value in the amount of the check when it was issued and has surrendered nothing until the check is actually paid by the drawee. Thus, discharge of the drawer for delay would provide the drawer with cost-free benefits, an unjust enrichment. Only when the drawer is deprived of funds as a result of the delay, *e.g.*, through the drawee's insolvency, can the drawer be discharged without unjust enrichment.

C. **Dishonor:** *Dishonor* of an instrument occurs when it is presented for payment or acceptance and *the party who is supposed to pay or accept refuses* to do so. The return of an instrument to obtain a proper indorsement, however, does not constitute a dishonor.

1. **What constitutes dishonor:** An act of dishonor varies with different instruments. U.C.C. § 3-502 establishes general rules that govern dishonor.

   a. **Dishonor of notes:** With respect to notes, dishonor occurs if the note is not paid on the date of presentment to the maker in the case of a demand note. A note that is payable at a definite time is dishonored if it is not paid on the date it becomes payable. No presentment is necessary to effect dishonor of such a note, unless it is payable at or through a bank or the terms of the note require presentment. In such a case, dishonor occurs if presentment is made and the note is not paid on the maturity date of the note or the day or presentment, whichever is later.

    b. Dishonor of checks: A check is dishonored if it is presented to the payor bank for payment and the check is returned by the bank in a timely manner consistent with the requirements of Article 4. Generally, dishonor occurs when the payor bank refuses to pay and returns the instrument by its ***midnight deadline***, which is defined as midnight on the banking day after the banking day on which it receives the item. U.C.C. § 4-104(a)(10). For analysis of the midnight deadline, see p. 117, *infra*. If the check is presented to the drawee bank for immediate payment, however, dishonor occurs if the draft is not paid on the day of presentment.

2. Refusal to certify: Refusal of a drawee bank to certify a check ***does not constitute dishonor***. U.C.C. § 3-409(d). One explanation for this result is that a check is a demand instrument calling for payment, not acceptance. Certification, however, is a form of acceptance; thus, it is not an act to which the holder of a check is entitled. Once a bank has certified a check, wrongful dishonor of the check permits the person entitled to enforce it to obtain compensation for expenses and loss of interest resulting from the nonpayment. Consequential damages are recoverable if the bank obligated on the check refuses to pay after receiving notice of the circumstances that give rise to the claim of damages. These damages may include attorney's fees. See U.C.C. § 3-411, Official Comment 2. A bank that has certified a check, however, may refuse payment when (i) it is uncertain of the presenter's identity; (ii) the bank asserts a claim or defense that it has reasonable grounds to believe is available against the person entitled to enforce the instrument; (iii) the bank has suspended payments; or (iv) payment is prohibited by law. U.C.C. § 3-411. Recall that a bank generally may only assert a claim or defense of its own; a claim of a third party may be asserted by a bank only if there has been compliance with U.C.C. § 3-305(c). These rules similarly apply to dishonor of cashier's checks and teller's checks.

3. When notice of dishonor required: Notice of dishonor is required in order to impose liability on an indorser. Notice of dishonor must be given to impose liability on a drawer only in the case of a draft that has been accepted by a party other than a bank. U.C.C. § 3-503(a).

4. Form of notice: Notice of dishonor may be given by any person and by any reasonable means. Oral and electronic communications are specifically permissible under U.C.C. § 3-503(b). The notice, however, must reasonably identify the instrument and indicate that the instrument has been dishonored or has not been paid or accepted. In the case of a bank that has received an instrument for collection, return of the item will constitute notice of dishonor.

5. **Time of notice:** A collecting bank must give notice of dishonor of an item taken for collection *before its midnight deadline*; any other person must give notice of dishonor of the instrument taken for collection within 30 days following the day on which the person receives notice of dishonor. With respect to any other instrument, notice of dishonor must be given within 30 days following the day on which dishonor occurs. U.C.C. § 3-503(c).

> **Example:** On June 1, Smith gave Jones a check for $500 in return for goods. The check was drawn on First Bank. Jones negotiated the check to Brown on June 2. Brown deposited the check in his account at Second Bank on June 3. Second Bank presented the check for payment to First Bank on June 4. On that same date, First Bank dishonored the check and returned it to Second Bank, which received it on June 5. Second Bank must inform its customer, Brown, of the dishonor by midnight of the next banking day. Brown has 30 days to inform Jones of the dishonor. Recall that failure to comply with the notice of dishonor requirements will discharge Jones as an indorser, but failure to give timely notice of dishonor will not generally discharge the drawer of a check. Nevertheless, Smith is entitled to have the instrument presented to the drawee and dishonored before his liability on his drawer's contract is triggered.

D. **Protest:** Prior to the Revision, protest of dishonor was required to hold drawers or indorsers liable on an instrument drawn or made payable outside the United States. U.C.C. PR § 3-509. Protest consists of a statement that identifies the instrument and certifies that presentment has been made (or why it has not been made) and dishonor has occurred. The certificate must be made under the hand and seal of an official, such as a notary, who is authorized to certify dishonor by the law of the place where the dishonor occurs. Under the Revision, protest is not mandatory and must be specifically requested by the holder. Even where such a request is made, protest is no longer a condition to liability of drawers or indorsers. U.C.C. § 3-505(b).

E. **Excuse:** Failure to make timely presentment or to give timely notice of dishonor may be excused. U.C.C. § 3-504. Presentment will be excused if the party seeking excuse can demonstrate that he or she could not make presentment with due diligence; that presentment would be futile because the maker or acceptor had repudiated the obligation to pay or is dead or in insolvency proceedings; that the terms of the instrument made presentment unnecessary; that the drawer or indorser had waived presentment or otherwise had no expectation that the instrument would be paid by the party primarily liable on it; or that the drawer instructed the drawee not to pay or the drawee had no obligation to pay the instrument. Notice of dishonor is excused if notice is unnecessary under the terms of the instrument, or the party whose obligation is being enforced waives notice of dishonor. Any waiver of presentment also serves as a waiver of notice of dishonor. Notice of dishonor may be excusably delayed if the delay was caused by circumstances beyond the control of the person giving notice and that person exercised reasonable diligence once the cause of the delay was eliminated.

> **Example 1:** Smith issued his check to Brown in payment of services rendered. Brown indorsed the check to the order of Jones in payment for goods. Immediately after depositing the check in her account, Jones left on business for three months. On her return, she discovered that the check had been returned to her because it was drawn on insufficient funds. Jones immediately seeks to recover from Brown on his indorser's contract. Brown claims that he did not receive timely notice of dishonor. Jones is excused for her delay if she could not reasonably have received earlier notice of the dishonor.

> **Example 2:** In *Makel Textiles, Inc. v. Dolly Originals, Inc.*, 4 U.C.C. Rep. Ser. 95 (N.Y. Sup. Ct. 1967), the payee of a note sought recovery against a corporate officer who had indorsed to guarantee the corporate obligator. The officer contended that his contract liability was excused because the payee had failed to make presentment or give notice of dishonor. The court determined that presentment and notice were superfluous to protect the rights of an indorser where, as here, he participated in the affairs of the corporation and was fully aware of its inability to pay the note. The court did, however, dismiss an action against a second indorser who also received no notice of dishonor but who was not involved in the operation of the corporate maker.

V. CONTRACT OF ACCOMMODATION PARTY

A. **Definition:** An accommodation party is a person who signs an instrument for the purpose of incurring liability on the instrument without being a direct beneficiary of the value given for the instrument. U.C.C. § 3-419(a). Typically, the accommodation party is signing to guarantee the obligation of the party accommodated. The accommodation party may sign in any capacity, e.g., as a maker or indorser.

Example 1: Smith applied to First Bank for a loan to start a new business. First Bank did not think that Smith was sufficiently creditworthy to receive the loan, but was willing to make the loan if Smith's cousin, Jones, would agree to become a co-maker of the note evidencing the loan. Jones has no role in the operation of the business. If Jones agrees, she is an accommodation party as she is signing the note for the purpose of lending her name to another party to it rather than of receiving the direct benefit of the instrument.

Example 2: Same as above, but Jones signed an independent agreement with First Bank guaranteeing payment of the loan to Smith. Jones is not an accommodation party for Smith as she has not signed the instrument to which he is a party. Jones may have various obligations to First Bank as a result of her guarantee. She will not, however, have either the rights or duties of an accommodation party. Instead, her rights and obligations will be governed by the ***law of suretyship***.

1. **Benefit:** Difficult issues may arise over whether the alleged accommodation party has received a benefit from the value given for the instrument. Where the signer has received the benefit of the value given, the signer cannot attain accommodation party status, and is instead liable on the instrument in the full capacity in which he or she signed. Benefit under the U.C.C. must be "direct," so that the satisfaction a parent receives from signing a note for an independent child will likely not qualify. In *FDIC v. Blanton*, 918 F.2d 524 (5th Cir. 1990), the court determined that a co-maker on a corporate promissory note was not an accommodation party where the co-maker owned 99% of the corporate stock. The court determined that ownership of the stock meant that the co-maker derived substantial benefit from the loan made to the corporation. Compare *Jones v. San Angelo Nat'l Bank*, 518 S.W.2d 622 (Tex. Civ. App. 1974) (individuals who borrowed money as working capital for a company they each half-owned could not qualify as accommodation parties, even if the name of the company had appeared on the note).

   Example: Brown asked his wife to sign a note that permitted him to obtain a bank loan to obtain additional inventory for his business. Brown's wife had her own business and did not participate in the management or operation of her husband's business. No part of the proceeds of the bank loan were used by the wife's business. The Browns, however, did not keep separate personal banking accounts and used their mutual assets for family purposes. Brown's wife can probably assert that she is an accommodation party on the note for her husband's business. See *El-Ce*

Storms Trust v. Svetahor, 724 P.2d 704 (Mont. 1986) (wife signed as accommodation party where sole purpose was to enable husband to get loan to buy business inventory and she did not participate in the business); *McCarthy v. Sessions*, 572 N.Y.S.2d 749 (N.Y. App. Div. 1991) (wife was not accommodation party where she signed note for farm equipment sold solely to her husband because she worked on the farm and benefitted from the equipment).

B. Liability: The accommodation party is *liable in the capacity in which he or she signed.* Thus, an accommodation party who signs as maker bears the same liability to a holder of the instrument as any other maker. An accommodation party who signs as an indorser bears the same liability to a holder as any other indorser. The person entitled to enforce the instrument is not required to show that any consideration was given to the accommodation party. U.C.C. § 3-419(b).

1. **Limit on liability:** The accommodation party, however, is *not liable to the party accommodated*. Instead, the accommodation party who pays the instrument has a right of recourse, often termed the *right of reimbursement*, against the party accommodated. U.C.C. § 3-419(e). If a person entitled to enforce an instrument cancels or renounces the obligation owed by an accommodated party, that act does not discharge the obligation of an accommodation party who has a right of recourse against the accommodated party. U.C.C. § 3-605(b).

    Example 1: Jones agrees to become an accommodation party for Smith in order that Smith may receive a loan from First Bank. Jones and Smith sign a promissory note to the order of First Bank as co-makers. First Bank negotiates the note to Second Bank. On the date that the note comes due, Second Bank makes a demand for payment on Jones. Jones pays the note in full. Jones is subrogated to the rights of the holder who has been paid, and has a right of reimbursement against Smith, the party accommodated, for the full amount of the payment.

    Example 2: Same as above, but Jones refuses to pay Second Bank. At this point, Second Bank may proceed against Jones on her maker's liability, or against Smith on his maker's liability, or against both. If Second Bank recovers the full amount from Smith, he has no recourse against Jones, as Smith, the party accommodated, has no reimbursement claim against the accommodation party.

2. **Exoneration:** The accommodation party also has the common law right of exoneration. This right allows the accommodation party to

require the party accommodated to pay the obligee should the obligee attempt to collect directly from the accommodation party. This right, however, does not affect the obligee's ability to recover from the accommodation party should the party accommodated refuse to pay.

3. **Contribution:** Under the common law, if there is more than one surety for an obligation and fewer than all make payment of the obligation, those who pay have a ***right to obtain pro rata contribution from those who do not pay.***

   > **Example:** In order to obtain a loan from First Bank to purchase a car, Smith has both his parents sign as accommodation indorsers of the note he makes to the order of First Bank. Subsequently, the mother and father obtain a divorce. Smith defaults on the note when $5,000 remains outstanding and First Bank collects that amount from his mother. The mother has a right of contribution against the father in the amount of $2,500. U.C.C. § 3-116.

C. **Establishing accommodation status:** The accommodation party may receive the ***benefit of certain defenses*** not available to parties without that status. Thus, it may be important for an accommodation party to be able to demonstrate that she signed the instrument in that capacity. The person purporting to be an accommodation party, however, will have the ***burden of proving*** that she signed the instrument in that capacity.

1. **Indorsement:** An indorsement that, on its face, is not in the chain of title (i.e., the indorser was never a holder of the instrument) constitutes ***notice of its accommodation character.*** Such an indorsement is called an anomalous indorsement. U.C.C. § 3-205(d).

   > **Example:** Smith made a note payable to the order of Jones. Jones required Smith to obtain Brown's signature on the note. Smith subsequently negotiated the note to Black. Black saw that the note was payable to Jones and was made by Smith, but that Brown's signature appeared on the back. Since the chain of title does not include Brown, to whom the instrument was never payable on original issue or through negotiation, Black has notice that Brown's signature was anomalous and was made for accommodation.

2. **Oral proof:** Prior to the Revision, as against a holder in due course who did not have notice of the accommodation status, "oral proof" — presumably the equivalent of parol evidence, even when written — could not be used to establish accommodation party status. In other cases, however, "oral proof" could be used for this purpose. U.C.C.

PR § 3-415(3). The Revision omits the holder in due course exception. Whether or not the accommodation party can receive a discharge based on conduct of the holder, however, will depend on the knowledge or notice available to the person attempting to enforce the instrument. See p. 77, *infra*.

> **Example:** The case of *T.W. Sommer Co. v. Modern Door and Lumber Co.*, 293 Minn. 264, 198 N.W.2d 278 (1972) presents the following type of fact situation: Assume that Smith issued a promissory note to the order of Brown in return for a loan to Smith's corporation. Smith signed the face of the note in his capacity as president of the corporation and personally indorsed the back of the note as an accommodation party. Brown negotiated the note to First Bank in return for a loan. At maturity, Smith's corporation failed to pay First Bank, but Brown paid the note and sought recovery against Smith in his capacity as indorser. (Note that since Smith's name is outside the chain of title, any holder has notice of Smith's accommodation party status.) Smith may attempt to prove by parol evidence that he signed the note to accommodate Brown in obtaining a loan from First Bank, rather than to accommodate Smith's corporation, in its attempt to obtain a loan from Brown. If successful, Smith has no liability to Brown, as Brown is the party accommodated.

D. Defenses and discharge of accommodation party: In addition to the defenses that can be raised by any party to an instrument, e.g., real defenses, there are some special defenses of which an accommodation party can take advantage.

1. **Consideration and statute of frauds:**   An accommodation party often attains that status gratuitously, as when one relative agrees to cosign a note for another. Prior to the Revision, U.C.C. § 3-408 provided that lack of consideration is a defense against any person not having the rights of a holder in due course; accommodation parties sought to avoid liability to a holder on the grounds that they received no consideration for signing the note. The Revision eliminates any doubt on the need for consideration by explicitly providing that the obligation of an accommodation party may be enforced "whether or not the accommodation party receives consideration for the accommodation." U.C.C. § 3-419(c). In addition, the contract of accommodation can be enforced even if there has not been compliance with a statute of frauds.

2. **Extension of obligation:** If the person entitled to enforce the instrument extends the due date of the principal obligor's obligation to pay the instrument, the accommodation party is discharged ***to the extent he or she can prove*** that the extension caused loss with

respect to the right of recourse. U.C.C. § 3-605(c). In most cases, the extension will assist the accommodation party, because the party who is obligated on the instrument will have more time to make payment.

3. **Material modification:** If the person entitled to enforce the instrument agrees to a material modification of the principal obligor's obligation other than an extension of the due date, the modification discharges an accommodation party *to the extent that the modification causes loss* with respect to that party's right of recourse. The amount of that loss is presumed to be the amount of the right of recourse, although *the party entitled to enforce the instrument may prove* that the loss suffered by the accommodation party and caused by the modification was of a different amount.

> **Example:** Jones loaned money to Smith's corporation, and requested Smith's husband to sign the note in his individual capacity. One of the terms of the note was that the corporation could not manufacture widgets, which was known to be a risky venture. Jones subsequently agreed that the corporation could manufacture a limited number of widgets. That venture failed and the corporation defaulted on the note. Jones sought recovery from Smith's husband, who claimed he was discharged by the modification. Smith is discharged in the amount of his right of recourse against the corporation, unless Jones can prove that the loss suffered as a result of the widget venture was a different amount.

4. **Impairment of collateral:** If a party entitled to enforce an instrument impairs collateral that secures the obligation of the principal obligor on the instrument, the obligation of the accommodation party with a right of recourse against the principal obligor is discharged *to the extent of the impairment.* U.C.C. § 3-605(e).

   a. **Means of impairment:** Impairment may occur through damage to the collateral, or through failure to obtain or maintain an effective security interest in the collateral, or failure to make proper disposition of the collateral in selling it after default by the principal obligor. U.C.C. § 3-605(g).

   b. **Extent of discharge:** The value of the interest in collateral is impaired to the extent that the value of the interest in collateral is reduced to an amount less than the amount of the right of recourse of the accommodation party, or to the extent that the reduction in the value of the interest causes an increase in the amount by which the amount of the right of recourse exceeds the value of the interest in the collateral.

Example 1: Jones loaned $10,000 to Smith in return for Smith's note, which Brown signed as an accommodation party. Smith also gave Jones a security interest in the inventory of his store. Jones failed to perfect the security interest. Smith subsequently obtained a $9,000 loan from Black. Black secured the loan by obtaining a security interest in the inventory of Smith's store. Black perfected the security interest. Smith subsequently defaulted on both loans. Black seized the inventory and sold it for its fair market value of $12,000. Black retained $9,000, owed to him by Smith, and paid the remaining $3,000 to Smith, who still owes $10,000 to Jones. Jones collects the $3,000 from Smith and now seeks to recover the additional $7,000 from Brown. The failure of Jones to perfect the first security interest impaired the value of the collateral, but to what extent? Prior to the impairment, the value of Brown's interest in the collateral was $10,000, the amount of his right of recourse against Smith. As result of the impairment, the value of Brown's interest is only $3,000, while the amount of Brown's right of recourse remains $10,000. Thus, the impairment reduced Brown's interest in the collateral to an amount $7,000 less than the amount of the right of recourse. Brown's interest was, therefore, impaired to the extent of $7,000, and Brown is discharged to that extent. While Brown remains obligated for $3,000 on the loan to Smith, Brown owes Jones nothing, since Jones has collected $3,000 on the loan.

Example 2: Jones loaned $10,000 to Smith in return for Smith's note, which Brown signed as an accommodation party. Smith also gave Jones a security interest in the inventory of his store. Jones failed to perfect the security interest. Smith subsequently obtained a $9,000 loan from Black. Black secured the loan by obtaining a security interest in the inventory of Smith's store. Black perfected the security interest. Smith subsequently defaulted on both loans. Black seized the inventory and sold it for its fair market value of $8,000. Black retained all $8,000, owed to him by Smith. The failure of Jones to perfect the first security interest impaired the value the collateral, but to what extent? Prior to the impairment, the value of Brown's right of recourse ($10,000) exceeded the value of the interest in the collateral ($8,000) by $2,000. In effect, Brown was undersecured by $2,000. After Black takes the proceeds of the sale of the collateral, nothing will be left for Brown in the event Jones recovers from Brown (because Black was owed $9,000 and only recovered $8,000). Hence, the value of Brown's right of recourse ($10,000) now exceeds the value of the interest in collateral ($0) by $10,000. This is an $8,000 increase in the amount by which the right of recourse exceeds the value of the interest (since the exceeded amount was previously $2,000), and it is to this extent that Brown is discharged. Brown, therefore, still owes Jones $2,000 on the accommodation contract.

5. **Discharge of indorser:** The above rules on discharge apply to discharge of indorsers, as well as to discharge of accommodation parties.

6. **Bankruptcy:** If the accommodated party's discharge results from circumstances over which the holder has no control, the accommodation party remains liable. This is most likely to occur when the accommodated party receives a discharge from its obligation in bankruptcy. It was presumably just this possibility that led the original creditor to require the additional security of an accommodation party in the first place. Thus, it would be anomalous to permit the discharge to terminate the accommodation party's liability.

7. **Defenses of accommodated party:** Notwithstanding the general bar in U.C.C. § 3-305(c) against the use of defenses of a third party, an accommodation party is generally understood to have ***no greater liability*** than that of the party accommodated. U.C.C. § 3-305(d) authorizes an accommodation party to assert defenses or claims in recoupment that the accommodated party could assert against the person entitled to enforce the instrument. The exceptions to this rule are defenses of discharge in insolvency proceedings, infancy, and lack of legal capacity.

> **Example:** Jones signed as an accommodation maker on a note issued by Smith to First Bank. The proceeds were used by Smith to purchase an automobile. First Bank took the note under circumstances that prevented it from becoming a HDC. Smith refused to pay First Bank because the automobile was not operating properly. If First Bank proceeds against Jones on her accommodation party contract, she should be able to assert Smith's claim against payment.

8. **Notice of accommodation party status:** The rules concerning discharge of an accommodation party apply only to a person entitled to enforce the instrument who has knowledge of the accommodation, or who has notice of it by virtue of explicit language in the instrument or by virtue of the anomalous indorsement. U.C.C. § 3-605(h). An accommodation party may also waive events or conduct that would otherwise constitute discharge. U.C.C. § 3-605(i).

E. **Contract of guarantor:** Words of guaranty may be added to a signature, typically to an indorsement, that impose additional obligations on the signer. Where the language used indicates that the signer is acting as guarantor of the obligation of another, the signer will be considered an accommodation party and will have the rights and obligations discussed above. At times, however, the signer may use language that indicates that the party is guaranteeing *collection*, rather than payment, of the instrument. Where the words of guarantee speak unambiguously of collection, the signer is obliged to pay the amount due on the instrument only where certain conditions are satisfied. Satisfaction of these conditions indicate that the principal obligor on the instrument will not make payment. The requisite conditions include obtaining an unsatisfied execution of judgment and the declaring of insolvency by the principal obligor. U.C.C. § 3-419(c). Once these conditions are satisfied, the liability of the party who guarantees collection remains the same as that of any accommodation party.

> **Example:** In order to obtain a business loan from First Bank, Smith signed a note in his capacity as corporate president and named the Bank as payee. The bank also required that Smith sign the note in his individual capacity. Smith agreed and indorsed the note, "Collection guaranteed: s/ Smith." Shortly before the note became due, Smith's business declared bankruptcy. On the due date of the note, First Bank presented the note to Smith for payment on his indorsement. Smith cannot insist that the bank first attempt to collect from the business, as any such effort would be useless.

VI. DISCHARGE OF CONTRACT LIABILITY

A. Introduction: A party who is contractually obligated on an instrument may be discharged from its obligation in a variety of ways. Some methods of discharge lie outside the scope of the Uniform Commercial Code, such as discharge through bankruptcy proceedings. Other events of discharge unique to indorsers and accommodation parties are discussed immediately above. The U.C.C. itself, however, provides for other methods of discharge, such as late presentment or notice of dishonor, discussed above, or payment.

B. Payment: A party obliged to pay the instrument may be discharged from the obligation by making payment or providing satisfaction to the person entitled to enforce the instrument. U.C.C. § 3-602(a). Recall that a person entitled to enforce includes a holder, a person with the rights of a holder (the shelter principle), and a person entitled to enforce a lost or stolen instrument.

> **Example:** In return for a $1,000 loan, Smith delivered to Jones a negotiable note in the amount of $1,000, payable on June 30 to

bearer. On June 1, while Jones was still in possession of the note, Smith paid her $1,000. Smith has no further obligation to Jones in respect of the instrument. In addition, under the principle of merger, the underlying obligation that led to creation of the note is incorporated into and merged with the instrument. Thus, discharge on the instrument constitutes a discharge on the underlying obligation. U.C.C. § 3-310.

1. **Personal defense:** Discharge is a personal, not a real defense; therefore, discharge by payment, or by any other method provided by the Uniform Commercial Code, is not effective against a holder in due course who does not have notice of the discharge when he takes the instrument. It is for this reason that it is essential for a payor of an instrument to obtain its return when he or she tenders payment.

    Example: In return for a $1,000 loan, Smith delivered to Jones a negotiable note in the amount of $1,000, payable on June 30 to bearer. On June 1, while Jones was still in possession of the note, Smith paid her $1,000. Smith, however, failed to obtain the instrument from Jones. On June 15, Jones negotiated the note to Green, who had no notice of the discharge, for value. On June 30, Green demanded payment from Smith. As Green is a holder in due course, Smith's prior payment to Jones is not a defense against Green's demand.

2. **Competing claim:** The discharge is effective even though payment is made with knowledge that some other person is asserting a claim to the instrument, as long as payment is not by someone who knows he or she is prohibited by judicial process from making payment or (in the case of instruments other than a cashier's check, teller's check, or certified check) by someone who accepted indemnity against loss resulting from refusal to pay the instrument. U.C.C. § 3-602.

    Example 1: Jones obtained a cashier's check from First Bank to purchase a car from Smith. The check was made payable to Smith's order. Immediately after Jones delivered the check to Smith and obtained the car, Jones realized that the car was not in the condition warranted. The cashier's check was not payable from Jones' account and thus she could not stop payment on it. She could, however, assert an adverse claim to the check and prevent First Bank from paying it if she provides indemnity or obtains an injunction.

    Example 2: In *Dziurak v. Chase Manhattan Bank*, 58 A.D.2d 103, 396 N.Y.S.2d 414 (1977), *aff'd*, 44 N.Y.2d 776, 406 N.Y.S. 2d 30, 377 N.E.2d 474 (1978), a bank customer obtained an official bank check or cashier's check from Chase Manhattan payable to his order and indorsed the check to the order of Staveris. Prior to the time the check cleared, the customer sought to stop payment on it. The bank's attorney advised that the payment on the check could not be stopped without a court order. The lower court determined that the drawer-bank of a cashier's check engages to pay the person who presents it for payment unless that person takes the instrument by theft or in violation of a restrictive indorsement. The court realized that the bank could have sought an indemnity bond or a court order to avoid payment, but did not require the bank to do so. The Court of Appeals affirmed holding that the check was a primary obligation of the issuing bank that was accepted at issuance. Since the check was not payable from the customer's account, the bank was under no legal obligation to honor the customer's request to stop payment.

Rationale: Permitting discharge in these circumstances initially appears appropriate because it reduces the concerns of holders about competing claims and increases the confidence of makers and payors that they have no liability on either the instrument or the underlying obligation. In addition, since payees are more comfortable with a bank's solvency than with an individual's solvency, making checks drawn on banks difficult to stop increases the confidence of sellers in the finality of transactions and makes them more willing to accept instruments. At the same time, some cases that do not fit the language of U.C.C. § 3-602 seem to fall within these rationales.

Example 3: Smith issued a negotiable note to the order of Jones in return for goods sold by Jones. Brown stole the note, forged Jones's signature, and transferred the note to Green for value. Green presented the note to Smith for payment at maturity. Jones contended that her indorsement had been forged, but did not obtain an injunction or provide indemnity. Smith did not believe Jones, and paid Green in good faith. A technical reading of U.C.C. § 3-602 suggests that Smith is not discharged. That provision permits discharge only when payment is made to a person entitled to enforce the instrument. Since Green took an instrument bearing a forged indorsement, he does not easily fit the definition of a person entitled to enforce so payment to him does not constitute a discharge. Nevertheless, it seems that this is just the type of case to which U.C.C. § 3-602 is directed, as failure to apply the U.C.C. rule places substantial burden on the payor to determine the proper payee.

C. Tender of payment: A party who tenders full payment to the person entitled to enforce the instrument is discharged of all subsequent liability in the amount of the tender. U.C.C. § 3-603.

D. Refusal of tender: If the person entitled to enforce the instrument refuses the tender, the party making the tender is discharged as against anyone who might otherwise have a right of recourse against him or her.

E. Cancellation and renunciation: The person entitled to enforce the instrument can discharge a party's liability on the instrument by cancellation of the instrument or by renouncing rights. U.C.C. § 3-604.

1. Cancellation may consist of suitably ***striking*** out the party's signature or by destroying the instrument.

2. Renunciation may consist of surrender of the instrument to the party discharged or execution of an independent writing.

VII. PROCEDURAL ISSUES

A. Accrual of cause of action: Prior to the Revision, Article 3 stated rules relating to the accrual of a cause of action for different types of instrument. See U.C.C. PR § 3-122. For instance, the time at which a cause of action for contract liability accrues against a maker or acceptor depended on the nature of the instrument. Where the instrument was due at a certain time, the cause of action accrues on the ***day after maturity***. In the case of a demand instrument, however, the cause of action accrued on its date or, if no date was stated, on the ***date of issue***. U.C.C. PR § 3-122(1). A cause of action against a drawer or indorser accrued when the instrument had been ***dishonored*** and a ***demand*** had been made on the drawer or indorser. These rules have been replaced in the Revision by statements of the various obligations of parties to an instrument that indicate the events that trigger liability, such as the giving of notice of dishonor to an indorser.

B. Statute of limitations: U.C.C. § 3-118 contains a detailed statute of limitations. An action on a note payable at a definite time must generally be brought within ***six years after the due date***. An action to enforce a note payable on demand must be brought within six years after the demand. Prior law was unclear as to whether the limitations period ran from the time of issue or demand. An action to enforce an unaccepted draft must be commenced within three years after dishonor of the draft or ten years after the date of the draft, whichever comes first. An action to enforce the obligation of the acceptor of a certified check, or the issuer of a teller's check, cashier's check, or traveler's check, must be brought within three years after demand for payment has been made.

VIII. WARRANTY LIABILITY

A. **In general:** Persons who deal with instruments make warranties to subsequent transferees of those instruments, just as sellers of goods make warranties of quality and title to purchasers. Typically, these warranties have the effect of *placing a loss that results from an unauthorized act or signature on the party who was in the best position to avoid that loss*. As a general rule, the party sustaining the loss will be the individual who took the instrument from the wrong-doer. Keep in mind, however, that there are important exceptions to this general rule. These warranties are found in U.C.C. §§ 3-416 and 3-417. With respect to items in bank collection, essentially the same warranties are provided for under U.C.C. §§ 4-207 and 4-208.

   1. **Presentment and transfer warranties:** Not all parties who deal with an instrument, however, make identical warranties. The warranties made to a payor by one who presents an instrument for payment (*presentment warranties*) are narrower than warranties made by one who transfers the instrument to a non-payor (*transfer warranties*). Hence, payors who suffer losses will have less ability than mere transferees to shift those losses to previous holders of the instrument.

   2. **Advantages:** While warranty liability and contract liability are not mutually exclusive, there may be reasons to favor one theory over another in particular circumstances.

      Example: In 1995, Jones purchased a note bearing Smith's signature as maker and Brown's name as indorser. The note had a maturity date of June 1, 2001. Shortly after making the purchase, Jones discovered that Smith's signature was forged. Jones has no immediate recourse against Brown on Brown's indorsement contract, as there has not yet been any dishonor of the note and likely will not be one until 1995. Jones, however, may have an immediate breach of warranty action against Brown as warranties concerning the validity of prior indorsements are made on transfer of the instrument.

   3. **Disclaimer of warranty liability:** Neither transfer nor presentment warranties can be disclaimed with respect to *checks*. U.C.C. §§ 3-416(c), 3-417(e). Warranty disclaimers by an indorser must appear in the indorsement with words that specifically refer to warranties. See U.C.C. § 3-416, Official Comment 5.

4. **Accrual and termination of cause of action:** Transfer warranties are deemed to be made *when the instrument is transferred*; presentment warranties are deemed to be made *when the instrument is presented* for payment or acceptance. No cause of action or claim for relief for breach of a transfer or presentment warranty arises, however, until the claimant has reason to know of the breach. U.C.C. §§ 3-416(d), 3-417(f).

5. **Statute of limitations:** Notice of a claim of breach of warranty must be given to the warrantor within 30 days after the claimant has reason to know of the breach and the identity of the warrantor. Failure to give notice within this period discharges the warrantor to the extent of any loss caused by delay in giving notice.

6. **Damages:** The measure of damages for breach of a transfer warranty is the *loss suffered as a result of the breach,* but not more than the amount of the instrument plus expenses and loss of interest incurred as a result of the breach. U.C.C. § 3-416(b). The measure for breach of a presentment warranty to a drawee who makes payment is the amount the drawee paid on the instrument, less the amount the drawee is entitled to or has recovered from the drawer. The drawee may also recover *expenses* and loss of interest resulting from the breach. U.C.C. § 3-417(b). If the presentment warranty is made to a drawer or indorser after dishonor of the instrument by the drawee, the measure of damages for any breach is the amount equal to the amount paid plus expenses and loss of interest resulting from the breach. U.C.C. § 3-417(d).

B. **Scope of transfer warranties:** Transfer warranties are made only by persons who both transfer an instrument and receive consideration for the transfer. A person who satisfies these criteria makes the transfer warranties to his or her transferee. If the transfer is made by indorsement, however, the transfer warranties also run to any subsequent transferee. Notwithstanding this broad scope of persons who benefit from the transfer warranties, only a transferee who takes the instrument in good faith is entitled to recover for breach of the transfer warranty. U.C.C. § 3-416(b).

1. **Shelter provision:** Initially it might seem that the limitation on transfer warranties to immediate transferees insulates one who does not transfer by indorsement from liability to subsequent holders. It is important to keep in mind, however, that the shelter provision of U.C.C. § 3-203 may have the effect of negating the limitation.

> **Example:** Brown transferred a bearer instrument to Jones by delivery without indorsement in return for valuable consideration. Keep in mind that no indorsement is necessary to negoti-

ate a bearer instrument. Jones subsequently transferred the instrument to Smith, again for consideration. Under U.C.C. § 3-416, Jones had the benefit of warranties made by Brown, but Smith, who was not Brown's transferee, did not. Under U.C.C. § 3-203, however, Smith was entitled to whatever rights his transferor, Jones, had. These included the right to bring an action against Brown for any breach of warranty.

C. Content of the transfer warranties: Transferors make five separate warranties. These warranties are most important in cases of forged signatures on checks and will be discussed in depth in the chapter dealing with forgery and alteration, *infra*, pp. 94-96. At this point, however, it is useful to understand the general scope of transfer warranties.

1. Warranty of right to enforce the instrument: A transferor warrants that he or she is a person entitled to enforce the instrument. The effect of this warranty is to provide the same right to the transferee under the shelter principle. In effect, this warranty provides that there are ***no unauthorized or missing indorsements*** on the instrument.

> **Example 1:** Brown makes a note payable to the order of Jones. Smith steals the note from Jones, forges her indorsement, and signs the note and transfers it to Green for consideration. Green subsequently signs the note and transfers it to Black, again for consideration. Green has breached the warranty that he is a person entitled to enforce the instrument. No one can be the holder or have the rights of a holder with respect to an instrument bearing a forged indorsement. Thus, every person who takes the instrument subsequent to the forgery and who transfers the instrument will necessarily breach the warranty of good title. The Revision clarifies an issue in the prior version of the Code that used the anomalous phrase that a transferor who transfers by indorsement makes a warranty of good title to any "subsequent holder." U.C.C. PR § 3-417(2). Since no one who takes in a chain of title that includes a thief can be a holder, U.C.C. § 1-201(20), there could be no subsequent holders of such an instrument to whom the warranty of title can be made. Nevertheless, it seemed clear that this warranty was intended to run to subsequent transferees of the instrument. The Revision clarifies the issue by making transfer warranties applicable to "any subsequent transferee."

> **Example 2:** Smith steals a blank form of promissory note, makes it payable to the order of Jones and forges Brown's name

as maker. Jones transfers the note to Green. Jones has not breached any warranty of title. Although the note contains a forgery and is unenforceable against Brown, recall that the forged maker's signature is effective as the signature of the forger, Smith. U.C.C. § 3-403(a). The note is considered a "rightful" note of Smith and contains no forged indorsement; thus, each subsequent transferee can obtain good title.

Example 3: Smith finds a bearer note issued by Jones on the street. Smith transfers the note to Brown for valuable consideration. Brown transfers the note to Green, also for consideration. There are no forged indorsements on the note and, thus, each transferee can become a holder. Therefore, the transferors were persons entitled to enforce the instrument. Prior to the Revision, a transferor warranted that the transfer was "otherwise rightful," and the transfers in this case might have been seen to have been other than rightful with respect to the original owner of the note. That language of warranty does not appear in the Revision, however.

2. **Warranty as to signatures:** A transferor warrants that all signatures on the instrument — whether indorsements, drawers' or makers' signatures, or accommodation signatures — are authentic and authorized. The pre-Revision language, which warranted that signatures were "genuine" or authorized was redundant, since U.C.C. § 1-201(43) defines "unauthorized" signatures to include forgeries and U.C.C. § 1-201(18) defines "genuine" signatures to exclude forgeries. Nevertheless, it is unclear what is added by the use of the adjective "authentic." Breach of this warranty is in the nature of strict liability. It is irrelevant that the warrantor neither did have nor should have had knowledge that the signature was unauthorized. Note, however, the limited scope of the term "unauthorized." It refers only to the capacity of the signer and not to the nature of the underlying transaction.

Example: Smith fraudulently induced Brown to issue to his order a check in the amount of $1,000 in payment for an "antique" desk that turned out to be of recent manufacture. Smith transferred the check to Jones. Smith has not breached the warranty that Brown's signature was not "authorized," as that term refers only to the signature being made by a proper party rather than made pursuant to a legitimate transaction.

3. **No alteration:** A transferor warrants that the instrument transferred bears ***no alteration*** as that phrase is defined in U.C.C. § 3-

407. An alteration is an unauthorized ***change in the contract of a party*** to the instrument in any respect. Alterations include:

a. changing the amount for which the instrument is payable;

b. changing the maturity date of the instrument;

c. completing the instrument in a manner other than as authorized; and

d. adding or removing parties to the instrument.

> **Example:** On January 2, 1996, Smith issued Jones a check in the amount of $100 in payment for some law books. Smith mistakenly dated the check "January 2, 1995," as he was not accustomed to writing the new year. Jones subsequently noticed the error and wrote "1996" over the incorrect date. This change may be implicitly authorized, since it reflects Smith's true intent, and thus not constitute an alteration.

4. **No defense or claim in recoupment:** A transferor warrants that the instrument is not subject to a defense or claim in recoupment that can be asserted against the warrantor. This warranty is made even to a transferee who is a holder in due course and thus not subject to the same defense. This result is justified by the desire to protect holders in due course from having to defend lawsuits. The holder in due course may proceed against the transferor on a breach of warranty claim rather than defend the lawsuit. U.C.C. § 3-416, Official Comment 3. Prior to the Revision, the transferor could, by transferring without recourse, limit this warranty to one of no knowledge of a defense. U.C.C. PR § 3-417(3). This option has been deleted. The transferor's knowledge of the defense is irrelevant to the making of the warranty.

5. **No knowledge of insolvency proceedings:** A transferor warrants that he or she has ***no knowledge of any insolvency proceeding*** that have been instituted with respect to the maker, acceptor, or drawer of an unaccepted instrument. The warranty, however, does not guarantee that the maker, acceptor, or drawer is, in fact, solvent.

D. **Scope of the presentment warranties:** A presentment warranty is made by a person (including, in the case of a U.C.C. § 4-208 warranty, a customer or collecting bank) who obtains payment or acceptance of an instrument. Each ***prior transferor***, however, also makes presentment warranties. Thus, while presenters for payment or acceptance make only presentment warranties, prior transferors may make both transfer and presentment warranties. The presentment warranty is made to ***any person*** who in good faith pays or accepts the instrument. No warranty is made to the drawer of an unaccepted draft when the draft is presented to the drawee. A warranty is made to the drawer only when presentment for payment is made to the drawer with respect to a dishonored draft. The decision of *Sun 'n Sand, Inc. v. United California Bank*, 582 P.2d 920 (Cal. 1978), in which the court found that a warranty was made to the drawer when a check was presented to the drawee, has been rejected by the Revision. See U.C.C. § 3-417, Official Comment 2.

E. Content of presentment warranties — unaccepted drafts: Presentment warranties contain subtle differences from transfer warranties that may affect the ultimate responsibility for an instrument, particularly in the case of forged maker's or drawer's signatures. As in the case of transfer warranties, these warranties are most important in cases of forged signatures on checks and will be discussed in depth on pages 90-113, *infra*, dealing with forgery and alteration. Presentment warranties vary, depending on the nature of the instrument. Where the instrument is an unaccepted draft, the warranties are as follows:

1. **Warranty of right to enforce:** A presenter or prior transferor warrants to the payor or acceptor that he or she was, at the time the warrantor transferred the draft, a person entitled to enforce the draft or a person authorized to obtain payment or acceptance on behalf of one entitled to enforce the draft. As in the case of transfer warranties, this warranty is breached where there is a forged indorsement on the instrument. As noted in the discussion of transfer warranties, however, no warranty of right to enforce is breached where the instrument bears a forged maker's or drawer's signature. In that case, the forgery is operative as the signature of the forger, and, thus, the instrument is a valid one. One who pays or accepts the instrument cannot claim that any presenter or prior party has breached a warranty with respect to the instrument.

2. **No alterations:** As in the case of the transfer warranty, a transferor or presenter warrants to the payor that the instrument contains no alteration.

3. **Authorized signatures:** A presenter or prior transferor warrants only that he or she has **no knowledge that the signature of the maker or drawer is unauthorized**. Note that this warranty differs from the transfer warranty, which vouches for the genuineness of all signatures, regardless of the transferor's knowledge.

   a. **Rule of *Price v. Neal*:** This provision is consistent with the common law rule of *Price v. Neal*, 3 Burr. 1354 (1762) and the finality rule of U.C.C. § 3-418. These principles preclude one who has paid or accepted an instrument from recovering the amount of the instrument from any holder in due course or other party who has changed position in reliance on the payment.

Example: Brown stole a blank check from Smith and forged Smith's name on a check payable to the order of Jones. The check was drawn on First Bank. Jones indorsed the check and deposited it in her account at Second Bank. Second Bank presented the check to First Bank, which did not notice the forgery and paid. Jones has breached a transfer warranty to Second Bank because the check contained an unauthorized signature of the drawer. Unless either Jones or Second Bank knew that the drawer's signature was unauthorized, however, neither breached a presenter's warranty because the unauthorized signature was that of a drawer. As Jones and Second Bank were holders in due course of the check, First Bank will be unable to throw the loss back on them.

F. **Content of presentment warranties — other instruments:** If a dishonored draft is presented for payment to a drawer or indorser, or another instrument other than an unaccepted draft is presented for payment and paid, warranties need be less broad. This is because these cases involve situations in which the payor is clearly in a superior position to avoid the loss, such as where the unauthorized signature is the payor's own. Thus, the person obtaining payment and prior transferors in these cases warrant to the payor only that the warrantor is, or was at the time of transfer, a person entitled to enforce the instrument or authorized to obtain payment on behalf of one so entitled. U.C.C. § 3-417(d).

G. **Warrantor's defenses:** A warrantor who is subject to a breach of presentment warranty claim based on an unauthorized indorsement on, or alteration of, a draft may defend by proving that the indorsement is effective as a result of a failure to use ordinary care or that the drawer in precluded as a result of negligence or failure to discover the unauthorized indorsement or alteration in a timely fashion. Thus, a drawee bank will, in effect, be required to proceed against its own negligent customer before proceeding against the warrantor.

IX. CONVERSION LIABILITY

A. **Introduction:** In addition to liability that may be incurred through a party's contract on the instrument or through a breach of warranty, in certain cases the Uniform Commercial Code imposes liability on a theory of conversion. Conversion most commonly occurs when a check is *paid over a forged indorsement*. Hence, much of the discussion of conversion will be delayed until pages 90-113, *infra*, which deal specifically with forgery and alteration. At this point, however, it is useful to understand the nature of conversion liability as an alternative to contract and warranty liability.

B. **Convertors:** For purposes of the Uniform Commercial Code, conversion usually occurs by an act of a drawee or other payor. The act that triggers liability is the exercise of rights over the instrument in violation of the interests of the true owner. Thus, U.C.C. § 3-420 applies the common law of conversion of personal property to instruments. Conversion is also defined as taking an instrument by a means other than negotiation from a person not entitled to enforce the instrument. An instrument is also converted by a bank when it makes or obtains payment with respect to an instrument for a person who is not entitled to enforce the instrument or to receive payment. Actions for conversion, however, may not be brought by issuers or acceptors of an instrument and payees or indorsees who did not receive delivery of the instrument. U.C.C. § 3-420(a).

> **Example 1:** Brown issued a note payable to the order of Smith, payable June 1, 1990, in return for Smith's sale to Brown of an automobile. Jones stole the note from Smith, forged Smith's indorsement, and transferred the note to Green, who did not know of the theft or forgery. On June 1, 1990, Green presented the note to Brown for payment. Brown did not know of the theft, paid Green the amount of the note, and received the note in return. Brown has exercised ***dominion and control*** over the note inconsistent with Smith's rights, and, therefore, has converted Smith's property.

> **Example 2:** Brown issued a check to the order of Jones and mailed it to her. The check was drawn on First Bank. Green stole the check from the mail, forged Jones' signature, and deposited the check in his account at Second Bank. Second Bank obtained payment of the instrument from First Bank. Brown has no action for conversion against Second Bank. (Brown may have other causes of action against First Bank.) Jones, who never received the check, has no action in conversion against any party.

C. **Damages:** If a conversion action is brought under U.C.C. § 3-420, the measure of damages is presumed to be the ***face amount*** of the instrument. Recovery is limited to an amount no greater than the amount of the plaintiff's interest in the instrument.

CHAPTER 5

LIABILITIES ON FORGED AND ALTERED INSTRUMENTS

I. INTRODUCTION

A. Principles of loss allocation: The U.C.C. creates an intricate scheme for allocating losses that occur as a result of forgery and alteration of negotiable instruments. For the most part, this scheme seeks to accomplish one of two objectives: to place the ultimate loss on the party who was in the best position to avoid it, and to allocate the loss to the party best able to spread it over persons and over time. These objectives frequently work in tandem; for instance, collecting banks often may fit both descriptions. Additionally, these objectives, particularly the first, generally have the effect of placing the loss on the party who took the instrument from the wrongdoer. This party, one may presume, is frequently in the best position to find the wrongdoer and recover against him.

B. Study hint: Keeping these objectives in mind will greatly assist interpretation of the loss allocation provisions of the U.C.C. It is important to understand, however, that certain provisions of the U.C.C. appear to deviate from these rationales and are justified instead on alternative grounds, *e.g.*, the desire to bring finality to a transaction.

C. Bases of liability: The scheme for accomplishing these objectives entails the three separate forms of liability that have been discussed earlier: warranty liability, contract liability, and conversion liability. The application of these rules varies with the capacity in which the forger signed the instrument and with the capacity in which the party from whom recovery is sought dealt with the instrument.

II. FORGED DRAWER'S SIGNATURES

A. Signature requirement: It is a basic rule of negotiable instrument law that *no party is liable* on an instrument unless his or her *signature* appears thereon. U.C.C. § 3-401. If the signature was forged by a person unauthorized to sign the drawer's signature, the signature is "ineffective" as the signature of the drawer. U.C.C. § 3-403(a). A discussion of what constitutes a signature for these purposes may be found *supra*, pp. 55-59. The signature does, however, operate as the signature of the unauthorized signer.

1. Charging drawer's account: For purposes of allocating losses resulting from forgery, the rule dictates that a drawee that pays a draft bearing a forged drawer's signature cannot charge the drawer's account. This rule is codified in U.C.C. § 4-401(a), which permits a bank to charge against a customer's account any item that is **"*properly payable*"** from the account. An item is only properly payable if it is authorized by the customer and is in accordance with any agreement between the customer and the bank. An item bearing a forged drawer's signature would not satisfy these requirements.

B. Holder's recourse: One who presents an instrument bearing a forged drawer's signature for payment has **no recourse against a drawee** that discovers the forgery <u>prior</u> to the time when the drawee accepts the instrument or otherwise becomes responsible for it, *e.g.*, by failing to meet the deadline for dishonoring the check, referred to as the "midnight deadline," *supra*, p. 68.

1. **Check not an assignment:** This principle is consistent with the rule that a check is not an assignment of funds in the drawer's account. U.C.C. § 3-408.

2. **Indorser's liability:** The presenter, however, will be able to recover the amount of the dishonored instrument from any prior indorser. This liability is based on either of two theories.

   a. **Contract:** Contract liability exists under the indorser's commitment to pay the amount of the dishonored instrument according to its terms at the time of the indorsement to a person who is entitled to enforce the instrument or to a subsequent indorser who paid the instrument. U.C.C. § 3-415(a).

   b. **Warranty:** Warranty liability exists, because an indorser who receives consideration for his or her indorsement warrants to any transferee who takes the instrument in good faith that "all signatures on the instrument are authentic and authorized." U.C.C. § 3-416(a)(2).

   Example: Brown stole a blank check from Green's checkbook, forged Green's name on it, and completed the check in the amount of $1,000. The check was drawn on First Bank. Brown gave the check to Jones in exchange for stereo equipment. Jones negotiated the check to Smith for $1,000. Smith indorsed the check and deposited it in his account in Second Bank. Second Bank presented the check for payment to First Bank, which noticed the forged drawer's signature and did not pay the check. Second Bank may revoke any provisional settlement it made with its customer, Smith, for the check. U.C.C. § 4-214. Second Bank also has an action against Smith on his indorser's contract under U.C.C. § 3- 415(a). Smith, however, has a similar contract action against Jones on her indorser's contract. In addition, Smith has a warranty action against Jones because she violated the transfer warranty that all signatures were authentic or authorized. Jones must bear the loss unless she can find Brown. Brown, of course, remains liable on his drawer's contract, as his signing of Green's name is operative as Brown's own signature, even though it is ineffective as the signature of Green.

C. Liability of drawee or payor who pays instrument over a forged drawer or maker's signature: As noted above, a drawee who pays over a forged drawer's signature cannot charge the drawer's account since the instrument is not properly payable. In addition, the drawee cannot recover the amount of the item from any holder in due course or person who has in good faith changed his position in reliance on the payment. Thus, the ***drawee will generally bear the loss*** even though it did not take the instrument from the forger.

1. Finality rule: This is the finality rule of *Price v. Neal*, 3 Burr. 1354 (1762), *supra*, p. 87 and it is codified at U.C.C. § 3-418. Under this doctrine, a drawee who accepts or pays an instrument bearing a forged drawer's signature is bound by that act and cannot recover the payment. See U.C.C. § 3-418, Official Comment 1.

   a. Justification: The initial justification for the rule was that the drawee was in the ***superior position to detect*** the forgery since it has access to the drawer's signature card. Thus, if the drawee were to compare the forgery with the drawer's actual signature, presumably the unauthorized nature of the signature would be apparent. Nevertheless, the rule is one of strict liability; there is no allowance even for a drawee who makes the comparison but reasonably fails to detect the forgery.

   b. Modern justification: In today's banking environment few banks will actually compare drawer's signatures to signature cards on all but the largest checks. Thus, more contemporary justifications of the finality rule adopt a less fictional explanation. First, the fact that the drawee bank has the opportunity to examine signatures gives it the incentive to determine when it is socially efficient to make such an examination. Presumably, the bank will have substantial historical information about the rate of check fraud, the kinds and amounts of checks that are most susceptible to fraud, and the means of fraud prevention. The bank, therefore, is in the ***best position to compare the costs and benefits*** of undertaking prevention in a particular situation. Drawee banks will presumably not invest more in the avoidance of check fraud than the expected losses that are likely to occur as a result of fraud. For example, a bank will not spend more than $10 to examine a check in the amount of $10,000 that has a .001 probability of being forged (and that, therefore, has an expected loss of $10). Since banks are in a better position than their customers to know the appropriate probabilities of check fraud and costs of fraud prevention, placing on drawee banks the risk of check fraud provides them with incentives to make cost-effective decisions. In addition, the information available to banks, combined with the imposition of strict liability on them, induces banks to make appropriate investments in new technologies that will detect or deter check fraud.

 c. Critique: Note, however, that the finality rule does deviate from the other U.C.C. provisions regarding fraud that place the ultimate loss on the party who took from the wrongdoer — such as where the drawee does not pay over the forgery — presumably on the theory that such a party was in the superior position to detect and avoid the wrongdoing. To the extent that the rule purports to bring the transaction to an end by preventing drawees from reopening the transaction once they have paid an item, it is unclear why this particular point is the appropriate one at which to end the loss allocation process.

2. Scope: The finality rule is effective only against one who took the instrument in good faith and for value or who in good faith changed position in reliance on the payment. It also does not preclude an action for breach of the warranty of presentment under U.C.C. § 3-417, but the drawee must prove that such a warranty has been breached.

 Example: Brown steals Smith's checkbook and forges Smith's name on a check drawn on First Bank to "bearer." Brown gives the check to Jones as a deposit on a television set that Brown wishes to purchase from Jones. Jones agrees that Brown may have the television set on tender of the balance of the purchase price. In the meantime, Jones deposits the check and it is paid by First Bank. First Bank discovers its error prior to the time that Brown tenders the remainder of the purchase price. If Jones has not spent the proceeds of the check or otherwise changed position in reliance on the payment, First Bank may recover the amount of the check from Jones, since Jones has not given value for it and, therefore, does not have the rights of a holder in due course.

3. No warranty: A drawee bank that pays over a forged drawer's signature generally has no warranty action against presenters or indorsers. Presenters warrant to one who pays or accepts the instrument only that they have no knowledge that the drawer's signature is unauthorized. U.C.C. §§ 3-417(a)(3); 4-208(a)(3). While indorsers who transfer items make the warranties of genuine or authorized signatures to any "transferee," a term that technically includes the drawee, that term is intended to exclude payors. U.C.C. PR § 4-207, Official Comment 4. If a drawer's signature turns out to be unauthorized, the drawee will not be able to throw the loss back upstream by virtue of warranty liability, unless the presenter (or a prior transferor) knew of the lack of authority.

4. **Signature of forger:**   Recall that <u>one in possession</u> of a check bearing a forged drawer's signature <u>can still be a holder</u> and, hence, a holder in due course entitled to the benefit of U.C.C. § <u>3-418</u>, because the forger's signature operates as the signature of the <u>unauthorized signer</u>, even though it is wholly ineffective as the signature of the proper drawer. U.C.C. § 3-403(a).

   > **Example:** Same as the previous example, except that First Bank pays the check only after Jones parts with the television. First Bank may not recover from any of the previous parties other than Brown, who is liable for defrauding the Bank. Recall that Brown is not liable on a drawer's contract, because there has been no dishonor of the check.

5. **Drawee recovery in other cases:** Cases of mistaken payment by drawees arising from circumstances other than payment of forged drawer's signatures and payment over stop payment orders are governed by the ***common law of restitution***. U.C.C. § 3-418(b). For instance, an effort by a bank to recover payments mistakenly made from an account that contained insufficient funds would be governed by these principles. The law of restitution generally permits a person who, because of mistake of fact, has paid money to another in the payment of a draft or note, to recover from the recipient of the money. Exceptions exist in the law of restitution, however, for payment over a forged signature to one who did not know of the forgery, and for payment by a drawee who mistakenly believed that it held sufficient funds of the drawer. See Restatement of Restitution, §§ 29-38.

III. FORGED INDORSEMENTS

A. **Rights of the drawer or maker:**   As in the case of a forged drawer's signature, the forgery of an indorsement is ***ineffective*** as the signature of the person whose name is signed. U.C.C. § 3-403(a). Additionally, the presence of a forged indorsement prevents the instrument from being "properly payable" from the drawer's account. Therefore, a drawee bank that pays an instrument bearing a forged indorsement ***cannot***

charge the drawer's account. This rule applies regardless of the degree of care exercised by the drawee bank. As we will see, however, the bank may have some defenses based on the drawer's level of care.

1. **No holder:** This conclusion is supported by U.C.C. § 3-501, which suggests that only a ***"person entitled to enforce the instrument"*** can make a presentment. Recall that this category includes only a holder, one with the rights of holders, and one who can enforce a lost or stolen instrument. No person who takes in a chain of title subsequent to a forger of an indorsement can be a "holder." No such person may make an indorsement, since an indorsement must be made by a holder. U.C.C. §§ 1-201(20), 3-201(b). Thus, a drawee that pays an instrument bearing a forged indorsement will not be able to charge the drawer's account the amount of the instrument.

2. **Drawee's recourse:** Unlike the case of a forged drawer's signature, where a drawee that pays will bear the ultimate loss, a drawee that pays an instrument bearing a forged indorsement will generally be able to shift the loss to others who dealt with the instrument.

3. **Warranty liability:** The drawee will be able to shift liability to the presenter, because the presenter was not a person entitled to enforce the instrument (since the instrument bears an unauthorized indorsement) and, thus, breached a presenter's warranty. U.C.C. §§ 3-417(a)(1), 4-208(a)(1). The presenter, in turn, will be able to impose liability on prior transferors, as their transfers were in violation of the transfer warranty that all signatures were authentic and authorized and that the warrantor was a person entitled to enforce the instrument. U.C.C. §§ 3-416(a)(1), (a)(2), 4-207(a)(1), (a)(2). This chain of shifting losses should end with the transferor who took from the forger. That individual may seek recovery from the forger and, having dealt with the forger, should otherwise bear the loss.

    > **Example:** Brown issued a check to the order of Smith, drawn on First Bank. Jones stole the check from Smith, forged Smith's signature, and transferred the check to Green. Green deposited the check in his account at Second Bank. Second Bank presented the check to First Bank for payment. First Bank paid the check, but subsequently was informed of the forgery by Brown. First Bank may recover the amount of the check from Second Bank under U.C.C. § 4-208(a)(1). Second Bank may recover the amount of the check from Green under U.C.C. §§ 4-207(a)(1), (a)(2). Green may recover from Jones if he can find her. Green cannot recover from Brown on the drawer's contract liability because Brown can raise the defense of theft against Green, who is not a holder in due course (or a holder at all). Thus, the party who takes from

the thief bears the loss unless that party can proceed directly against the thief.

4. **Rationale:** The party who takes from the thief is usually in the *superior position*, among those who dealt with the instrument, *to ascertain the proper identity of the forger and, thus, to detect and prevent the forgery*. It is obviously more difficult for subsequent parties to the instrument to determine the identity or good faith of prior parties with whom they have not dealt.

B. **Rights of the party whose indorsement has been forged:** The party whose indorsement has been forged generally will wish to obtain a replacement instrument from the drawer or maker, or to obtain the funds from a party who paid the instrument.

1. **Right to recover on the underlying contract:** If the instrument was stolen *prior to the delivery of the instrument* to the party whose indorsement is forged, then the underlying obligation still exists. A note or uncertified check suspends the underlying obligation only where the instrument is "taken" for the obligation. U.C.C. § 3-310(b). If a certified check, teller's check, or cashier's check is taken for the underlying obligation, the obligor is discharged as if an amount of money equal to the amount of the instrument had been taken. U.C.C. § 3-310(a). (The issuer or acceptor of the instrument, of course, remains liable on the instrument). In either case, if there was no delivery, then the underlying obligation remains intact.

   Example: Jones delivered her car to Smith in return for his promise to pay her $1,000 the following week. Smith wrote out a check payable to the order of Jones and placed it in his desk. Brown stole the check from the desk. Smith's obligation to Jones has not been suspended even though the check was drawn, since it was not "taken" for the obligation.

2. **Right to enforce the instrument:** The person whose indorsement is forged is no longer a holder, as the thief will generally have relieved that person of possession. Nevertheless, that person may remain a person entitled to enforce the instrument. The person may enforce the instrument if (i) the person was in possession of the instrument and entitled to enforce it when loss of possession occurred, (ii) the loss of possession did not result from a transfer by the person or from a lawful seizure, and (iii) the person cannot reasonably obtain possession of the instrument because it has been destroyed, lost, or stolen. U.C.C. § 3-309(a). Even where these conditions are satisfied, the person must prove the terms of the instrument and his or her right to enforce it. A court may require the

person to provide ***adequate protection*** to the person required to pay the instrument. This protection insures the obligor against double liability. For instance, if the instrument subsequently were to fall into the hands of a holder in due course, such as where the instrument was a bearer instrument, the obligor could be required to pay twice if a court had allowed the person who lost it to recover from the drawer, acceptor, maker, or prior transferor. Thus, a court may require that the person claiming the right to enforce ***indemnify*** the liable party from any further claims on the instrument. U.C.C. § 3-309(b). Adequate protection is a flexible concept, however, and may be satisfied by arrangements other than indemnity.

> **Example:** Jones delivered her car to Smith in return for his check, drawn payable to her order, for $1,000. Brown stole the check from Jones prior to the time that Jones indorsed it. Jones is no longer a holder of the instrument. She does, however, remain a person entitled to enforce the instrument under U.C.C. § 3-309. Jones may recover the amount of the instrument from Smith if she can prove possession at the time of the theft, the fact of the theft, and the terms of the instrument. Smith, of course, may fear that Jones has negotiated the check so that any payment he makes to Jones will subject him to double liability when a holder presents the check for payment. Of course, if Jones did not indorse the check prior to the theft, no one may subsequently become a holder. But Smith may be unsure whether Jones did indorse, and thus seek adequate protection just in case she did. Thus, Smith may ask a court to require Jones to indemnify him against further claims on the instrument.

a. **Lost or stolen cash equivalent checks:** Different rules apply in the case of the loss or theft of a check that serves the function of a cash equivalent, i.e., a cashier's check, teller's check, or certified check. A drawer or payee of a certified check or the remitter or payee of a cashier's or teller's check may make a claim to receive the amount of the check by filing a ***"declaration of loss,"*** made under penalty of perjury, to the effect that the declarer lost possession of the check through some means other than transfer or lawful seizure and that the declarer cannot reasonably obtain possession of the check. U.C.C. § 3-312. A claimant who communicates his or her claim to the bank that has issued the cashier's or teller's check or that has accepted the certified check (denominated the ***"obligated bank"***) and who submits the declaration of loss to the bank is entitled to recover the amount of the check 90 days after the date of the issuance or acceptance or when the claim is asserted, whichever is later. Until that time, the claim has no legal effect and the obligated bank may make or permit payment of the check. An obligated bank that makes payment prior to the time that the claim is payable is ***discharged*** of all liability on the instrument. Once the claim does become enforceable, the obligated bank must pay the amount of the check to the claimant if payment has not previously been made to a person entitled to enforce the check. As long as the obligated bank has satisfied the Article 4 requirements for timely action with respect to payment of checks, payment to the claimant discharges the obligated bank of all liability on the check. If a person with the rights of a holder in due course should subsequently present the check, however, the claimant must either refund the amount of the check to the bank that pays, or pay the amount of the check to the holder after dishonor by the obligated bank. For instance, a stolen cashier's check that has been issued to bearer may ultimately fall into the hands of a holder in due course, and that party does not lose his or her right to enforce the instrument by virtue of the submission of a declaration of loss by a claimant. The assumption of the Code, however, is that the instruments to which this provision applies will be presented for payment within 90 days after issuance or acceptance, so that instances of later presentment will be sufficiently rare to make payment to the claimant at that time relatively riskless.

b. Alternative actions: A claimant who qualifies for recovery under both Sections 3-309 and 3-312 may proceed under either. Claimants should prefer the latter provision, since it avoids the need for giving adequate protection to the bank. It is important to note, however, that not all parties to certified, cashier's or teller's checks will be able to make claims under U.C.C. § 3-312. For instance, assume that a payee of a cashier's check negotiates it to a third party and that the check is stolen from that party. Since a declaration of loss may ***only be made by a drawer, payee, or remitter,*** the victim of the theft cannot qualify under the special provisions of U.C.C. § 3-312. This limitation allows the obligated bank to determine which persons are clearly entitled to assert a claim with respect to the bank. In addition, any declaration of loss constitutes a warranty of the truth of the statements made in the declaration, so that the bank has additional protection against fraudulent claims. In addition, there may be circumstances under which a party to an instrument cannot qualify for recovery under Section 3-309, but is entitled to recovery on satisfaction of the conditions of U.C.C. § 3-312.

For instance, a remitter of a cashier's check who suffers a loss before delivery of the instrument would not qualify under U.C.C. § 3-309, because a remitter is not a "person entitled to enforce" the check.

Example: Jones purchased a cashier's check made payable to the order of Brown and delivered it to him. Green stole the check from Brown. Brown submitted a declaration of loss to the issuing bank prior to the time that the check was presented for payment and within time for the bank to take action on the check before paying it. A week later, the check was presented to the bank by a depositary bank which received the check from its customer, Black. Black, however, took the check from Green, who had forged the payee's indorsement. Since the instrument bears a forged indorsement, neither Black nor the depositary bank is a person entitled to enforce it. Should the obligated bank pay the depositary bank, it will not be discharged of its liability to Brown under U.C.C. § 3-312, because discharge requires payment to a person entitled to enforce. The obligated bank, however, will have claims against the depositary bank for both breach or warranty and conversion.

3. **No discharge:** A payor who makes payment to a party who presents an instrument bearing a forged indorsement is not discharged, since discharge requires payment to a person entitled to enforce the instrument, and the possessor of an instrument bearing a forged indorsement generally will not have that status. U.C.C. § 3-602(a).

4. **Right to recover from drawee for conversion:** An instrument that has been paid over a forged indorsement has been ***converted by the payor***. The ***payor's knowledge of or negligence regarding the forgery*** is irrelevant. Once the check has been received by the payee, the payee is considered its owner, so that interference with the rights of the payee by paying the proceeds to another person constitutes conversion.

Example: Brown issued a check to the order of Smith, drawn on First Bank. Jones stole the check from Smith, forged Smith's signature, and transferred the check to Green. Green deposited the check in her account at Second Bank. Second Bank presented the check to First Bank for payment. First Bank paid the check. First Bank is liable to Smith in conversion.

5. **Right to recover from collecting banks for conversion:** U.C.C. § 3-419(3) provides that a ***representative,*** other than a depositary bank, who has in ***good faith*** dealt with an instrument

or its proceeds on behalf of one who was not a person entitled to enforce the instrument is not liable in conversion beyond the amount of any proceeds that the representative retains. This provision resolves a difficult debate that existed prior to the Revision. Under U.C.C. PR § 3-419(3), a representative, including a collecting bank, was not liable in conversion for dealing with an instrument or its proceeds on behalf of someone who was not the true owner, as long as the representative acted in good faith and in accordance with reasonable commercial standards, and retained no proceeds.

a. **Limits of immunity:**   On its face, the pre-Revision provision appeared to limit severely the liability of collecting banks to a payee or other true owner whose indorsement has been forged. That party had to prove that a collecting bank that met the definition of a ***representative***, and that acted ***in good faith*** and in accordance with reasonable ***commercial standards***, still retained ***proceeds*** of the forged instrument. Nevertheless, courts struggled mightily to construe the language of this provision in a manner that permitted recovery in conversion against collecting banks.

Example: Brown issued a check in the amount of $500 to the order of Smith, drawn on First Bank. Jones stole the check from Smith, forged Smith's signature, and transferred the check to Green. Green deposited the check in her account at Second Bank. Second Bank presented the check to First Bank for payment. First Bank paid the check. Green subsequently withdrew $250 of the $500 from her account. Smith brings an action against Second Bank in conversion. Second Bank claims that U.C.C. PR § 3-419(3) limits its liability to the $250 remaining in its hands on the grounds that it has dealt with the check in good faith and in accordance with reasonable commercial standards. Smith may claim that allowing this direct action avoids the circuity of actions that would otherwise occur if he is required to sue First Bank and they then sue Second Bank on its presenter's warranty. Resolution of this dispute depended on a number of issues.

b. **"Representative":** Some courts limited the scope of U.C.C. PR § 3-419(3) by defining narrowly the concept of "representative" as used in that section. These courts argued that a bank is a "representative" only when it is acting as a ***true agent***, such as when engaged in brokerage activities, rather than when it is ***engaged in the normal practice of check collection***. If this were the case, a bank that collected or was the depository of a check bearing a forged indorsement would not get the benefit of the limited immunity provided by U.C.C. PR § 3-419(3). This argument was rejected in *Knesz v. Central Jersey Bank & Trust Co.*, 97 N.J. 1, 477 A.2d 806 (1984). Knesz owned a cooperative apartment and engaged a New York attorney to act as his financial agent with respect to the property. The attorney, who was later disbarred, instead sold the property and received checks that had been made payable to or indorsed to the order of Knesz. The attorney forged Knesz's indorsement and indorsed some of the checks to a third party in satisfaction of the attorney's debt. These checks were deposited by the attorney's creditor in the defendant bank and were subsequently paid by the various drawees. The creditor later issued checks, paid by the defendant bank, in the full amount of the deposited funds.

The Superior Court had permitted Knesz to recover against the defendant bank in conversion. The lower court determined that a collecting bank that allowed withdrawals against deposited checks was dealing with its own funds and was not acting in a representative capacity. The court considered that an alternative holding would require the payee to bring conversion suits against numerous and distant drawee banks rather than against a single depository. The Supreme Court of New Jersey reversed. That court held that under U.C.C. PR § 4-201, a bank handling an item for collection was the agent of the owner. Since the forger could not be the owner of the item, that term was interpreted to cover the payee whose indorsement was forged. Thus, notwithstanding the possible desirability of avoiding circuitous actions, the court was unwilling to ignore the plain meaning of the provision. The proposed revisions to Article 3 would permit a conversion action to be brought against a depositary bank.

c. **"Proceeds":** Some courts have argued that a collecting bank that permits a customer to withdraw funds traced to a check bearing a forged indorsement ***parts with its own funds*** rather than the "proceeds" of the check, or that the funds represented by the check are held "in trust" for the true owner. On either of these theories, Smith would be able to recover the entire $500 from Second Bank in the above example, notwithstanding Green's $250 withdrawal. The court in *Knesz* rejected any broad interpretation of "proceeds" and defined the term as "the amount, if any, the bank actually has left in its control as a consequence of dealing with the forged check." The Revision does not resolve the debate over the scope of "proceeds."

Example: In *Cooper v. Union Bank*, 9 Cal.3d 123, 507 P.2d 609, 107 Cal. Rptr. 1 (1973), an attorney's secretary had stolen checks intended for the attorney and forged his indorsement as payee. She cashed some of the checks and deposited the others in her personal account. Prior to discovery of the forgery she withdrew the entire amount of these deposits. The checks were ultimately paid by the drawee banks. The court held that the attorney could recover from the depositary in conversion notwithstanding the withdrawals. The proceeds of the deposits, the court held, became commingled with the bank's own funds. Thus, the bank retained the proceeds of the deposits, even if they had paid out the amounts stated in the checks. Those proceeds were held in constructive trust for the true owner.

    d. "Good faith": Some courts have gone to substantial lengths to find that a collecting bank failed to comply with commercial standards or to act in good faith. Recall that "good faith" is defined objectively for purposes of Article 3. U.C.C. § 3-104(a)(4) requires a bank to observe reasonable commercial standards of fair dealing as well as to be honest in fact. Thus, a depositary bank may still be liable for conversion if it behaves in a manner inconsistent with what similarly situated banks would have done to discover a forgery. Prior to the Revision, however, "good faith" was defined subjectively. Thus, courts that wanted to impose conversion liability on a collecting bank that had been honest in fact had to determine that the bank failed to comply with reasonable commercial standards.

    Example: Smith was the vice president of the XYZ Corporation, which had its account with First Bank. The bank was aware that XYZ Corporation made daily deposits of large amounts from its debtors. Smith also had a personal account at First Bank. Smith forged the signature of the XYZ Corporation's Treasurer on some checks made out to the order of the corporation in large amounts and deposited them in his personal account. Smith then withdrew the funds. First Bank arguably had a duty of inquiry with respect to the checks and its failure to make inquiry constituted the absence of good faith conduct and, therefore, removes the immunity of U.C.C. § 3-420(c).

C. Rights of drawer against depositary or collecting bank: Prior to the Revision, there was conflict in the cases concerning the ability of the drawer of a check that has been paid over a forged indorsement to recover directly from the depositary bank. In *Stone & Webster Engineering Corp. v. First National Bank & Trust Co.*, 345 Mass. 1, 184 N.E.2d 358 (1962), the plaintiff drew three checks that were stolen by one of its employees prior to delivery to the payee. The employee received cash for the checks at the defendant bank, which collected the amount of the checks from the drawee. When the drawee refused to re-credit the plaintiff's account, the plaintiff brought an action directly against the defendant on a theory of conversion. The Supreme Judicial Court held that no cause of action existed. The Revision explicitly adopts the holding of *Stone & Webster*. It **precludes actions** for conversion by the issuer or acceptor of the instrument. It also precludes such actions by a payee or indorsee who did not receive delivery of the instrument. U.C.C. § 3-420(a).

> **Example:** Jones drew a check payable to the order of Smith in payment for goods purchased from Smith. Jones mailed the check to Smith. Brown stole the check from the post office, forged Smith's signature, and cashed the check at First Bank, the drawee. Smith brought a conversion action against First Bank. Smith loses. Smith did not have any rights in the check until receipt. Until that time, Smith is entitled to recover from Jones on the underlying obligation. That obligation has not been suspended, because Smith has not "taken" an instrument for it. U.C.C. § 3-310.

1. **Arguments against direct action:** In *Stone & Webster*, the court maintained that the drawer was not a holder and had no valuable rights in the forged check. In addition, some courts and commentators resist a direct action on the claim that the drawee is in a better position to know whether the drawer delayed in giving notification of the forgery or was otherwise negligent in contributing to the forgery.

2. **Arguments for direct action:** Permitting a direct action by the drawer against the depositary would avoid the circuity of actions that would otherwise result when the drawer recovers from the drawee and the drawee recovers from the depositary bank on its warranty. In order to reach this result, the Supreme Court of California, in *Sun 'n Sand, Inc. v. United California Bank*, 211 Cal.3d 671, 148 Cal. Rptr. 329, 582 P.2d 920 (1978), avoided U.C.C. § 3-419(3) altogether and asserted that the **drawer is the ultimate "payor"** to whom warranties of good title are made by a presenting bank. Thus, a collecting bank, such as the depositary, breached this warranty by seeking payment from the drawer's account on a check bearing a forged indorsement and was liable to the drawer for the breach. The **Revision reverses this result** by providing that presentment warranties are made to the drawee, and not ultimately to the drawer.

IV. EFFECT OF NEGLIGENCE ON ALLOCATION OF LOSS FOR FORGERY

A. Introduction: To this point, the discussion has assumed that no party negligently contributed to the forgery or alteration of the instrument. The presence of negligence, however, may shift the liability from the party who would otherwise bear it and place the liability on the negligent actor.

Rationale: If the objective of the Uniform Commercial Code's loss allocation rules is to place the loss on the party in the superior position to prevent that loss from occurring in the first place, allocation of responsibility may be placed on a party who is demonstrably negligent rather than on the party who took from the forger. Care on the part of the negligent party could have prevented the forger from succeeding in his or her wrongful conduct. Notice, however, that this principle conflicts with the **strict liability** principle embodied in the final payment rule of U.C.C. § 3-418.

B. General rule: Any person whose failure to exercise ordinary care, substantially contributes to alteration of an instrument or to the making of a signature is precluded from asserting the alteration or the forgery against one who, in good faith, pays the instrument, takes it for value, or takes it for collection. U.C.C. § 3-406.

> **Example 1:** Brown drew a check to the order of Smith in the amount of $10.00. Brown wrote the amount of the check in pencil. Smith erased the $10.00 amount in the right hand corner of the check and the words in the center of the check and replaced them with the figure $100.00 and the words "one hundred dollars." The drawee bank, First Bank, paid the check for $100. Brown is precluded by his negligent use of pencil from claiming the check was not properly payable for $100.

> **Example 2:** Brown was the treasurer of XYZ Corporation. The Corporation was expecting a delivery of goods during a time when Brown had a business meeting. Brown, therefore, left a signed but incomplete corporate check with his secretary, Green. When the delivery was made, Green gave the deliverer a personal check for the amount of the delivery. Green then completed the corporate check to his own order and inserted an amount greater than the delivery amount. Green cashed the check with the drawee bank. Brown and XYZ Corporation are precluded by Brown's negligence from denying that the check is properly payable from the Corporation's account.

Example 3: Brown owed Smith $100. Brown drew a check to the order of Smith and negligently mailed it to the wrong Smith. The recipient indorsed the check and deposited it; the drawee bank, First Bank, ultimately paid the check. Brown is precluded by his negligence in misaddressing the check from claiming the check was not properly payable. A court, however, may determine that Brown's negligence did not "substantially contribute" to the forgery and, thus, does not preclude him from shifting the loss to First Bank. See *Behring International, Inc. v. Greater Houston Bank*, 662 S.W.2d 642 (Tex. Civ. App. 1983).

1. **Ordinary care:** For purposes of U.C.C. § 3-406, negligence consists of the failure to use ordinary care. U.C.C. § 3-103(a)(7) defines ordinary care, in the case of a business, as observance of reasonable commercial standards prevailing with respect to that business in the area in which the business is located. In the case of a bank that takes an instrument for collection or for payment through ordinary means, reasonable care does not necessarily require the bank to examine the instrument. Examination may be costly in light of the expected benefits. Thus, *examination will not be required* unless it is called for by the bank's own procedures or by general banking usage or by state or federal law. Of course, there may be particular situations in which the circumstances under which the bank is acting are sufficiently suspicious to require the bank to undertake investigation of the instrument. The Code does not define "ordinary care" in the case of a person who is not a business. Presumably, common law definitions would apply. Ordinary care is considered to be a different concept than *failure to deal fairly* in conducting the transaction, which is the essence of the definition of good faith in U.C.C. § 3-103(a)(4). See U.C.C. § 3-103, Official Comment 4.

2. **Comparative negligence:** A negligent party will not be precluded from asserting the alteration or unauthorized signature if the person asserting the preclusion, e.g., the payor bank, failed to exercise ordinary care in paying or taking the instrument.

   a. **Payor negligence:** Prior to the Revision of Article 3, any such party was unable to assert any preclusion against the negligent party. This limitation was similar to the last clear chance doctrine in tort law by imposing on the last party capable of avoiding the loss the obligation to do so, if it recognized or should have recognized the contributory negligence of a prior party. U.C.C. PR § 3-406.

   Example: Jones drew and delivered a check to Smith in the amount of $1,000, drawn on First Bank. Jones negligently left sufficient space in the body of the check that Smith was able to alter the amount to "one thousand one hundred" dollars. Nevertheless, Smith's alteration was so sloppy that it would have raised suspicion in the mind of a reasonable person. First Bank, however, paid the check in the amount of $1,100. When Jones sought to have First Bank recredit her account in the amount of $100, First Bank refused, claiming that Jones was precluded by her negligence from asserting the alteration against the drawee. Jones wins. Although she was negligent, First Bank's own negligence prevents them from asserting a defense under U.C.C. PR § 3-406.

3. **Rationale:** A drawee that pays an instrument under such circumstances as to constitute negligence or departure from reasonable commercial standards has surrendered an *opportunity to prevent success* by the wrongdoer. At this stage of the transaction, prior negligent parties have already *underinvested in precautions* against forgery. Thus, some incentive for the drawee to act is necessary to avoid the loss, and threat of liability on the instrument constitutes that incentive.

   a. **Allocation between negligent parties:** U.C.C. § 3-406 changes the allocation of losses when both the person asserting the preclusion (generally the drawee or payor) and the party against whom the preclusion is asserted have been negligent. The last clear chance doctrine has been replaced with a principle of comparative negligence. Under this doctrine, the loss is allocated between the parties according to the extent to which the failure of each to exercise ordinary care contributed to the loss. U.C.C. § 3-406(b). The person against whom the preclusion is asserted must prove the other party's failure to exercise ordinary care. U.C.C. § 3-406(c).

C. **Availability to depositary bank of claim that drawer was negligent:** Parties who can assert the preclusion of U.C.C. § 3-406(a) include one who takes the instrument for value or for collection. Nevertheless, this provision does not appear to authorize a direct action against a negligent drawer by a depositary bank that has been successfully sued by a drawee for breach of warranty.

1. **Common law:** The depositary bank may, however, retain a common law negligence action against the drawer. U.C.C. § 1-103.

2. **Customer negligence:** The depositary bank may still seek to require the drawee bank to assert any U.C.C. § 3-406 rights the drawee might have against its customer before proceeding against the depositary bank. In *Girard Bank v. Mount Holly State Bank,*

474 F. Supp. 1225 (D.N.J. 1979), a depositary bank that collected a check bearing a forged indorsement sought to avoid warranty liability to a drawee bank that had paid the check. The depositary alleged that the drawee's failure to assert a U.C.C. § 3-406 defense against its customer prevented it from proceeding affirmatively against a collecting bank. The court disagreed. Even though the U.C.C. does bar a drawee that fails to assert certain defenses against a customer from proceeding against collecting banks, U.C.C. § 4-406 (discussed below), the court determined that these explicit bars should not be extended where no such express provision exists. Further, the court prevented the depositary from raising a U.C.C. § 3-406 claim directly against the drawer, as that provision applies only to drawees, payors, and holders in due course.

D. Judicial construction: Some courts will go to substantial length to find negligence on the part of a bank. In *Medford Irrigation District v. Western Bank*, 66 Or. App. 589, 676 P.2d 329 (1984), a customer of a bank negligently failed to supervise a bookkeeper or audit its accounts, so that the bookkeeper was able to forge checks in excess of $68,000. None of these checks had a face amount in excess of $5,000. The drawee bank followed a banking custom of not examining signatures on checks in amounts less than $5,000 and introduced evidence that examination of smaller checks would impose costs in excess of expected detection of forgeries. Nevertheless, the court found that the bank had failed to exercise ordinary care by not making an examination of the drawer's signatures. Note that the definition of "ordinary care" in U.C.C. § 3-103(a)(7) provides that failure to examine is not necessarily negligent conduct.

V. CUSTOMER'S OBLIGATION TO INSPECT BANK STATEMENTS

A. General rule: Even where a forgery or alteration has occurred without any negligence on the part of the drawer, the drawee's liability for subsequent forgeries or alterations may be limited if the customer fails to discover and report the initial offenses. U.C.C. § 4-406.

1. **Bank duties:** A bank that sends or makes available to a customer a *statement of account* showing payment of items for the account must either return the items, make them available to the customer, or provide information that allows the customer to identify the paid items. Notice, however, that the bank is not required to send a statement of account to its customer. The duties imposed by U.C.C. § 4-406 apply only to a bank that sends or makes available a statement of account. Additionally, the bank is not required to return to

the customer items presented for payment against the customer's account, such as checks. A bank that does not return items must either retain them or maintain the ability to furnish legible copies for seven years after receipt of the items.

2. **Customer duties:** A customer who receives a statement of account or items must exercise reasonable promptness in ***examining the statement*** or the items to determine whether there are any unauthorized signatures or alterations. The customer must ***promptly notify*** the bank of any discrepancies. Promptness is measured from the time the customer ***should have discovered*** the unauthorized payment. U.C.C. § 4-406(c).

3. **Customer inaction:** A customer who fails to comply with his or her obligation of examination and notification is ***precluded*** from asserting against the bank an ***unauthorized signature*** of the customer or ***alteration*** of the item, if the failure caused the bank to suffer a loss. Additionally, the customer is precluded from asserting against the bank an unauthorized signature of the customer or alteration by the same wrongdoer on any other item paid by the bank in good faith if the payment was made before the bank received notice from the customer of the discrepancy and after the customer had a reasonable period of time, not exceeding 30 days, in which to examine the item or statement of account and to notify the bank. U.C.C. § 4-406(d)(2).

> **Example:** Brown stole Smith's checkbook on January 1. On January 5, Brown drew a check for $100 and forged Smith's signature as drawer. The drawee, First Bank, paid this check on January 10 and returned the check with Smith's monthly statement on January 31. Smith never examined the statement and did not realize that the returned items included a check with a forged drawer's signature. On March 1, Brown drew another check from the same checkbook for $500. First Bank paid this check on March 5. Smith may require First Bank to recredit his account for the $100 check which was not properly payable because it bore a forged drawer's signature. Since Smith did not comply with his obligations of examination and notification, however, Smith is precluded from asserting his unauthorized signature against First Bank with respect to the $500 check.

4. **Bank negligence:** If the customer proves that the bank failed to exercise ordinary care in paying the item and that the failure substantially contributed to the loss, the loss will be allocated between the customer and the bank according to the extent to which the failure of each to exercise ordinary care contributed to the loss. U.C.C. § 4-406(d). This comparative negligence principle changes the rule

that applied previously. Prior to the Revision, delay by a customer would not aid a bank that pays a check unreasonably. A customer who could establish that the bank **lacked ordinary care** in paying the item was not precluded from asserting an unauthorized signature or alteration, notwithstanding the customer's failure to make proper examination or notification. Here, again, the **last clear chance** principle operated to place the loss on a party that failed to detect and cure the negligence of a prior party.

> **Example:** Same as above, but the second check was drawn for $5,000 and reasonable care in First Bank's geographical area requires all drawees to make visual comparison of drawer's signatures and signature cards on checks in excess of $1,000. First Bank would have realized that Smith's signature was forged had it made such a comparison, but it negligently failed to do so. Smith is not precluded from asserting the unauthorized signature against First Bank, notwithstanding his failure to make prompt inspection of returned items and report forgeries to First Bank. Under U.C.C. § 4-406(d), however, the loss would be allocated between Smith and First Bank. Thus, Smith would not be able to avoid some loss as a result of his negligence.

5. **Absolute bar:** A customer who does not discover and report an alteration or his own unauthorized signature within **one year** after the statement or items are made available is precluded from asserting against the drawee the unauthorized signature or alteration. This preclusion is in the nature of **strict liability**; it operates regardless of the level of care of the bank or the customer. U.C.C. § 4-406(f). The effect of this provision is to prevent the payor bank from choosing to recredit the account of its customer and passing the loss to upstream collecting banks on breach of warranty theory.

   a. **Need to proceed against customer:** Under prior law, a payor bank that **could claim that a customer has failed to make proper examination** or notification and failed, on request of a prior party to the check, to assert that claim against the customer could not assert the unauthorized signature or alteration as a basis for recovery from any collecting bank or other prior party. U.C.C. PR § 4-406(5). U.C.C. § 4-406(f) now prevents actions against upstream banks only where the one-year bar is in effect.

      Example: Over a series of months, Green, Brown's bookkeeper, stole a series of checks that had been properly drawn to Brown's creditors, forged the payee's indorsements, and deposited the checks in his account at Second Bank. Second Bank transferred the checks to the drawee bank, which paid them. Brown received statements from the drawee that contained the checks with the forged indorsements. Brown did not inspect the statements, but learned of the forgeries some months later when creditors complained that they had not been paid. Brown demanded that the drawee bank recredit his account as the checks bearing forgeries were not properly payable. The drawee bank agreed to do so and brought an action against Second Bank for breach of the presentment warranty. Under U.C.C. PR § 4-406(5), Second Bank could avoid liability by demanding that the drawee resist Brown's claim for credit with respect to checks forged after the statement containing the first forgeries were available to Brown.

    b. Difference from § 3-406:   Notice that this explicit requirement varied from the holding of the court in the *Mount Holly* case, *supra*, p. 106, with respect to the drawee's ability to proceed against a depositary rather than make a negligence claim under U.C.C. § 3-406 against its customer. Unlike U.C.C. § 3-406, U.C.C. PR § 4-406(5) expressly required that a drawee proceed against its customer before it attempted to impose warranty liability on a prior party.

6. Reporting of forged indorsements: U.C.C. § 4-406 imposes ***no duty*** on drawers to look for unauthorized indorsements. Thus, there is no time period within which customers must report forged indorsements to their banks.

VI.   IMPOSTORS AND FICTITIOUS PAYEES

    A. General rule: In some situations, unauthorized signatures will be effective as the indorsement of the payee or the signature of the drawer, notwithstanding the general rule of U.C.C. § 3-403(a). These cases tend to involve either likely negligence on the part of the party whose signature is forged or cases in which the Uniform Commercial Code appears to allocate losses to parties in superior positions to avoid the loss.

    1. Effect: The "effectiveness" of these signatures means persons with an interest in the instrument will have rights not otherwise available to parties who hold instruments bearing forged indorsements.

    2. *Good title* to such an instrument may pass just as if no forgery existed, so that person with interests them are persons entitled to enforce these instruments. Thus, subsequent transferees may be holders and holders in due course.

3. The "effectiveness" of the signature will bar any claim that the item is not ***properly payable***, and, thus, a drawee that pays the item may charge the drawer's account.

B. Impostor rule: If an impostor induces the issuer of an instrument to issue the instrument ***to the impostor,*** or to a person acting in concert with the impostor, by impersonating the payee or a person authorized to act for the payee, an indorsement in the name of the payee by any person, including a forger, is effective as the indorsement of the payee in favor of a person who, in good faith, pays the instrument or takes it for value or for collection. It does not matter whether the imposture is ***through the mails or face to face***. U.C.C. § 3-404(a).

> **Example 1:** Smith knew that Brown had performed work for Jones. Smith told Jones that his name was Green, that he was Brown's employee, and that he had been sent by Brown to pick up the check for the work done. Smith asked Jones to make the check payable to the order of Green. Jones complied with Smith's wishes. Smith indorsed the check by signing "Green" on the reverse and the drawee, First Bank, paid the check. Since Smith had no interest in the instrument but presented himself as a party entitled to it he is an impostor and his signature is effective.

> **Example 2:** Same as above, but Jones made the check payable to the order of Brown. Smith forged Brown's indorsement on the check. Smith's signature is again effective. Where the impostor is impersonating an agent the effect is the same as if the impostor was impersonating the payee. This is a change from prior law, which made an impostor's indorsement of a principal's signature ineffective on the theory that the impostor had not impersonated the payee, but had only misrepresented his authority.

> **Example 3:** Smith knew that Brown had performed work for Jones. Smith sent a bill to Jones for the work that Brown had done. Smith's bill requested payment for the work in the name of "Smith, Inc.," which has no relationship to Brown. Smith's indorsement in the name of "Smith, Inc." is effective, even though Smith's representation was made through the mail.

1. **Scope of "impostor":** Not every forgery will constitute an imposture. If a thief steals a check and indorses it in the name of the payee, that forgery will not constitute an imposture. The forger must have ***actively impersonated the payee*** by holding himself out to be that person. Otherwise, the forgery rule would apply to

virtually any forgery situation. *Dominion Bank v. Household Bank,* 827 F. Supp. 463 (S.D. Ohio 1993).

2. **Comparative negligence:** If the person paying an instrument bearing an impostor's signature or taking it for value or for collection fails to exercise ordinary care, the issuer may recover from that person to the extent that the failure contributed to the loss. U.C.C. § 3-404(d).

C. **Fictitious payees and "persons without interest":** In some circumstances, an indorsement on a check issued by or in the name of a drawer to a fictitious person or to a person who is not intended to have any interest in the check will be effective. These rules typically apply in situations where employees have engaged in misconduct by providing names of payees to their employer or issuing checks of their employer. The loss allocation scheme of the Code is predicated on the belief that such losses are ***best allocated to the employer*** who could have supervised the employee.

1. **Effective indorsements:** Anyone in possession of an instrument made payable to a fictitious person is a ***holder of the instrument***. An indorsement of the instrument by any person in the name of the payee stated in the instrument is effective as the indorsement of the payee in favor of one who, in good faith, pays the instrument or takes it for value or for collection. These same rules apply if the person whose intent determines to whom the instrument is payable (a concept defined in U.C.C. § 3-110) names an actual payee, but does not intend that party to have any interest in the instrument. U.C.C. § 3-404(b).

   Example 1: Jones was the corporate treasurer of A Company. Jones drew a check payable to Smith, an actual creditor of A Company, in the amount owed. At the time Jones drew the check, however, she intended to steal it before it was mailed to Smith. When Jones steals the check and indorses it as Smith, she is a holder of it and her indorsement is effective as that of Smith, since Jones was a person whose intent determines to whom an instrument is payable. It is irrelevant whether Smith was an actual creditor, since Jones did not intend Smith to have any interest in the check. This resolves a dispute under prior law concerning whether the fictitious payee doctrine applied where a check was issued to a true creditor.

   Example 2: Same as above, but Jones did not initially have the intent of stealing the check. Instead, Jones formed that intent only after she signed the check in order to pay Smith. As a technical matter, the "person without interest" rule would not apply to make her indorsement effective, since she did initially intend the payee to have an interest in the instrument.

Example 3: A Company uses a check-writing machine to issue its checks. Brown, a thief who has no affiliation with A Company, obtains access to the machine and causes it to produce a check payable to X Corp., a real company, which is not a creditor of A Company. Brown's indorsement in the name of X Corp. is effective to make Brown a holder and a person entitled to enforce the instrument. Under U.C.C. § 3-404(b)(ii) and U.C.C. § 3-110, Brown was the person whose intent determined to whom the instrument was payable. It is irrelevant that Brown was without authority to supply the name of X Corp.

2. **Depositary banks and "effective" fraudulent checks:** For purposes of the impostor rule, the persons without interest rule, and the fictitious payee rule, an indorsement is made in the name of a payee if it is made in a name substantially similar to that of the payee or if the instrument is deposited in a depositary bank to an account with a name that is substantially similar to that of the named payee. A depositary bank may be a holder of the instrument even if the instrument has not been indorsed, since U.C.C. § 4-205 makes such indorsements unnecessary. U.C.C. § 3-404(c).

3. **Comparative negligence:** If the person paying an instrument bearing an indorsement made under the conditions stated in U.C.C. § 3-404(b) or taking it for value or for collection fails to exercise ordinary care, the issuer may recover from that person to the extent that the failure contributed to the loss. U.C.C. § 3-404(d).

D. **Employer supervision:** An indorsement of an instrument, whether issued by or issued to an employer, by an employee who has ***responsibility*** with respect to the instrument is effective as the indorsement of the person to whom the instrument is payable. This rule applies as long as the indorsement is made in the name of the payee. U.C.C. § 3-405(b).

1. **Responsibility:** This rule does not cover all employees who engage in fraud. It applies only to an employee who has authority to sign or indorse instruments on behalf of the employer, or to process instruments received by the employer for bookkeeping or for deposit, or to prepare instruments to be issued by the employer, or to supply information concerning payees of instruments to be issued by the employer, or otherwise to deal with the employer's instruments in a responsible capacity. Having access to blank or incomplete instruments does not, of itself, constitute responsibility. Nevertheless, employees who gain such access may be able to issue

effective instruments under the "person without interest" rule of U.C.C. § 3-404(b).

Example 1: Jones, an employee of A Company, is charged with receiving incoming checks, preparing them for a bookkeeper who places A Company's indorsement on the checks, and depositing them in A Company's account at First Bank. Jones steals a check received by A Company from Brown, drawn on Second Bank. Jones forges A Company's indorsement on the check, makes it payable to herself, and deposits it to her own account at Third Bank. Third Bank sends the check to Second Bank, which pays. A Company demands another check from Brown, who claims that she has already paid A Company. Prior to the Revision, no provision imposed liability on the employer with respect to incoming checks unless the employer was negligent under U.C.C. PR § 3-406. Under U.C.C. § 3-405, Jones would be a responsible employee, and, thus, her indorsement in the name of the payee would be effective as that of A Company. Brown's obligation to A Company has, therefore, been discharged. Third Bank breached no warranty to Second Bank and Second Bank may charge Brown's account. This result is more consistent with the rationale that employers are superior supervisors of their employees. To the extent that employers can supervise, there does not seem to be a basis for distinguishing between supervision of the treatment of incoming and outgoing checks.

Example 2: Same as above, but the theft of the check is made by Green, a mailroom employee at A Company, whose tasks are limited to delivering mail to addressees within the company. Green's indorsement is not effective under U.C.C. § 3-405 because he is not an employee who has responsibility with respect to the instrument. The check is not effective under U.C.C. § 3-404, because it does not involve the issuance of a check to a fictitious person or a person whom the issuer does not intend to have an interest in it. Rather, it involves an incoming check. If A Company had been negligent in leaving the check where Green could get access to it, A Company could be precluded from asserting the unauthorized signature against one who paid the instrument or took it for value or for collection. U.C.C. § 3-406.

Example 3: Jones was the corporate treasurer of A Company. Jones drew a check payable to Smith, an actual creditor of A Company, in the amount owed. At the time Jones drew the check, she did not have the intent of stealing the check. Instead, Jones formed that intent only after she signed the check in order to pay Smith. Jones stole the check and indorsed it with Smith's name. Recall that in the discussion of the "person without interest" rule above, this scenario did not qualify to make the indorsement effective, since Jones did initially intend the payee to have an interest in the instrument. Nevertheless, under the employer supervision rule of U.C.C. § 3-405(b), the indorsement would be effective as that of the named payee.

Example 4: Green was a bookkeeper of A Company, entrusted with placing the company's indorsement stamp on incoming checks. The stamp read "A Company." Green stamped a check received by A Company from Brown. Green then stole the check and deposited in his account at First Bank. U.C.C. § 3-405(b) does not apply to this case because there is no forged indorsement. A Company only has an action against First Bank if it knew of Green's fiduciary status and had notice of the breach of fiduciary duty. See U.C.C. § 3-307(b).

2. **Comparative negligence:** A person who pays or takes for value or for collection an instrument bearing an indorsement by a responsible employee, but who fails to exercise ordinary care, is liable to the person who would otherwise bear the loss to the extent that the failure contributed to the loss. U.C.C. § 3-405(b).

Chapter 6

CHECKS AND CHECK COLLECTION

I. INTRODUCTION TO ARTICLE 4

A. General principles: Article 4 of the U.C.C. governs *bank deposits and collections*, and, thus, defines the legal obligations between a bank and its customer. Article 4 is not the only source of legal principles that affect this relationship, however. Financial institutions are heavily regulated by state and federal officials, and these parties issue numerous regulations that limit the ability of banks to enter into specific contractual provisions with their customers. Within these limits, however, a bank may negotiate the terms of its relationship with a customer, such as what types of writings will be accepted as drafts, interest rates, and fees for services. Under Article 4 a bank may not, however, enter into an agreement that disclaims responsibility for its own lack of *good faith* or failure to exercise *ordinary care*, or that limits *damages* for such lack or failure. The bank and its customer may agree on *reasonable standards* by which to measure the bank's responsibilities. U.C.C. § 4-103(a).

II. BASIC CONCEPTS IN ARTICLE 4

A. Relationship with Article 3: Article 4 governs the deposit and collection of any *"item."* An "item" can be a negotiable instrument or any non-negotiable promise or order to pay money that a bank handles for collection or payment. U.C.C. § 4-104(a)(9). Payment orders for electronic funds transfers that are governed by Article 4A of the U.C.C. do not constitute items. Neither do credit or debit slips generated by use of a credit or debit card. Items that constitute negotiable instruments within the meaning of Article 3 are also subject to the provisions of that Article. In the event that there is a *conflict* between Article 3 and Article 4, Article 4 governs. U.C.C. § 4-102(a).

B. Relevant parties: Article 4 uses special nomenclature that often corresponds to names used under Article 3. Care should be taken to use these special names only in their proper context.

1. Article 4 refers to the drawee of a draft **as the *payor bank*.** U.C.C. § 4-105(3).

2. A *depositary bank* is the first bank to take an item for collection. If the item deposited for a purpose other than immediate payment over the counter, e.g., collection and subsequent credit to the customer's account, or credit against an outstanding debt owed by the customer to the bank, the bank that first takes the item is a deposi-

tary bank, even if it is also the payor bank. If the item is taken by the payor for immediate payment over the counter, however, the bank is not considered a depositary bank. U.C.C. § 4-105(2).

3. Any bank that handles an item in the course of collection between (but not including) the payor bank and the depositary bank is an *intermediary bank*. U.C.C. § 4-105(4).

4. Any bank that handles an item for collection other than the payor bank is a *collecting bank*. U.C.C. § 4-105(5). If an item is "payable through" a particular bank, that bank is a collecting and not a payor bank. U.C.C. § 4-106(a). In the case of an item that is "payable at" a particular bank, the U.C.C. explicitly authorizes each adopting jurisdiction to determine whether the named bank should be treated as a collecting bank or as a payor bank. U.C.C. § 4-106(b), Alternative A and B.

5. Any bank that presents an item (the demand for acceptance or payment, U.C.C. § 3-501(a)) is a *presenting bank*, but the payor bank is not itself a presenting bank.

6. Any party who has an account with a bank and for whom the bank has agreed to collect items is a *customer* of that bank. U.C.C. § 4-104(a)(5). Thus, a bank that maintains an account with a second bank is a customer of that second bank.

C. **Computation of time for bank action:** Under Article 4, a bank that receives an item for deposit, collection, or payment must act on the item (decide whether to pay the item, dishonor it, or send it further along in the collection chain) within specific time periods. Failure to do so may cause the bank to be liable for the amount of the item even if it cannot collect the amount from another party to the item or a customer. In addition, federal law regulates the timing of the return of checks that have been dishonored by payor banks. Failure to comply with these regulations, which are authorized by the Expedited Funds Availability Act and Regulation CC of the Federal Reserve Board, may render the bank liable for any damages incurred by the depositary bank or the bank's customer as a result of tardiness. See 12 C.F.R. § 229.38(A). These time limitations become particularly important with respect to the granting of credits to depositors, the stopping of payments, and liability for forgeries and alterations. Thus, they will be discussed in some detail in sections describing those situations. There are, however, some general principles that should be considered throughout the study of Article 4.

1. **Midnight deadline:** Action that, under the U.C.C., is required to be taken by a bank's midnight deadline generally must be taken by *midnight on the next banking day* following the banking day on

which the bank receives the relevant item or notice. U.C.C. § 4-104(a)(10). See *supra*, p. 68 and p. 91. These limits, however, may be altered by federal regulations, clearing house rules, or other agreements.

2. **Multi-branch banks:** If an item is handled by different branches of the same bank during the collection process, each branch is considered a *separate bank* for purposes of computing the time within which and determining the place at or to which action may be taken or orders must be given under Articles 3 and 4. U.C.C. § 4-107.

> **Example:** Jones received a check from Green on June 1. The check was drawn by Green on his account at First Bank. On June 2, Jones deposited the check at the Main Street Branch of First Bank, where she maintained her account. On June 3, the check was forwarded to the State Street branch of First Bank, where Green maintained his account. For purposes of determining the midnight deadline by which First Bank must determine whether to pay Green's check, First Bank received the check on June 3, even though the check was received at a different branch of the same bank on June 2. Although the rule was written to allow branches of banks to be treated as separate entities when those branches operate with substantially different procedures, such as where the branches are in different jurisdictions, the rule does not require any investigation into whether or not substantial variation exists. In an age of computerization, one might think that branches of the same bank would be sufficiently linked to permit all branches to be treated as a single bank. U.C.C. § 4-107, Official Comment 1 gives some basis for deviating from the rule. It states that the decision not to draft a more specific rule "leaves to the courts the resolution of the issues arising under this section on the basis of the facts of each case." Thus, in the above example, a court might find that the two branches should be treated as the same bank. Permitting courts to exercise such discretion, however, imposes significant doubt on a process of check collection that is highly dependent on certainty.

3. **Bank rules:** A bank may establish a rule that treats items received no earlier than 2:00 p.m. as having been received at the opening of the next banking day. This provision permits banks an opportunity to process items, prove balances, and make necessary entries on its books each banking day. U.C.C. § 4-108.

III. FEDERAL OVERLAY ON THE CHECK COLLECTION SYSTEM

A. **Expedited check clearing:** One recurring problem in the check collection system has been the uncertainty of a depositary bank about whether a check will ultimately be paid by the drawee. Since most checks are paid, the Uniform Commercial Code requires notification only of non-payment, not of payment. Yet, if checks are drawn on banks distant from the depositary bank, notification of nonpayment may take a substantial period of time as the check is routed through a series of collecting banks prior to presentment and then must be re-routed back to the depositary bank after dishonor. Compliance with the U.C.C. requires only that banks return checks in a reasonably prompt manner. Timeliness has been judged from the time the bank returns the check, not the time at which the depositary receives notice of dishonor. The result, traditionally, has been that depositary and collecting banks have not wanted to release funds (grant final credit to their customers) until several days after a check has been deposited. In addition to fears that the check will ultimately be dishonored, depositary banks have little incentive to release funds early as banks may be able to use the funds in the interim while paying little or no interest to the customer.

B. **Federal law:** The federal government, through regulations issued by the Federal *Reserve Board* and additional legislation, has affected the methods and times of check collection. These regulations have the effect of *"agreements"* under the Uniform Commercial Code, which permits parties to enter into agreements that vary the provisions of Article 4. U.C.C. § 4-103(b). As provisions of federal law, they also preempt the U.C.C. in any case of conflict.

   1. **Regulation J:** The Federal Reserve Board, through Regulation J, empowers Federal Reserve Banks to issue operating circulars that govern the handling of checks and other items. These circulars are binding on those interested in a check that is collected through the Federal Reserve System, whether as owner of the check or as a party in the collection and payment process. Regulation J attempts to expedite the check collection process by requiring payor banks to give *prompt notice* of nonpayment of checks that have been collected through the Federal Reserve System.

   2. **Expedited Funds Availability Act:** In 1987, Congress passed the Expedited Funds Availability Act, which attempts further to expedite the check collection process and reduce the period between when a customer deposits an item in his or her account and when the funds can be withdrawn as a matter of right. The Act also requires depositary banks to pay interest due on deposited amounts

when the bank receives a provisional credit for the item. The Act further divides checks into "local," "non-local," and an unnamed category that covers items unlikely to be dishonored (wire transfers, government checks, "on us" checks) and establishes a **schedule** that requires that funds in respect of these deposits be available for withdrawal as of right within specific periods after the deposit is made. The effect of the Act is to shift some of the risk of dishonor from the customer to banks within the collection chain. The Act applies to the entire payment system, not just to payment mechanisms that pass through a Federal Reserve Bank.

3. **Regulation CC:** The Expedited Funds Availability Act also grants the Federal Reserve Board general regulatory authority over the entire check collection system, not just the Federal Reserve check collection process. The Federal Reserve has responded with Regulation CC ("Reg CC"), 12 C.F.R. § 229, which addresses the issue of funds availability by setting schedules for making deposits available to customers. The Regulation also requires all banks to give **prompt notice of dishonor** of certain checks, even if the bank has a longer period of time for return of the actual check. The notification requirement applies to all checks in amounts exceeding $2,500, and the period for notice is less than that provided in Regulation J. Reg CC also governs the physical return of the check in a manner intended to ensure **expeditious treatment** of the item and abolishes the practice of giving provisional credits between banks. Thus, credits need not be "undone" when checks are dishonored. Reg CC, however, governs only checks. Article 4 governs items that are collected by banks in addition to checks, such as remittance drafts.

IV. OVERVIEW OF CHECK COLLECTION PROCESS

A. **Mechanics of collection:** Checks are typically written by drawers to payees in exchange for goods or services. A payee or subsequent indorsee of a check will typically deposit that instrument where the depositor has an account. The depositary bank may be, but usually is not, the same bank as the payor bank. Check collection involves the means by which the check is sent from the depositary bank to the drawee or payor bank and the decision-making process by which the payor bank determines whether to pay the item and charge the drawer's account the amount of the check. The payor bank, however, may determine that the check will not be paid. This might occur, for instance, if the payor bank discovers that the drawer's account contains insufficient funds to support the check. Alternatively, the payor bank may discover that the drawer has issued a stop payment order against the check. Should the payor bank decide not to pay the item, it must take action to inform the depositary and collecting banks that the check has been dishonored. This process involves the return of checks.

B. Types of checks: The process by which checks are collected varies with the identity and location of depositary and drawee banks.

1. **"On us" checks:** "On us" checks are checks that are deposited or cashed *at the bank on which they were drawn*. Either act constitutes presentment of the check for payment at the payor bank. U.C.C. § 3-501(a). A presenter who is a customer of the payor bank may either cash the check or deposit it in his or her account. A presenter who is not a customer will present the check for cash.

2. **Clearing house items:** Clearing house items are checks drawn on banks other than the depositary bank but that are *within the same local area*. Representatives of these banks may meet at a local clearing house on a daily basis and present checks drawn on each other. Each clearing house bank will settle its account with the other participating banks through a series of debits and credits in accounts maintained through the clearing house.

   Example: Smith receives a check, payable to his order, from Jones for $1,500. The check is drawn on First Bank. Smith deposits this check in his account at Second Bank. Second Bank provisionally credits $1,500 to Smith's account. The same day, Brown draws a $1,000 check drawn on Second Bank to the order of Green and Green immediately deposits the check in his account at First Bank. First Bank provisionally credits $1,000 to Green's account. The next day, representatives from First Bank and Second Bank meet at the local clearing house. Smith's check is given to First Bank and Brown's check is given to Second Bank. If these are the only checks that the two banks have to exchange on that day, Second Bank will receive a net credit on the books of the clearing house in the amount of $500, the difference between the two checks. First Bank will, correspondingly, receive a $500 debit. First Bank will then debit Jones's account $1,500 and Second Bank will debit Brown's account $1,000.

3. **Out-of-town checks:** Checks drawn on banks distant from where they are deposited may be *cleared through the Federal Reserve*. Each of the 12 regional Federal Reserve banks may clear checks within its district or, if necessary, transmit checks to the payor bank's district. Depositary banks using the Federal Reserve to collect checks will submit a package of checks with a list of the individual items known as a cash letter. The Federal Reserve sorts the

checks, makes the appropriate debits and credits in accounts maintained with that Federal Reserve bank by depositaries and payors, and delivers the sorted checks to their respective institutions, or to their correspondent banks or clearing house.

> **Example:** Smith purchases an antique vase from Jones while on vacation in San Francisco. Smith pays for the vase with a check drawn on First Bank in Boston. Jones deposits the check in her account with Second Bank in San Francisco. Second Bank deposits the check for credit in its account at the Federal Reserve Bank in San Francisco. That Federal Reserve Bank transmits the check to the Federal Reserve Bank in Boston. The Boston Federal Reserve Bank sends the check to First Bank and debits the amount of the check from First Bank's account at the Boston Fed. Settlement for the item between the two Federal Reserve Banks is made through the Interdistrict Settlement Fund and is reflected in a credit given by the San Francisco Fed. to Second Bank. Second Bank then finalizes the credit given to Jones.

C. **Provisional settlement:** When a check is deposited in a customer's account to be forwarded to the drawee bank (the "forward collection process"), the U.C.C. provides for the customer to receive a ***provisional settlement or credit*** for the item from the depositary bank. U.C.C. § 4-201(a). At this point, the depositary bank may, but is not required to, permit withdrawal of the deposited funds by its customer. As a matter of protecting itself against exposure on uncollected funds, the depositary bank will not want the customer to have a right to withdrawal until that bank is assured that the drawee will pay the check. Thus, the depositary must send the check to the drawee. Alternatively, in a process known as ***check truncation***, presentation for payment will be made electronically, rather than through physical delivery of the check. Whether presentation is made through physical presentation or electronically, typically the drawee pays the amount of the check, debits the drawer's account, and returns the check to the drawer with a statement of checks drawn on the drawer's account during the statement period. Should the drawee dishonor the check, however, the process of transferring the check must be reversed so that the depositary will know that the check remains unpaid (the "return process"). This reversal may occur either by sending the item back through the collection chain, or by returning it directly to the depositary bank, or by sending information about the check to the depositary bank. This last means of providing notice is required for some checks under federal law. On receiving such notice, the depositary will reverse the provisional credit given to its customer. That reversal may occur by charging the customer's account on the bank's books or by seeking a refund directly from the customer.

1. **Reg CC and "final settlement":** Reg CC changes the language, but not the substance, of this forward check collection process. Reg CC provides that settlements between banks are final when made, even during the forward collection process. 12 C.F.R. § 229.36(d). The Commentary to Reg CC, however, makes clear that this technical change was not intended to change the ability of depositary and collecting banks to reverse credits given for checks that are subsequently dishonored. The language of finality was intended to permit the payor bank to return unpaid checks expeditiously, which typically means by some route other than undoing the forward collection chain step-by-step. Thus, direct returns to the depositary bank are possible. At the same time, the payor bank will have a ***right of revocation and recovery of settlement,*** under U.C.C. § 4-301, against collecting banks to whom it gave a "final" settlement. See page 133, *infra*. This will be possible because the final settlement called for by Reg CC does not constitute ***final payment*** for purposes of the U.C.C., which makes final payment binding on the payor bank. In the words of the Commentary to Reg CC, "[12 C.F.R. § 229.36(d)] provides that settlement between banks during the forward collection chain is 'final' rather than 'provisional.' Settlement by a paying bank is not considered to be final payment for purposes of [the] U.C.C. . . . because a paying bank has the right to recover settlement from a returning or depositary bank to which it returns a check under this subpart."

V. RIGHTS AND OBLIGATIONS OF COLLECTING BANKS

A. **Agency:** The rights of parties during the collection process apply regardless of whether a bank is considered owner of the item or agent of the owner. Thus, pre-Code debates about whether a collecting bank actually owns an item are generally irrelevant to issues that arise under the Code. Nevertheless, for resolution of those issues that remain contingent on the status of actors, the Code provides that, during the collection process, each bank that handles an item serves as *agent* or *sub-agent* of the owner of the item. U.C.C. § 4-201(a).

1. **Liability for care:** While each collecting bank must use ordinary care in presenting an item or sending it for presentment, no bank is otherwise liable for the conduct of another bank or person in the collection chain. U.C.C. § 4-202(c). These provisions codify the ***"Massachusetts rule"*** of the common law, which made each bank liable

only for its own negligence. The provisions reject the **"New York rule,"** which made each bank in the collection chain an agent for banks prior in the chain, and, thus, subjected the initial collecting bank to liability for the conduct of subsequent banks. A collecting bank must, however, exercise ordinary care in the selection of intermediary banks and agents through which it transmits items to the payor bank.

2. **Distinction:** The difference is important if a bank acts negligently with respect to an item. Under U.C.C. § 4-201, only that bank is liable to the owner of the item. Under the New York rule, prior banks would also be liable for selection of the negligent bank as their agent. See U.C.C. § 4-202(c), which limits a bank's liability to its own negligence.

3. **Scope of agency status:** The agency status of a collecting bank prevails regardless of the presence or form of indorsement and even if credit given for the item can or has been withdrawn. U.C.C. § 4-201.

B. **Collecting bank obligation of ordinary care**: A collecting bank is required to exercise ordinary care in each of the following activities:

1. *presenting* an item or *sending* it for presentment;

2. sending *notice of dishonor* or non-payment or returning an item to a transferor after learning that the item has not been paid or accepted;

3. *settling* for an item after receiving final settlement; and

4. *notifying* its transferor of any *loss or delay* in transit after the collecting bank has discovered it. U.C.C. § 4-202(a).

5. In addition, *no bank may disclaim its responsibility* for good faith and ordinary care, although it may by agreement reasonably define its standard of responsibility. U.C.C. § 4-103(a).

C. **What constitutes ordinary care:** The U.C.C. provides certain standards by which the reasonableness of a bank's conduct or its compliance with the obligation of ordinary care during the collection process may be measured.

1. **Midnight deadline:** A collecting bank has exercised ordinary care if it takes any required action before its *midnight deadline* following receipt of the item, notice, or settlement. If the bank takes a longer period of time, it bears the burden of establishing that it has acted in a timely fashion, consistent with its obligation of ordinary care. U.C.C. § 4-202(b).

Example: On May 1, Brown deposited in his account at First Bank a check drawn by Jones on her account at State Bank. First Bank sent the check to Second Bank on May 2. Second Bank was to send the check to State Bank, but misplaced it and did not send it until May 10. On May 9, Jones withdrew all her funds from State Bank. State Bank refused to pay the check and so notified Second Bank on May 11. Second Bank notified First Bank of the check's dishonor on May 12, and First Bank notified Brown on the same day. Second Bank may be liable for lack of ordinary care in misplacing the check and not acting seasonably in presenting the check. First Bank bears no liability as it is not the principal of Second Bank (recall that banks are not agents for each other in the collection process) and acted reasonably and with ordinary care in sending the check to Second Bank and giving notice of dishonor to its customer, Brown.

2. **Sending items:** A collecting bank must send items for collection by any *reasonably prompt method*, given the nature of the item and the circumstances of collection, such as cost and custom. The collecting bank is authorized to send the item directly to the payor bank, but is not obligated to do so. U.C.C. § 4-204.

3. **Damages:** Damages for failure to exercise ordinary care in handling an item will normally be the *amount of the item* less any amount that could not have been realized even if the bank had exercised ordinary care, e.g., where the drawer has valid defenses to payment of the owner. If the bank's failure to exercise due care rises to the level of bad faith, the owner may recover other proximately caused damages. U.C.C. § 4-103(e).

D. **Collecting bank's right of charge-back or refund:** Under U.C.C. § 4-214, a collecting bank that has made a *provisional settlement* with a customer but fails to receive payment for the item may *revoke* the settlement with its customer. The collecting bank may make the revocation by *charging* the customer's account the amount of any credit or by obtaining a *refund* from the customer.

Example: Jones stole Smith's checkbook and forged Smith's signature on a check made payable to Brown in the amount of $100 and drawn on First Bank. Brown deposited the check in his account at Second Bank. Second Bank credited Brown's account $100 and sent the check to First Bank for collection. First Bank noticed the forged signature, refused to pay the check, and returned it to Second Bank in a timely fashion. Second Bank may charge back $100 against Brown's account if it returns the item to him or notifies him of the dishonor within a reasonable time. The fact that a depositor uses the provisional credit initially given on deposit of the item does not affect the right of the collecting bank. Thus, if Brown has withdrawn the $100, Second Bank may obtain a refund from him.

1. **Timely action:** The collecting bank must return the item or send its depositor or transferor notification of the facts by the collecting bank's **midnight deadline** or within a **reasonable longer time** after it learns the facts. A bank that does not act within this deadline may still exercise its right to revoke, charge back, or obtain a refund, but is liable for any loss that results from the delay. U.C.C. § 4-214(a). Thus, if the depositor has withdrawn funds during the period of delay, and the depositary bank is unable to recover funds from its customer, the collecting bank that failed to exercise a timely right of charge back will bear the loss.

2. **Termination:** The collecting bank's right of charge-back or refund **terminates** on final payment of the item. Of course, when the payor bank makes final payment, the collecting bank is entitled to the amount of the draft.

3. **"On us" items:** If the depositary bank is also the payor bank and has made a provisional settlement with the depositor, it may charge back the amount or obtain a refund from the depositor if it returns the item to the depositor before it has made final payment and before its midnight deadline. U.C.C. §§ 4-214(c), 4-301. The provisional settlement must be made by midnight of the banking day of receipt.

> **Example 1:** Jones received a check from Smith drawn on First Bank. On Monday, Jones deposited the check in her own account at First Bank and received a provisional credit. That night, during the process of posting, the clerk at First Bank noticed that Smith's account had insufficient funds to cover the check. The clerk immediately mailed the check back to Jones and reversed the provisional credit. First Bank was entitled to revoke the settlement and charge Jones' account.

> **Example 2:** Same as above, but Jones cashed the check at First Bank instead of depositing it at her account. After the clerk realized that Smith's account had insufficient funds, First Bank sought to obtain a refund from Jones. She is not required to provide a refund, as payment of the check in cash by the payor bank constitutes "final payment" which cuts off the right of refund.

E. **Obligations on return of item:** A collecting bank has returned an item when it **sends the item or delivers it** to the bank's customer or to the transferor of the item. U.C.C. § 4-214(b). Reg CC, however, preempts this rule with respect to checks.

1. **Direct return:** The Regulation permits direct return of checks to the depositary bank or to another bank that can handle the return expeditiously, even if that bank was not involved in the forward collection process. Either a payor bank or an intermediary bank can make direct return to the depositary. It is in order to accommodate this direct return process that Reg CC makes settlements final rather than provisional. 12 C.F.R. §§ 229.30(a)(2), 229.31(a)(2).

2. **Timing of return:** A collecting bank or other bank that handles an item between the payor bank and the depositary bank during the return process (designated as a "returning bank" under Reg CC) must return a check received during the return process in an expeditious manner. 12 C.F.R. § 229.31. The "expeditious manner" requirement may be satisfied by either of two tests:

   a. **Two-day/four-day test:** A returning bank acts expeditiously if it sends the returned check in a manner such that the check would normally be received by the depositary bank not later than 4:00 p.m. (local time) of

      -- the *second business day* following the banking day on which the check was presented to the paying bank if the paying bank and the depositary bank are located in the same check processing region (local paying bank), or

      -- the *fourth business day* following the banking day on which the check was presented to the paying bank if the paying bank and the depositary bank are not in the same check processing region (nonlocal paying bank). 12 C.F.R. § 229.31(a)(1). For these purposes, the paying bank is in the same check processing region as the depositary bank if the paying bank is in the same check processing region (the geographical area served by an office of a Federal Reserve bank for purposes of check collection) as the physical location of the branch or proprietary automated teller machine of the depositary bank in which the check was deposited, or the physical location of both the branch of the depositary bank at which the drawer's account is held and the nonproprietary automated teller machine in which the check is deposited.

   b. **Forward collection test:** A returning bank acts expeditiously if it sends the returned check in a manner that a similarly situated bank would normally handle a check of a similar amount, drawn on the depositary bank, and received by the similarly situated bank for forward collection at the time the returning bank received the returned check. 12 C.F.R. § 229.31(a)(2). This test essentially allows returning banks to satisfy the requirement of expeditious return if they treat returned checks no worse than checks received for forward collection. The underlying assumption is that collecting banks will act expeditiously with respect to checks handled for forward collection out of self-interest in order to collect money from downstream banks as quickly as possible.

3. **Special provisions:** In some cases, a returning bank may be unable to identify the depositary bank of a returned check. The returning bank may then return the check to any collecting bank that handled the check for forward collection. If the returning bank itself was a collecting bank with respect to the unidentifiable check, it must return the item to a collecting bank that handled the check prior to the time that the returning bank handled it. 12 C.F.R. § 229.31(b). Where the dishonored check is unavailable, a copy of the check or proper written notice may be substituted. 12 C.F.R. § 229.31(f).

4. **Obligations of depositary bank:** Reg CC requires a depositary bank that has received a returned check to satisfy specific obligations. These include *acceptance* of the returned checks and written notices of nonpayment at designated locations, and *payment* to the returning or paying bank that returns the check to it for the amount of the check by the close of business on the banking day that the depositary bank received the check. 12 C.F.R. § 229.32. A bank that receives a returned check or notice because the returning bank or paying bank mistakenly believes the recipient is the depositary bank must promptly send the returned check or notice to the proper depositary bank directly or by means of a returning bank, or send the returned check or notice back to the bank from which it was received. 12 C.F.R. § 229.32(c).

VI. OBLIGATIONS OF THE PAYOR BANK: THE FINAL PAYMENT RULE

A. **Overview:** A payor bank that finally pays an item becomes accountable for the amount of the item. U.C.C. § 4-302. At that point, provisional settlements become *final*, and the payor bank will be *unable to give effect* to any *notice, stop orders, legal process*, or *setoffs* with respect to the item. Customers will be able to *withdraw* as a matter of right any funds represented by the finally paid item. U.C.C. § 4-215(d). If a payor bank is accountable for an item, it must disburse the funds that the item represents. A bank's ability to recover mistaken final payments depends on the nature of the bank's mistake and the conduct of the recipient in taking the instrument and expending the proceeds.

B. What constitutes final payment: Final payment occurs when the *payor bank* takes or fails to take any one of a variety of actions. It is important to remember, however, that final payment refers only to the action of payor banks.

1. **Payment in cash:** Final payment occurs if the payor bank pays the item in cash. U.C.C. § 4-215(a)(1). Only a payor bank may pay an item in cash. A bank that receives for deposit a check drawn on another bank and then gives the depositing customer cash for the check has not "paid" the check. Rather, the depositary bank has taken the check for collection and has made a provisional settlement with its customer. Frequently, a bank that makes such a settlement will place a hold on the customer's account in the amount of the cash given to the customer and maintain that hold until the check is finally paid by the payor bank. Technically, this form of making final payment does not make the bank "accountable" for the item (as that phrase is used in U.C.C. § 4-302), since the cash payment itself constitutes the necessary accounting.

   Example: In *Kirby v. First & Merchants National Bank*, 210 Va. 88, 168 S.E.2d 273 (1969), Kirby took a $2,500 check to the plaintiff bank and deposited $2,300 of it in her checking account, receiving $200 in cash. The bank subsequently discovered that the check was drawn against insufficient funds and sought to charge Kirby's account $2,500. The court held that the check had been cashed at the bank and, thus, final payment had been made. Therefore, the bank was not entitled to charge back Kirby's account. The court further held that, even if the settlement for the check had only been provisional, the bank was responsible for the item because it failed to revoke settlement prior to its midnight deadline.

2. **Settlement without right of revocation:** Final payment occurs if the payor bank settles for the item but does not have a *right to revoke* the settlement under statute, clearing house rule, or agreement. U.C.C. § 4-215(a)(2).

   a. **Provisional or final:** Under the U.C.C., a bank may settle for an item either provisionally or finally. A bank makes settlement by payment in cash, by clearing house settlement, in a charge or credit, or by remittance. U.C.C. § 4-104(a)(11). Final settlement constitutes final payment for purposes of U.C.C. § 4-215. In order to make the settlement provisional, the bank must have a right to revoke through statute or agreement when the settlement is initially made. Such agreements are frequently found in clearing house rules.

b. Statutory right: U.C.C. § 4-301 constitutes a ***statutory*** right to revoke a settlement. That section permits a payor bank that has settled for an item before midnight of the day of receipt to revoke the settlement if it returns the item (or, where the item is unavailable, sends written notice of dishonor) prior to the midnight deadline. This provision authorizes the practice of "deferred posting," by which a payor bank receives items on one day but does not post the items to the customer's account until the next day. Any dishonored items, therefore, would not be returned until the day after receipt.

c. Effect of Reg CC: Recall that under Reg CC, all settlements are final. A payor bank that desires to return a check must act expeditiously. See p. 135, *infra*. Expeditious return may affect the timing requirements of U.C.C. § 4-301. A bank that acts subsequent to the midnight deadline requirements of U.C.C. § 4-301, but that still is able to satisfy the requirements of expeditious return will not be liable for the delay. See U.C.C. § 4-301, Official Comment 1. This extension deters banks from using a slower system of return, such as the mail, for dishonored checks in order to meet the midnight deadline where the same bank could make a faster return by waiting an extra day and using its courier service.

3. **Passage of time:** Final payment occurs when the payor bank fails to revoke a provisional settlement within the time limits permitted by statute, clearing house rule, or agreement. U.C.C. § 4-215(a)(3).

   a. Midnight deadline: In the absence of a clearing house rule or agreement that provides a longer period, the period in which a payor bank can revoke a provisional settlement ends at its ***midnight deadline***. U.C.C. § 4-301.

   Example: Smith stole Brown's checkbook and forged Brown's signature on a check made out to the order of Jones in the amount of $1,000. The check was drawn on First Bank. Jones deposited the check in her account at Second Bank. Second Bank forwarded the check to First Bank. First Bank received the forged check on Monday morning. Due to a large volume of checks received on that day, it was unable to complete the process of posting until Wednesday morning. At that time, the clerk at First Bank discovered the forgery and returned the check to Second Bank. The return comes too late, as the midnight deadline passed at midnight on Tuesday. Thus, First Bank became accountable for the item under U.C.C. § 4-302. First Bank may attempt to argue that the high volume of checks resulted from circumstances beyond its control and that its delay should be excused under U.C.C. § 4-109, discussed p. 132, *infra*. In order to succeed, First Bank must be able to show the cause for the delay, the inability of the bank to control the cause, and its due diligence once the cause materialized.

b. **Time of receipt and data processing centers:** For purposes of the midnight deadline, is a check received by a payor bank when it reaches the bank itself or when it reaches a data processing center used by the bank? In *Idah-Best, Inc. v. First Security Bank of Idaho*, 584 P.2d 1242 (Idaho 1978), the depositary bank sent a check to a branch of the drawee bank. That branch sent the check to the data processing center used by the drawee branch. The center encoded the check and debited the amount of the check from the drawer's account. During the night, the computer rejected the check for insufficient funds. The next day the check was forwarded to the drawee branch for examination and determination whether to pay. The bank dishonored the check the following day. The court held that the drawee had complied with the midnight deadline on the grounds that receipt of the check by the data processing center was not the same as receipt by the drawee branch. Hence, the midnight deadline did not begin to run until receipt by the drawee branch. Subsequent cases have rejected this holding. See, e.g., *Central Bank of Alabama v. Peoples National Bank*, 401 So.2d 14 (Ala. 1981). Reg CC explicitly defines "receipt" of a check by a paying bank to include receipt at an off-premises data processing center. 12 C.F.R. § 229.36(b)(1). That regulation, however, is concerned with the expeditious return of checks and does not necessarily govern the timing issues related to the midnight deadline.

4. **Process of posting:** Prior to the adoption of amendments to Article 4, the point at which final payment occurred was defined to include the completion of the "process of posting." U.C.C. PR § 4-213(1)(c). This process consisted of a series of steps that led to a determination of whether or not to pay the item.

a. **Procedure for deciding to pay:** The process of posting was considered the usual procedure followed by the payor bank in determining whether to pay an item and recording the payment. It was defined in U.C.C. PR § 4-109 to include the following steps:

i. *verifying* the drawer's signature,

ii. *ascertaining* that funds were available in the drawer's account

iii. *stamping* the item "paid,"

iv. *charging* the drawer's account, and

v. *correcting* any erroneous action.

b. Uncertainty of time of satisfaction: This definition, and the provision making completion of the process of posting a measure of when final payment had occurred, were deleted because of substantial uncertainties about the time when the requisite steps had been taken, particularly in the area of stop payment orders.

Example 1: Smith stole Brown's checkbook and forged Brown's signature on a check made out to the order of Jones in the amount of $1,000. The check was drawn on First Bank. Jones deposited the check in her account at Second Bank. Second Bank forwarded the check to First Bank. First Bank received the check, sorted it, stamped it "paid," encoded the amount by machine, and determined that Brown had sufficient funds in his account to cover the check. First Bank had a rule that signatures on all checks in excess of $500 were to be visually examined by a clerk, but the clerk failed to notice the forgery. The process of posting has been completed and the check has been finally paid. Recall that if Jones is a holder in due course, First Bank will be unable to recover funds from her once payment to her has been made. U.C.C. § 3-418. In addition, First Bank will be unable to charge Smith's account as an item bearing a forged drawer's signature is not properly payable, *supra,* p. 90.

Example 2: Same as above, but First Bank has a policy of checking signatures only on checks in excess of $1,500. Thus, no verification of signatures will have occurred. While First Bank may argue that the absence of any signature verification means the process of posting has not been completed under U.C.C. PR § 4-109, if First Bank has done all it normally does with respect to this check, it is likely that posting would have been deemed completed.

C. Excuse from midnight deadline rules: A collecting bank or payor bank may be excused for exceeding the time limits of Articles 3 and 4 if a delay was caused by interruption of communication or computer facilities, suspension of payments by another bank, war, emergency conditions, or other *circumstances beyond its control*, provided it *exercised diligence* under the circumstances. U.C.C. § 4-109.

Example: First Bank was the drawee bank on a check drawn by Smith to the order of Jones in the amount of $1,000 and deposited by Jones in her checking account at City Bank. City Bank forwarded the check to First Bank on July 1. That evening, First Bank's computer that was responsible for processing checks malfunctioned. First Bank did not have a backup system and failed to seek assistance from other data processing centers. The computer did not function properly again until July 7. At that time, First Bank discovered that Smith only had $50 in his checking account and returned the check to City Bank. First Bank may be liable on the check for failure to act within the midnight deadline. In *Sun River Cattle Co., Inc. v. Miners Bank of Montana, N.A.*, 164 Mont. 237, 521 P.2d 679 (1974), the court held that failure to anticipate a computer malfunction or to seek assistance elsewhere when the breakdown occurred constitutes a lack of due diligence. Thus, a court that followed this holding would conclude that First Bank may not be excused for its delay. The court in *Sun River Cattle* also suggested that the scope of excuse could be expanded by agreement under U.C.C. § 4-103, but that no such agreement had been entered into by the parties. The explicit addition, in the 1990 amendments to Article 4, of the interruption of "computer facilities" as a basis for excusable delay might be considered an effort to reverse or relax the holding in *Sun River Cattle*. Nevertheless, the failure to anticipate such a breakdown might cause a bank to fail that prong of the test that requires any excusable interruption to be "beyond the control" of the bank.

D. Consequences of final payment: Once final payment has occurred, the ability of the payor to recover or obtain reimbursement of even improperly paid funds will depend on the circumstances of the recipient of the funds and the basis for the mistaken payment. U.C.C. § 3-418. See discussion of final payment, *supra*, pp. 128-129.

1. **Right of recovery and restitution:** The Revision specifically incorporates common law rights of restitution in certain circumstances. If a drawee pays a draft in the mistaken belief that the draft was not subject to a stop payment order or that the draft did not bear an unauthorized drawer's signature, the drawee may recover the amount of the draft from the person who received payment. In any other cases, the drawee may recover the payment to the extent permitted by state law governing mistake and restitution. These remedies, however, are not available to a drawee who has made payment to a person who took the instrument in good faith and for value or who has changed position in reliance on the payment. If a drawee has the right to recover funds under U.C.C. § 3-418, the fact that final payment has occurred under U.C.C. § 4-215 does not alter that right. Prior to the Revision, some courts and

commentators suggested that final payment itself cuts off the right of reimbursement by virtue of the "accountability" language of U.C.C. PR §§ 4-213, 4-302. The Revision made clear that the effect of final payment on the right of the drawee to recover a mistaken payment is governed by U.C.C. § 3-418, rather than U.C.C. § 4-215.

Example 1: Jones stole Smith's checkbook and forged Smith's signature on a check made payable to Brown in the amount of $100. Brown took the check without notice of the forgery, in good faith, and gave value for it. The drawee, First Bank, paid the check without detecting the forged drawer's signature. After Jones notified First Bank of the forgery, First Bank attempted to recover the $100 payment from Brown. First Bank should be unsuccessful because it made final payment to a holder in due course and Brown made no warranty concerning the authenticity of the drawer's signature.

Example 2: In *Morgan Guaranty Trust Co. v. American Savings & Loan Ass'n*, 804 F.2d 1487 (9th Cir. 1986), the court considered the circumstances under which a payor that had finally paid a note could recover for mistaken payment under U.C.C. PR § 3-418. In that case, the holder in due course of a note presented it for payment to Morgan Guaranty, even though the holder knew that the maker had declared bankruptcy, an event that would have given the payor the right to dishonor the note. Morgan Guaranty failed to dishonor the note within the time limits set by U.C.C. § 4-213, and, thus, made final payment. When Morgan Guaranty subsequently realized that payment should not have been made, it sought a restitutionary recovery. The district court stated that once final payment had occurred, its effect was governed by U.C.C. § 3-418, which prohibited restitution where final payment had been made to a holder in due course. The Court of Appeals noted that there had been a split in judicial decisions about whether U.C.C. PR § 4-213 (the pre-Revision section that defined "final payment") had independent substantive effect or only defined final payment and left its consequences to U.C.C. PR § 3-418. The appellate court held that U.C.C. PR § 3-418 governed as to effect, but was augmented by common law principles, including a common law restitutionary right to recover mistaken payments. That right could be exercised here, a majority of the court concluded, because the holder knew of the maker's bankruptcy and knew that the payor "could have dishonored" the note. Thus, the holder had no expectation of final payment, even though the payor did not dishonor. One member of the court vigorously dissented on the theory that

U.C.C. PR § 3-418 had displaced the common law right of restitution for mistaken payment.

2. **Presentment warranties:** The limitations on the right of restitution do not affect any claim that the drawee may have for breach of a presentment warranty.

3. **Accountability:** A payor bank that is not also the depositary bank is accountable for an item, whether properly payable or not, if the payor bank retains the item beyond midnight of the banking day of receipt without making a provisional or final settlement for it. In addition, any payor bank, i.e., even one that is the depositary bank, is accountable for the item if it does not pay or return the item or send notice of dishonor until after its midnight deadline. U.C.C. § 4-302(a). "Accountability," however, does not mean absolute liability. A party seeking to hold a payor bank accountable must demonstrate that it suffered injury as a result of the delay and is subject to defenses of fraud or breach of warranty. See U.C.C. § 4-302, Official Comment; *First National Bank in Harvey v. Colonial Bank*, 831 F. Supp. 637 (N.D. Ill. 1993).

E. **Obligations on return of item under Reg CC:** A payor bank (designated a "paying bank" under Reg CC) that determines not to pay a check has additional obligations under Reg CC, and, as noted above, these obligations may conflict with (and, therefore, pre-empt) obligations under the U.C.C. Primarily, the paying bank has an obligation to return the check in an expeditious manner. This obligation, however, does not apply to a party that breached a presentment warranty under U.C.C. § 4-208. 12 C.F.R. § 229.30(a).

1. **Direct return:** The Regulation permits direct return of checks to the depositary bank or to another bank that can handle the return expeditiously, even if that bank was not involved in the forward collection process. A paying bank can make direct return to the depositary. It is in order to accommodate this direct return process that Reg CC makes settlements final rather than provisional. 12 C.F.R. § 229.30(a)(2).

2. **Timing of return:** A paying bank must return a check received during the return process in an expeditious manner. 12 C.F.R. § 229.30. The "expeditious manner" requirement may be satisfied by either of two tests.

   a. **Two-day/four-day test:** A paying bank acts expeditiously if it sends the returned check in a manner such that the check would normally be received by the depositary bank not later than 4:00 p.m. (local time) of

-- the **second business day** following the banking day on which the check was presented to the paying bank if the paying bank, where the paying bank and the depositary bank are located in the same check processing region (local paying bank), or

-- the **fourth business day** following the banking day on which the check was presented to the paying bank if the paying bank and the depositary bank are not in the same check processing region (nonlocal paying bank). 12 C.F.R. § 229.30(a)(1). For these purposes, the paying bank is in the **same check processing region** as the depositary bank if the paying bank is in the same check processing region (the geographical area served by an office of a Federal Reserve bank for purposes of check collection) as the physical location of the branch or proprietary automated teller machine of the depositary bank in which **the check was deposited**, or the physical location of both the branch of the depositary bank at which the **drawer's account is held** and the nonproprietary automated teller machine in which the check is deposited.

b. **Forward collection test:** A paying bank acts expeditiously if it sends the returned check in a manner that a similarly situated bank would normally handle a check of a similar amount, drawn on the depositary bank, and received by the similarly situated bank for forward collection at the time the returning bank received the returned check. 12 C.F.R. § 229.30(a)(2). This test essentially allows returning banks to satisfy the requirement of expeditious return if they treat returned checks no worse than checks received for forward collection. As in the case of returning banks, the underlying assumption is that collecting banks will act expeditiously with respect to checks handled for forward collection out of self-interest in order to collect money from downstream banks as quickly as possible.

3. **Notification on dishonor of large checks:** Under Reg CC, a bank that determines not to pay a check in the amount of $2,500 or more must provide notice of nonpayment to the depositary bank by 4:00 p.m. on the second business day following the banking day on which the check was presented. Notice may be made by any reasonable means and need not include the returned check. Thus, a telephone call or facsimile message is sufficient. 12 C.F.R. § 229.33. The depositary bank must send its customer notice of the dishonor by midnight of the banking day following the banking day on which it

received the returned check or notice, or within a longer reasonable time.

4. **Warranties on return:** A paying bank that returns a check and receives a settlement or other consideration for it warrants that it returned the check within the deadlines established by the U.C.C., Reg J, and Reg CC extensions; that it is authorized to return the check; that the check has not been materially altered; and that, where a notice in lieu of return has been made, the original check has not and will not be returned. Similar warranties are made with respect to any notice of nonpayment. 12 C.F.R. § 229.34.

5. **Warranties to paying bank:** Any bank that presents a check to a paying bank and receives a settlement or consideration for it warrants to the paying bank that the total amount of checks presented is equal to the total amount of the settlement demanded.

6. **Warranty on encoding:** In addition, *each bank that presents or transfers* a check or returned check warrants to any bank that subsequently handles it that, at the time of presentment of transfer, the information encoded after issue in magnetic ink on the check or returned check is correct. 12 C.F.R. § 229.34(c)(3). This warranty supersedes, with respect to checks, the warranty of U.C.C. § 4-209(a), which provides only that *the person who encodes* information on an item after issue warrants the accuracy of the information to a subsequent collecting bank and to the payor bank or other payor.

F. **Liability under Reg CC:** Reg CC requires banks to exercise ordinary care and to act in good faith in complying with its provisions.

1. **Damages:** A bank that fails to exercise ordinary care or to act in good faith may be liable to an injured party in the amount of the loss incurred, up to the amount of the check. Causal relationship between the failure to exercise due care and the loss must also be shown. A bank that fails to act in good faith may also be liable for other proximate damages. 12 C.F.R. § 229.38(a).

2. **Comparative negligence:** The Regulation adopts a comparative negligence scheme. Damages otherwise available to a person who itself fails to exercise ordinary care or to act in good faith will be diminished in proportion to the amount of negligence or bad faith attributable to that person. 12 C.F.R. § 229.38(c).

3. **No double liability:** A paying bank that fails to comply with Reg CC's return requirements and the midnight deadline of the U.C.C. with respect to a particular check may be liable under either Reg CC or the U.C.C., but not both. 12 C.F.R. § 229.38(b).

CHAPTER 7

BANK'S RELATIONSHIP WITH ITS CUSTOMER

I.   RIGHT TO CHARGE CUSTOMER'S ACCOUNT

A. Properly payable: A bank may charge a customer's account only for items that are "properly payable." U.C.C. § 4-401(a). In order to be properly payable, an item must be authorized by the customer and be in accordance with any agreement between the customer and its bank. Thus, the phrase excludes items that bear forgeries or alterations, items that are not yet due for payment, and items that do not bear the customer's signature.

1. **Overdraft:**   If an item is otherwise properly payable, the bank may charge the customer's account even if the charge creates an overdraft in the account. The draft itself constitutes a promise by the drawer to reimburse the drawee. U.C.C. § 4-401. It was unclear prior to the Revision whether a bank could charge either party to a joint account, or only the party whose order caused the overdraft when one party authorized a withdrawal that created an overdraft. The amendments to Article 4 provide that a customer is not liable for the amount of an overdraft if the customer neither signed the item nor benefited from its proceeds.

    Example: John and Mary held a joint account at First Bank. The account had a balance of $1,000. John wrote a check at the bank to the order of cash for $5,000 and the bank paid the check. John lost the proceeds of the check at the track. First Bank cannot recover the amount of the overdraft from Mary as she neither signed the check nor benefited from its proceeds, even though she is a customer on the account.

2. **Alteration and completion:**   If the item has been altered, a bank may still charge the customer's account for a good faith payment made consistent with the original tenor of the item, or consistent with a completed item, even though the bank knows that the item was left incomplete by the drawer. The bank does not have this right, however, if it knows that the completion was improper. U.C.C. § 4-401(d).

3. **Antedating and postdating:**   While drafts may be antedated or postdated without affecting their negotiability, an item is not properly payable until its stated date. U.C.C. § 3-113. In order to accommodate increased computerized treatment of checks, however, Article 4 treats postdated checks as properly payable at the time of

presentment, unless the customer has given notice to the bank of the postdating. U.C.C. § 4-401(c). The notice, which will be treated essentially as a stop payment order until the date of the check, must describe the check with reasonable certainty and be received at a time that permits the bank to act on it before the bank takes any action towards payment of the check. A bank that makes an early payment of a postdated item, however, will be subrogated to the rights of the holder who is paid and may be able to recover from the customer on that basis. U.C.C. § 4-407.

II. STOPPING PAYMENT ON AN ITEM

A. **Customer's right to stop payment:** A ***customer or any person authorized to draw on an account*** has the right to order the bank to stop payment of any item payable from the account or to close the account as long as the bank receives the order in time to act on it before becoming accountable for the item. U.C.C. § 4-403. If the signature of more than one person is required to draw on an account, any of the authorized signatories may stop payment or close the account.

1. **Form:** The customer's order may be ***oral or in writing***, but an oral order is effective only for 14 days.

> **Example 1:** John and Mary are married and have a joint account in First Bank. Mary learns that John has issued a check for a stereo system with funds that were supposed to be used to pay the mortgage. Mary may order First Bank to stop payment on the check even though she did not issue it, as the check is payable from her account.

> **Example 2:** City Savings Bank issues teller's checks payable through its account at First Bank. Jones has purchased a teller's check in the amount of $1,000 to pay for a stereo system Jones is buying from Brown. When Jones returns home with the stereo system, she immediately realizes that it is inoperable. Jones may not stop payment on the teller's check at First Bank, as the item is not payable from her account at that institution. She may, however, request City Savings Bank to issue a stop payment order to First Bank. City Savings Bank may do so, as a "customer" includes "a bank that maintains an account at another bank."

> **Example 3:** Jones is a seller of furniture. Brown endorses his paycheck from his employer over to Jones in payment for a table that Jones represents to be an antique. The check is drawn on First Bank. Brown has no account at First Bank. Immediately

after bringing the table home, Brown realizes that the table has been newly manufactured. Brown cannot order First Bank to stop payment on the paycheck as Brown is not a customer of the payor bank.

Note: In the two preceding examples, the aggrieved party may set up adverse claims to the check or request the drawee's customer to attempt assertion of the *jus tertii* doctrine.

2. **Liability:** Issuing a stop payment order does not relieve the drawer or maker of liability on the instrument. If the item has fallen into the hands of a holder in due course, or if a holder is not otherwise subject to a defense in the drawer's or maker's contract, the drawer or maker is still subject to contract liability.

> **Example:** Smith bought a $500 suit from Brown on a whim and gave Brown a personal check in return. After wearing the suit, Smith realized that he really could not afford it and sought to return it to Brown. Brown rightfully refused to take the suit back, so Smith issued a stop payment order to the drawee bank which, consistent with the order, dishonored the check. Smith remains liable to Brown (or any subsequent holder of the check) on the drawer's contract.

B. **When stop payment order comes too late:** A customer's stop payment order comes too late if the drawee bank does not have a reasonable time to act on it. That time expires if, at the time the drawee receives the order, it has taken any one of a series of actions. These actions essentially indicate that the bank has paid or intends to pay the item or is accountable for it. Thus, these actions are basically the same as those that allow a determination that the item finally has been paid under U.C.C. § 4-213. They include

1. *acceptance* or *certification* of the item,

2. *payment* of the item in *cash*,

3. *settlement* of the item *without having a right to* revoke the settlement under statute, clearing house rule, or agreement,

4. making a provisional *settlement without* revocation within the midnight deadline,

5. with respect to checks, passage of a cutoff hour, which may be no earlier than one hour after the opening of the next banking day after the banking day on which the bank received the check and no later than the close of that next banking day, or

6. where no such cutoff hour has been established, the close of the next banking day after the banking day on which the bank received the

check. In addition to their consequences for stop payment orders, these same time limits apply to foreclose the effectiveness of any ***knowledge, notice, legal process, or setoff*** that would otherwise terminate, suspend, or modify the bank's right or duty to pay an item or to charge the customer's account for the item. U.C.C. § 4-303(a).

C. **Process of posting:** Prior to the Revision, Article 4 also provided that stop payment orders, knowledge, notice, legal process, or setoff came too late to be effective with respect to a bank's duty or right to pay an item if received after completion of the "process of posting." That process involved the procedure that a bank follows in determining whether to pay an item and in recording the item. For purposes of when a stop payment order comes too late, the process of posting included:

1. *verification of signatures*,

2. ascertaining that ***sufficient funds*** are available in the customer's account,

3. ***charging*** the customer's account, and

4. ***correcting or reversing*** an entry or erroneous action. U.C.C. PR § 4-109.

Interpretation: The better interpretation of "process of posting" was that "correcting or reversing" erroneous action involves only correction of technical errors, such as debiting the customer's account in the wrong amount. In the controversial case of *West Side Bank v. Marine National Exchange Bank*, 37 Wis.2d 661, 155 N.W.2d 587 (1968), however, the Wisconsin Supreme Court held that the "reversing erroneous action" clause permitted a payor bank to honor stop payment orders received up to its midnight deadline, even though it had previously determined to pay the item. This interpretation makes superfluous the condition that stop payment orders come too late on completion of the "process of posting," as that process would never be completed until passage of the midnight deadline, which is an independent measure of the time when stop payment orders come too late. U.C.C. PR §§ 4-303(1)(e), 4-213. Additionally, a stop payment order comes too late even if it precedes completion of the process of posting if the payor bank has otherwise "evidenced by examination ... and by action its decision to pay the item." U.C.C. PR § 4-303(1)(d). This latter period clearly had passed in the *West Side Bank* case. Uncertainties about when the process of posting had been completed led to the elimination of the test from Article 4.

D. Certified and cashier's checks: Certified checks, cashier's checks or personal money orders issued by the bank on which they are drawn may be considered accepted on issuance and, thus, are not subject to stop payment orders. U.C.C. §§ 3-409, 3-412, 4-303(a)(1).

E. Effect of paying over stop payment order: A bank that pays an item over its customer's stop payment order is *prima facie liable* for the amount of the item.

    1. Subrogation: Nevertheless, the bank will be subrogated to the rights of any holder in due course of the item or to the rights that the payee or other holder had on the instrument or under contract law. Thus, if the payee or holder could have recovered the amount of the item from the drawer, either on the instrument or the underlying transaction, the bank will not have to recredit the customer's account. U.C.C. § 4-407.

        a. Customer burden: The customer bears the *burden of proof with respect to any loss suffered as a result of payment over a stop payment order*. U.C.C. § 4-403(c). This requirement implies that even a bank that has negligently paid an item over a stop payment order need not recredit the customer's account until the burden of proving loss has been met, notwithstanding that the bank was in the superior position to avoid the loss to the customer. Where the customer can prove losses, however, he or she can recover damages for wrongful dishonor of subsequent items.

        Example: Jones purchased a stereo system from Brown for $1,000 and issued Brown her check, drawn on First Bank, in that amount. Jones subsequently decided that she did not want to keep the system and sought to return it to Brown. Brown rightfully refused to take back the system or to return the check to Jones. Jones ordered First Bank not to pay the check. First Bank negligently paid the check over the stop payment order. First Bank need not recredit Jones' account since it is subrogated to Brown's right to the $1,000 payment and Jones cannot prove that she suffered any loss as a result of the bank's payment.

        b. Conflict: Notice, however, that U.C.C. § 4-407(2) allows a payor bank that has paid an item over a stop payment order to assert the rights of the payee or other holder against the drawer. A payor bank that sought to take advantage of this provision would have the burden of proving that its customer had not lost anything by virtue of payment over the order, since the customer would otherwise still have been liable to the payee or other holder whose rights the book is now asserting. But this allocation of the burden of proof conflicts with the above implication of U.C.C. § 4-403(c). Perhaps one way to resolve this conflict is to recognize that drafters of the Code have subsequently removed an original comment to U.C.C. § 4-403(c) that explicitly provided that the bank is not obligated to recredit the customer's account after paying over a stop payment order until the customer satisfied his or her burden of proof under that subsection. Thus, in the above example, Jones would assert that the bank had to credit her account until it could prove that it had the right of a holder to payment.

2. **Subrogation against holder:** A bank that pays an item over a stop payment order is also subrogated to the rights of the drawer or maker against any holder with respect to the transaction from which the item arose.

> **Example:** Same as above, but Jones seeks to return the stereo because it is not functioning as warranted. If First Bank fails to honor the stop payment order, it must recredit Jones' account, but is subrogated to Jones' breach of warranty claim against Brown and may recover the $1,000 from Brown. If the customer has the burden of proving loss, a bank that in good faith under U.C.C. § 4-403(c) refuses to recredit its customer's account after paying over a stop payment order will not be liable for damage suffered by the customer prior to the time when the customer satisfies his or her burden. Thus, if Jones, believing that the $1,000 check to Brown would not be paid, drew additional checks that were dishonored because payment of the $1,000 check left insufficient funds in her account, dishonor of those checks would not be wrongful prior to the time that Jones proved her loss. Jones, therefore, will assert that the bank has the burden of proving the rights of the holder to payment and must credit her account until it satisfies that burden.

3. **Limits:** The bank's right of subrogation exists "only to the extent necessary to prevent loss to the bank by reason of its payment of the item." U.C.C. § 4-407.

> **Example:** Same as above, but Jones returns the stereo because a wiring defect caused a fire in Jones's home and destroyed her property. First Bank is not subrogated to any claim Jones might have with respect to those damages as they were not caused by the Bank's payment of the item.

4. **No waiver:** Any attempt by a bank contractually to waive its liability for negligent payment in violation of an effective stop pay-

ment order is invalid. See U.C.C. §§ 4-103(a), 4-403, Official Comment 7. The Comment also notes, however, that an agreement to the contrary would have to be evaluated in the light of the general obligation of good faith.

III. ADVERSE CLAIM

A. General rule: A non-customer who cannot order a bank to stop payment may still be able to prevent the drawee bank from honoring the check as presented by asserting an adverse claim to the instrument.

   1. Intervention: The conditions for asserting an adverse claim are set forth in the discussion of the rights of holders, *supra*, pp. 42-47. Essentially, they require intervention of the claimant in an action brought by the holder against the maker or drawer for payment. U.C.C. § 3-305(c).

   2. Indemnity or injunction: Alternatively, the adverse claimant may seek to forestall payment to the holder. In order to accomplish this, the adverse claimant must either supply *indemnity* deemed adequate by the party seeking the discharge or obtain an *injunction* against payment, *supra*, p. 50.

IV. WRONGFUL DISHONOR OF AN ITEM

A. General rule: A payor bank is liable to its *customer* for damages proximately caused by the wrongful dishonor of an item. U.C.C. § 4-402. Thus, if a bank fails to honor a properly payable check drawn on an account that contains sufficient funds, the bank must pay any damages that the customer suffers as a result of the dishonor. The bank's liability is limited to actual damages, but these need not be financial. A customer who suffers nonfinancial damages, such as arrest or prosecution, may recover if she can prove they proximately were caused by the wrongful dishonor. Consequential damages may be recovered should they be justified in the particular case.

B. Punitive damages: The U.C.C. rejects the *"trader rule"* which allowed a merchant to recover damages with a showing of actual damages on the assumption that such a person was necessarily injured by a wrongful dishonor. The statutory limitation to actual damages may also be interpreted to displace any claim for punitive damages.

   Example: Jones maintained two checking accounts at First Bank, a personal account and an account for the corporation of which she was president. The treasurer of the corporation drew a $500 check against insufficient funds in the corporate checking account, but First Bank paid the check and charged the funds to Jones's personal checking account. This left Jones with a $100 balance in her personal account. On learning the above, Jones notified First Bank that the $500 check was a corporate obligation and asked them to recredit $500 to her personal account. The bank failed to do so. Jones subsequently wrote a check for $150 to Smith's Autos as a deposit on a new automobile. The bank dishonored the check. On return of the check to Smith's Autos, they cancelled the transaction with Jones. Jones brings an action against First Bank for harm to her reputation, but cannot prove any actual damages. Does the dishonor of her check after she notified First Bank that the $500 check was not a personal obligation constitute an absence of good faith that may support an independent claim for punitive damages? See *Loucks v. Albuquerque National Bank*, 76 N.M. 735, 418 P.2d 191 (1966).

C. Customer: Only a customer has rights under U.C.C. § 4-402. A customer is a person having an account with a bank or for whom a bank has agreed to collect items. U.C.C. § 4-104(a)(5). A "person" may be either an individual or an organization. U.C.C. § 1-201(30).

> **Example:** Assume in the example above that Jones had written a check against insufficient funds in her personal account and that First Bank paid the check against the corporate account. If First Bank subsequently wrongfully dishonored checks against the corporate account and the dishonor caused Jones personal damages, she would have no cause of action under U.C.C. § 4-402 because the "customer" that suffered the wrongful dishonor was the corporation, not Jones. See *Loucks v. Albuquerque National Bank*, 76 N.M. 735, 418 P.2d 191 (1966).

> Thus, a payee who is the holder of a check wrongfully dishonored cannot bring an action against the payor bank. This is consistent with the rule that a draft, including a check, does not operate as an assignment of funds in the drawee's hands and the drawee is not liable on the instrument until acceptance. U.C.C. § 3-408. Clearly, a payor bank that dishonors a check has not accepted it. The holder may, however, attempt to bring an action against the payor bank for common law negligence.

V. OTHER DOCTRINES AFFECTING BANKS AND THEIR CUSTOMERS

A. Agreement with customers: A bank may agree with its customer that certain provisions of Article 4 will not be binding on their relationship. No agreement, however, can disclaim validly a bank's responsibility for good faith conduct or failure to exercise ordinary care or limit damages for bad faith or negligence. The bank and customer, however, may agree on standards by which responsibility of the bank is to be measured as long as those standards are not manifestly unreasonable. U.C.C. § 4-103(a).

B. Stale checks: A bank is under no obligation to pay a check that is presented more than *six months* after its date, unless the check has been certified. U.C.C. § 4-404. Thus, dishonor of such a check is not wrongful, even if the customer has sufficient funds to cover the check. If the bank in good faith decides to pay such a check, it may charge its customer's account. Certified checks are exempt from this rule because the certifying bank has become the primary obligor under U.C.C. §§ 3-411, 3-413.

C. Death or incompetence of customer: U.C.C. § 4-405. A payor or collecting bank's authority to accept, pay, or collect an item or to account for proceeds of collection is not rendered ineffective by the customer's incompetence unless the bank knows of an adjudication of incompetence. The death or incompetence of a customer does not *automatically revoke* authority to pay, collect, or account for items. Revocation occurs only when the bank *knows* of the death or adjudication of incompetence and has a reasonable opportunity to act on it.

   1. Pre-death items: Even a bank that knows of a customer's death may pay or certify checks drawn on or before the date of death if it acts within 10 days of that date.

CHAPTER 8

ELECTRONIC FUNDS TRANSFERS AND CREDIT CARDS

I. INTRODUCTION

A. Types: Recent years have seen the growth of payment systems that involve mechanisms other than checks and notes. In the consumer area, these systems are dominated by two payment methods. A consumer who utilizes an ***electronic funds transfer*** authorizes debits from or credits to his or her account through the use of a terminal and an access device, such as a card. A consumer who utilizes a ***credit card*** authorizes the card issuer to make payments on the consumer's behalf. In return, the card user promises to repay the issuer.

B. Federal law: These areas are not directly regulated by the U.C.C., although some analogies do exist. Instead, these areas are regulated by federal law and regulations.

C. Disclosure: The federal law in these areas does not deal comprehensively with all aspects of electronic funds transfers and credit cards. Instead, federal laws and regulations are primarily concerned with consumer protection. Thus, these laws and regulations require certain disclosures, error resolution procedures, and limitations on when a consumer can be charged.

II. ELECTRONIC FUND TRANSFER ACT ("EFT ACT")

A. Introduction: Congress passed the EFT Act, 15 U.S.C. §§ 1693 et seq., in 1978 to provide consumer protection with respect to electronic payment systems. The Federal Reserve Board has enacted Regulation E to implement the EFT Act, 12 C.F.R. § 205.

    1. Mechanisms: While the EFT Act does not define electronic payment systems, common mechanisms include automatic teller machines, through which a consumer may make deposits, withdrawals, or payments without the intervention of a human teller, and point-of-sale terminals, through which the seller of a good may debit the account of the purchaser at the point of sale or at the seller's financial institution. The latter payment mechanism eliminates the need for the buyer to make payment by cash or check.

    2. Consumer accounts: In order to be covered by the EFT Act, an electronic fund transfer must involve a debit from or credit to an account "established primarily for personal, family or household purposes." 12 C.F.R. § 205.2(b). Thus, the EFT Act covers only consumer accounts.

3. **Transfers covered:** Under Regulation E, an "electronic fund transfer" includes all transfers resulting from debit card transactions, including those that do not involve an electronic terminal at the time of the transaction. Thus, if a purchaser executes an invoice at the point of sale, but the seller collects funds electronically at the seller's financial institution rather than at the point of sale, the transaction is covered, according to Regulation E.

B. **Disclosure requirements:** Regulation E requires disclosure of certain terms prior to a consumer's first electronic funds transfer. These disclosures include the consumer's liability for unauthorized charges, right to receive documentation of transfers, right to stop payment of an order, the financial institution's liability for wrongful dishonor, a notice of error resolution procedures, and a statement listing interest charges.

III. UNAUTHORIZED ELECTRONIC FUNDS TRANSFERS

A. **Definition:** Regulation E defines an unauthorized electronic funds transfer as a transfer "from a consumer's account initiated by a person other than the consumer without actual authority to initiate the transfer and from which the consumer receives no benefit." The term "unauthorized" excludes any transfer initiated by a person who was furnished with and authorized to use the access device to the account by the consumer, a transfer initiated with fraudulent intent by the consumer, or a transfer that is initiated by the financial institution or its employee.

> **Example 1:** Brown asks Smith for a loan of $100. Smith gives Brown his card and personal identification number ("PIN") that allows access to Smith's account at First Bank. This constitutes an "access device" that permits electronic access to Smith's account. Brown takes the card to an automatic teller machine of First Bank and uses it to withdraw $500 from Smith's account. Since Smith provided Brown with the access device, the transfer is not unauthorized and Smith is responsible for the full withdrawal.

> **Example 2:** Smith withdraws $100 from his account at First Bank using his access card and PIN at an automatic teller machine. As he leaves the machine, Smith is robbed by Brown, who demands that Smith hand over his card and inform Brown

of his PIN. Smith complies with Brown's demand. Brown withdraws an additional $500 from Smith's account. The Federal Reserve contends that handing over a PIN under such circumstances does not constitute "furnishing" of the access device and, thus, the transfer of the $500 is unauthorized. The $100 initial transfer by Smith is, of course, authorized.

Example 3: Same as above, but Brown never requests Smith to provide Brown with the access device. Instead, Brown forces Smith at gunpoint to make an additional $500 withdrawal with his access device and hand it over to Brown. Again, the Federal Reserve position is that the transfer is unauthorized.

Example 4: Same as above, but Brown only robs Smith of the $100 that Smith had withdrawn. The transfer was not unauthorized and, thus, the bank bears no liability for it.

Example 5: Brown holds up Smith at gunpoint and forces Smith to make out a check to bearer in the amount of $100. Brown cashes the check at the drawee bank before Smith can issue a stop payment order. It would be difficult for Smith to contend that his own signature was unauthorized under U.C.C. § 3-403, and, thus, Smith is likely to bear the loss. Notice here the difference between negotiable instruments and the Federal Reserve interpretation of unauthorized electronic funds transfers.

B. Limitations: If an unauthorized electronic fund transfer is made with an access device that is requested, authorized, or validated by the consumer (an "accepted access device"), then the consumer's liability for the transfer is severely limited.

1. **General rule:** As a general matter, the consumer's liability for an unauthorized electronic fund transfer will not exceed $50 or the amount of unauthorized transfers that occur before notice to the financial institution. The extent of the consumer's liability is not affected by any negligence or lack of ordinary care on the part of the consumer.

Example: Smith keeps the card that allows him electronic access to his account at First Bank in a paper sleeve provided by First Bank. Smith has negligently written his PIN on the paper sleeve. Smith loses the paper sleeve and card. Brown finds the card, notices the PIN written on the paper sleeve, and uses the card to withdraw $500 from Smith's account. Smith timely notifies First Bank of the lost card, but does not do so until Brown has already made the withdrawal. Since Regulation E and the

EFT Act make no exception for consumer negligence, unlike the case with U.C.C. § 3-406 with respect to checks, Smith is liable only for $50 of the $500 withdrawal.

2. **Notification:** If the consumer fails to notify the financial institution within two business days after learning of the loss or theft of the access device, the consumer's **liability may be increased**, but still will not exceed the lesser of $500 or the sum of

   a. $50 or the amount of unauthorized electronic funds transfers that occur before the close of the two business days, whichever is less, and

   b. the amount of unauthorized electronic fund transfers that the financial institution establishes occurred more than two business days after the consumer learns of the loss or theft of the access device, and only because the consumer failed to notify the institution.

3. **Failure to report:** If the consumer fails to report within 60 days of transmittal of the periodic statement sent by the financial institution any unauthorized electronic funds transfer that appears on the statement, the consumer's liability again can be increased, but will not exceed the sum of

   a. the lesser of $50 or the amount of unauthorized electronic funds transfers that appear on the periodic statement or that occur during the 60-day period, and

   b. the amount of unauthorized electronic fund transfers that occur after the close of the 60 days and before notice to the financial institution, and that the financial institution establishes would not have occurred but for the failure of the consumer to notify the financial institution within that time.

4. **Excuse:** If the consumer's delay in notifying the financial institution of loss or theft of an access device was caused by **extenuating circumstances**, such as extended travel or hospitalization, the time periods specified above are extended to a reasonable time.

5. **State law:** Any **state law that reduces the consumer's liability** below that imposed by the federal law or regulations concerning unauthorized electronic fund transfers has priority over the federal standard.

IV. CREDIT CARDS

A. **Nature of the transaction:** Unlike drafts and electronic funds transfers, credit cards do not involve a pre-existing fund of a customer.

Instead, the issuer of a credit card agrees to **honor requests for payment** submitted on behalf of sellers of goods or services that have been sold or rendered to the customer. The customer, in turn, agrees to repay the issuer. Thus, while the customer who has a deposit account with a bank is a creditor of that bank, a customer who uses a credit card becomes a **debtor** of the issuer.

1. **Means of collection:** A seller who accepts a credit card will send invoices that include the credit card number, seller's account number with the issuer, and, in face-to-face transactions, the customer's signature to the seller's bank. Typically, that bank will credit the seller's account and electronically transmit the relevant data, (including credit card number and amount of invoice), through banking channels to the issuer. The issuer makes payment to the transmitting bank and sends a periodic statement to the customer of charges against his or her account. The customer makes payment (either in full or, in the case of some credit cards, amortized over a payment period) directly to the issuer.

B. **Law:** The relationship between the issuer and the customer is governed in part by the **Federal Truth in Lending Act ("TILA"), Regulation Z** of the Federal Reserve Board issued under TILA (12 C.F.R. § 226) and the **Federal Fair Credit Billing Act**. Most of these provisions are directed at disclosure to the customer of terms and conditions of the relationship. Some of the provisions, along with the judicial gloss placed on them, dictate substantive elements of the relationship. For instance, Regulation Z requires that credit for payment be given as of the date of receipt in most circumstances.

1. **Cancellation:** While a condition of many credit card relationships is that the issuer may cancel the card at any time, at least one court has determined that cancellation must be preceded by an attempt to notify the customer, especially in the case where the customer seeks payment for goods or services already consumed (*e.g.*, a restaurant meal). The failure to provide notice precludes the card issuer from refusing charges and makes any such refusal equivalent to the wrongful dishonor of a check. *Gray v. American Express Co.*, 743 F.2d 10 (D.C. Cir. 1984).

2. **Applicability of federal law:** TILA and Regulation Z are directed primarily at use of credit cards by **consumers**. In determining whether a consumer transaction is involved, the primary purpose of the account rather than the particular transaction that gave rise to the dispute will govern. Nevertheless, Regulation Z prohibits issuance of credit cards for all purposes, including business, except in response to a request or application by the customer or as a renewal of an existing card. 12 C.F.R. § 226.12.

C. Disclosure requirements:

1. **Initial disclosure statement:** Regulation Z requires the issuer to disclose certain terms of the agreement to the consumer before the first use of the credit card. These include:

   a. the circumstances under which a finance charge will be imposed,

   b. an explanation of how that charge will be determined,

   c. the periodic rate that may be used to compute the finance charge,

   d. the method used to determine the balance on which the finance charge will be computed,

   e. the amount of any other charges,

   f. a statement that outlines the customer's rights to assert claims and defenses,

   g. a statement of error resolution procedures, and

   h. the existence of any security interest that the issuer purports to retain in property purchased by the customer with the card.

2. **Periodic statement disclosure:** The issuer must supply additional disclosures to the customer with periodic billing statements. These disclosure items include the account balance at the beginning of the billing cycle, an identification of each credit transaction, any credit to the account during the billing cycle, the rate used to compute any finance charge, the balance on which the finance charge is computed, the amount of the finance charge, the annual billing rate, the date by which payments must be received to avoid additional finance charges, and an address for notice of billing errors.

D. Unauthorized use:
A customer is ***strictly liable*** for the unauthorized use of a credit card, but the extent of that liability is ***sharply limited***.

1. **Defined:** Unauthorized use consists of the use of a credit card by a person other than the customer and who ***does not have actual, implied, or apparent authority*** for such use and from which the customer receives no benefit. Thus, an issuer may argue that it can charge a customer for use made without the customer's actual authority, but with respect to which the user had implied or apparent authority.

   > **Example:** Jones gave her teenage son her credit card to purchase a $25 shirt at a department store. The son also sought to purchase stereo equipment worth $200 with the card at the same store. The store transmitted the $225 charge to the issuer,

which charged Jones. If Jones objects to payment, the store may contend that she clothed her son with apparent authority to use the card for both purposes.

2. **Notification:** If the customer notifies the issuer of loss, theft, or possible unauthorized use of the card, the customer bears ***no liability*** for any subsequent use. Notification may be made by telephone or in writing, but is effective only when received or at the time ordinarily required for transmission.

3. **Use prior to notification:** If a card has been used without authorization of the customer prior to notification, the customer's liability is limited to the lesser of $50 or the amount of goods or services obtained with the card. Both the imposition of liability and the limitation apply without reference to the culpability of the customer.

4. **Limits on recovery:** The issuer may charge the customer the $50 liability cost only if

   a. the card has been ***accepted*** by the customer; and

   b. the issuer has previously provided the customer with ***notice*** of the maximum liability, the means by which the issuer may be notified of loss or theft, and a means to identify the customer or authorized user of the card.

   Example 1: Smith purchased some goods from Jones and paid for them with a credit card. Smith negligently left his credit card on the counter at Jones's store. Brown, another customer, picked up Smith's card and used it to purchase a $500 camera. Smith did not realize that he had lost his card, and, thus, did not notify the issuer until after Brown's transaction had been completed. Smith is liable for $50 of Brown's transaction.

   Example 2: Same as above, but Brown purchased the $500 camera with a telephone order to a mail-order seller. The Federal Reserve Board has taken the position that in these circumstances there is no means of identifying the user of the credit device and, thus, the customer has no liability at all.

   Example 3: Brown robbed Smith of his wallet which included Smith's credit card and his checkbook. Before Smith had a reasonable opportunity to notify the issuer or his bank of the robbery, Brown had used the card to purchase a $500 camera and had forged Smith's signature on a check for $500 payable to bearer. Brown cashed the check at the drawee bank. Smith is responsible for $50 of Brown's camera transaction. Smith is not responsible for any of the check transaction.

5. **Business use:** If an issuer has issued 10 or more cards to a business for the use of its employees, the business and the issuer may agree that the latter will bear greater than $50 liability for unauthorized use of the card. Neither the bank nor the business, however, may impose greater liability on an employee.

6. **No offset:** The issuer may not collect any amount owing from a credit card transaction against any deposit account held by the issuer for the same customer.

7. **Assertion of claims and defenses:** If a customer has a dispute with a seller who has honored a credit card, the customer may assert against the issuer all claims, other than tort claims, and defenses arising out of the transaction if the amount of the initial transaction *exceeds $50*. In effect, the card issuer may not claim the rights of a holder in due course with respect to the charge. 15 U.S.C. § 1666i.

   a. **Effort to seek resolution:** A customer may assert against the card issuer the claims and defenses it has against the seller only if the customer has made a good faith attempt to obtain satisfactory resolution of the problem from the seller.

   b. **Geographical limitation:** In addition, a customer may assert against the card issuer the claims and defenses it has against the seller only if the initial transaction occurred in the same state as the mailing address previously provided by the customer or within 100 miles from such address.

   c. **Exceptions:** The limitations on amount and geographical distance do not apply to any transaction in which the person honoring the credit card is the same person as the card issuer, is controlled by the card issuer, is under common control with the card issuer, is a franchised dealer of the card issuer's goods or services, or has obtained the order through a solicitation participated in by the card issuer.

   Example 1: While on vacation in New York, Smith, who resided in Indiana, purchased a computer from Brown's Computers in Manhattan for $2,000. Smith paid for the computer with a credit card that had been issued to her by First Bank of Indiana, which had its home office in Smith's city of residence. When Smith returned home, she discovered that the computer did not operate as promised by the salesman. Smith called the store to complain, but the salesman contended that Smith may have mishandled the computer on the way home. The store, therefore, refused to issue a credit to Smith's credit card or otherwise to exchange the product or refund her money. Smith does not have a right under the Federal Consumer Credit Protection Act to assert against First Bank the claim she has against Brown's Computers.

Example 2: Smith, a resident of Indiana, heard that Brown's Computers in Manhattan sold a computer that Smith wanted for the relatively low price of $2,000. She called Brown from Indiana and ordered the computer, paying for it with a credit card that had been issued to her by First Bank of Indiana, which had its home office in Smith's city of residence. When Smith received the computer, she discovered that it did not operate as promised by the salesman. Smith called the store to complain, but the salesman contended that Smith may have mishandled the computer after it arrived. The store, therefore, refused to issue a credit to Smith's credit card or otherwise to exchange the product or refund her money. If state law governing the transaction provides that this telephonic transaction occurred in Indiana, Smith will be able to assert against First Bank the claim she has against Brown's Computers.

CHAPTER 9

DOCUMENTARY DRAFTS AND LETTERS OF CREDIT

I. INTRODUCTION

A. Distant transactions: In face-to-face sales transactions, performance by the buyer and seller is frequently simultaneous, so the risk of non-performance is small. Payment is due when the buyer receives the goods and tender of payment is a condition of the seller's performance. U.C.C. §§ 2-310, 2-511. Where the parties do not face each other, however, each may be concerned about nonperformance by the other. The seller will be concerned that shipment of conforming goods prior to receiving payment will leave the goods in a distant market, and thereby preclude an easy remedy, such as resale, should the buyer either fail to pay or reject the goods on arrival. Thus, seller will want payment prior to shipment. Buyer, on the other hand, will fear that once he or she makes payment, seller has less incentive to send conforming goods and a distant seller will be more difficult to sue. Documentary draft and letter of credit transactions help to reduce each party's uncertainty in these situations and to provide each party with sufficient security about the performance by the other that each is willing to engage in the transaction.

II. NATURE OF DOCUMENTARY DRAFT TRANSACTIONS

Introduction: One way in which the parties can avoid the problem of distant transactions is to provide for a documentary transaction. In this form of transaction, the seller will be required to obtain certain documents from the carrier at the same time that the goods are shipped. These documents generally include a ***bill of lading*** that describes the goods that have been shipped. The bill of lading constitutes a ***document of title***, and is the mechanism by which the buyer can get access to the goods. U.C.C. § 1-201(15). It functions much in the same way as a safe deposit box key is the means of access to a safe deposit box. The buyer will be able to obtain goods from the carrier only by presenting the bill of lading when the carrier arrives to deliver the goods. After the seller has obtained the bill of lading from the carrier, he or she will attach to it a ***sight draft***, which is a draft drawn by the seller to his or her own order and payable by the buyer when presented or at "sight." The seller will then send the bill of lading with the sight draft attached to an agent of the seller in the buyer's area. The agent, in turn, will present the bill of lading and sight draft to the buyer. By inspecting the bill of lading and comparing it to the contract description of goods, the buyer can obtain assurance that the seller has shipped conforming goods. The buyer will only be able to retain the bill of lading for presentment to the carrier, however, if the buyer pays the sight draft. Thus, the seller receives assurance of payment for conforming goods.

III. NATURE OF LETTER OF CREDIT TRANSACTIONS

A. Introduction: A letter of credit is typically used when the distance between buyer and seller is sufficiently great that seller is not even willing to trust a documentary transaction. The seller, for instance, may fear that once he or she ships goods he or she will face such substantial difficulties getting payment or reclaiming the goods that the transaction is not worthwhile at the price the buyer is willing to pay. Thus, the parties may agree to a form of transaction that increases the security of the seller by providing a payment commitment from a third party. The letter of credit transaction, therefore, attempts to reduce the concerns of both buyer and seller by providing the buyer with assurances that goods conforming to the contract have been shipped before payment is released to the seller, while providing the seller with assurances that payment is forthcoming if a conforming tender is made.

B. Parties: In the letter of credit transaction, the buyer requests the bank of which it is a *customer* to *issue* a letter of credit naming the seller as *beneficiary*. The letter of credit states that on presentation of certain documents, the issuer bank will *honor* a *demand for payment* from the beneficiary.

1. Documents: The documents required typically include an *inspection certificate* attesting that goods shipped by the beneficiary conform to the contract of sale between the customer and beneficiary, an invoice that describes the goods, and a bill of lading that evidences shipment of the goods to the customer. In a documentary letter of credit transaction, the documents will also include a draft drawn by the beneficiary on the customer's account at the issuer bank. Documents are sent through banking channels at the same time the goods are shipped from the beneficiary to the customer. Generally, documents arrive prior to the goods. When the documents and draft are presented at the issuer bank, the documents are inspected to determine whether they conform to the requirements of the letter of credit. If they do conform, the issuer will pay the draft and debit the customer's account the corresponding amount.

2. **Effect:** Since the letter of credit constitutes an ***engagement to pay*** by a financial institution that the seller is likely to trust, the seller will be willing to ship goods, confident that payment will be forthcoming if the goods conform to the contract. Since payment will be made only if there is documentary evidence that the goods will be conforming, the buyer will be willing to permit the issuer to make payment, even though the goods have not yet been physically received.

3. **Independent contracts:** The letter of credit transaction, thus, involves three separate contracts: the contract between the customer and the beneficiary that sets forth the terms for the sale of goods between them, the contract between the customer and the issuer that permits the issuer to charge the customer's account on presentation of appropriate documents, and the contract between the issuer and the beneficiary that allows the beneficiary to obtain payment from the issuer. This independence principle, for instance, means that a beneficiary cannot avail himself or herself of the contractual relationship between the issuer and customer. Nor can the issuer generally invoke any contractual claims of its customer against payment of the credit to the beneficiary. Thus, the transaction consists of the following parts:

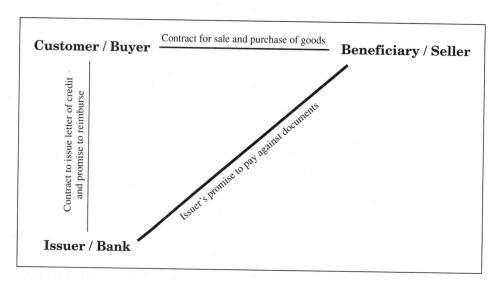

4. **Revocability:** A credit may be either revocable or irrevocable. U.C.C. § 5-103(1)(a).

5. **Assignment**: The beneficiary can transfer or assign the right to draw under a letter of credit only when the credit is expressly designated as transferable or assignable. U.C.C. § 5-116. Thus, any

drafts drawn under the credit will have to be signed by the beneficiary unless transferability or assignability is provided for in the credit. The beneficiary, however, may assign the right to proceeds under the credit. Any such assignment is generally governed by Article 9 as the assignment of an account.

6. **Other parties to the transaction:**

   a. The letter of credit is **not itself a** negotiable instrument. The draft that is drawn under the letter of credit, however, may be a negotiable instrument and may be negotiated to a subsequent holder or holder in due course. Frequently, the beneficiary discounts the draft with his or her own bank, thereby making the bank a holder of the draft. Additionally, if the beneficiary received from the shipper a negotiable document of title as evidence that conforming goods have been shipped, that document may also be negotiated.

   b. The beneficiary of the letter of credit may wish to have its own bank **confirm** the issuer's letter of credit. The issuer, for instance, may be well-known in banking circles, but unknown to the beneficiary. The confirming bank may either commit that it will itself honor a credit previously issued or that the credit will be honored by the issuer or by a third bank. U.C.C. § 5-103(1)(f). The confirming bank becomes directly liable on the credit to the extent of its confirmation, but also acquires the rights of the issuer. U.C.C. § 5-107(2).

   c. An issuer may also employ an **advising** bank to give notification of the issuance of a credit. U.C.C. § 5-103(1)(e). The advising bank does not assume any obligation to honor drafts or demands for payment made under the letter of credit. It does, however, bear liability for its own inaccuracies in giving advice about the credit. U.C.C. § 5-107(1). If the advising bank gives incorrect advice, the credit remains effective against the issuer according to its original terms. U.C.C. § 5-107(3).

C. **Sources of law:**

   1. **The U.C.C.:**   Article 5 of the U.C.C. governs two types of letter of credit transactions. The first involves a situation where the credit is issued by a bank and requires a documentary draft or documentary demand for payment. The second involves a situation where the credit is issued by a person other than a bank and the credit requires that the draft or demand be accompanied by a document of title.

   2. **Applicability to nondocumentary credits:** Banks may issue letters of credit that do not require documentation for payment. These

letters of credit are typically used to guarantee performance of the customer and include "standby" letters of credit. While commercial or documentary letters of credit require the issuer to assume primary liability on the presentation of documents, ***standby letters of credit*** require the issuer to pay only on delivery of documents showing that a party primarily responsible has failed to satisfy his or her obligation. The issuer will not be required to review the existence of the alleged default as long as a certificate of default corresponding to the terms of the credit is presented. Article 5 of the U.C.C. will apply to such a credit if it conspicuously states that it is a letter of credit or if it is entitled a letter of credit. U.C.C. § 5-102(1).

3. **UCP:** Letters of credit may also be subject to the Uniform Customs and Practice for Commercial Documentary Credit, issued by the International Chamber of Commerce ("UCP"). The most recent edition of these principles, known as UCP 500, were revised in 1993. By the terms of the UCP, its provisions apply to all documentary credit transactions where the UCP is incorporated into the text of the credit. See UCP Article 1. The UCP also explicitly recognizes the independence of credits from the sales or other contracts on which the credits are based. UCP Article 3. For most purposes, the provisions of the UCP are consistent with those of the U.C.C. In New York and a few other jurisdictions, U.C.C. Article 5 does not apply to a letter of credit that by its terms or by agreement or course of dealing or usage of trade is subject to the UCP.

IV. ISSUER'S RIGHTS AND OBLIGATIONS UNDER THE CREDIT

A. **Strict compliance and payment:** The letter of credit transaction is governed by principles of strict compliance. The independence principle implies that the obligation of the issuer to pay has nothing to do with the nature of the goods that are the subject of the contract between buyer and seller. The issuer's obligation to pay depends solely on documents called for under the credit. If the issuer is presented with a draft or demand for payment that complies with the credit, the issuer must make payment. U.C.C. § 5-114(1). As a matter of judicial interpretation of the law underlying credits, however, those documents must strictly comply with the conditions set forth in the credit. Any noncompliance with the terms of the credit justifies dishonor. UCP Article 13 provides that compliance "shall be determined by the international standard banking practice ..." which typically requires strict compliance. Proposed revisions to Article 5 endorse the strict compliance standard.

1. **Function of strict compliance rule:** Strict compliance is a useful standard to prevent issuers from making judgments about whether there has been sufficient compliance with the requirements of the credit. There are two reasons to avoid giving issuers discretion. First, they are generally only financers of the transaction between customer and beneficiary rather than experts with respect to the goods or services that constitute the subject of the transaction. Thus, issuers will have difficulty determining whether variations between the required documents and those presented are material. Second, issuers may have interests in satisfying their customers rather than distant beneficiaries. Thus, a bright-line rule that tells beneficiaries that they will receive payment as long as they do not vary from the requirements of the credit increases the certainty of the transaction and lowers its costs.

2. **"Strict" versus "absolute" compliance:** Strict compliance does not require that the documents presented contain no variation from what is required. Obvious errors may be tolerated. A misspelling of a name, e.g., "Smith" instead of "Smithe," would not violate the strict compliance rule as long as the variation left little room for confusion.

3. **No discretion:** Once the obvious error threshold is crossed, no interpretation should be necessary by the issuer. Even small differences between the documents required under the credit and documents presented permit the issuer to dishonor the draft or demand for payment.

    > **Example:** Brown enters into a contract to purchase wool coats from Smith. The terms of the contract require Brown to obtain a letter of credit from First Bank for Smith's benefit, with payment to be made against a draft bill of lading showing shipment of 50 cartons of wool coats. Smith presents a bill of lading that shows shipment of "50 cartoons of wool coats." First Bank may dishonor the draft. Nevertheless, the proposed revisions to Article 5 suggest that some discretion may be permitted, e.g., by allowing a draft referring to letter of credit "No. 188-S" to be paid although the requirement was that the draft refer to letter of credit "No. 188-5."

4. **Nonconforming goods:** If the documents required under the terms of the credit are presented in conformity with the contract between the issuer and the beneficiary, the issuer must pay even if it knows that goods or documents required under the contract between the customer and the beneficiary are non-conforming. It is in this sense that the letter of credit is independent of the contract

for the sale of the goods. Failure to pay would constitute wrongful dishonor of the credit under U.C.C. § 5-115.

5. **Satisfaction:** The issuer may, however, require that specified documents, such as the bill of lading or inspection certificate, be satisfactory to it. U.C.C. § 5-114(1), Official Comment 1. The issuer may modify the terms of the credit without notice to or consent from the customer or beneficiary if the issuer has established a revocable credit. U.C.C. § 5-106.

6. **Standard of care:** The issuer is required to observe good faith, and a bank issuer must comply with general banking usages in deciding whether to pay the credit and must examine the documents with care to determine whether they comply with the terms of the credit. U.C.C. § 5-109; UCP Article 13.

   a. An issuer is not otherwise responsible for performance of the underlying contract between the beneficiary and the customer.

   b. If the issuer has discharged its responsibility for careful examination it is not otherwise liable for the genuineness, falsification or effect of any document that appears regular on its face. U.C.C. § 5-109(2).

7. **Time for honor or rejection:** U.C.C. § 5-112.

   a. **Deferral of payment:** A bank may defer honor of the draft or demand for payment until the close of the third banking day following receipt of the documents. This period allows the issuer time for careful examination of the documents. If the presenter consents, the bank may defer honor for a further period. The UCP provides for a reasonable period, not to exceed a seven-banking-day period following receipt of the documents, to examine the documents and determine whether to pay. UCP Article 13.

   b. **Dishonor:** Failure to honor within these time limits constitutes dishonor.

   c. **Return of draft and documents:** Dishonor of a draft usually requires the drawee to return the draft and the documents to the presenter. U.C.C. § 4-302. Since the documents in letter of credit transactions frequently involve documents of title that control the possession of goods, a requirement that they be returned to a distant seller could impose hardship and make resale difficult. Thus, the issuer who has dishonored the draft may retain the documents as bailee for the presenter and notify the presenter that it has so acted. U.C.C. § 5-112, Official Comment 2. Under UCP Article 14(d), an issuer that decides to refuse documents must give notice of that fact and state all discrepancies in respect of which it made the refusal.

B. Exceptions to strict compliance rule:

1. Fraud or breach of warranty:

a. If

    i. a document required under the terms of a letter of credit does not conform to warranties made on negotiation or transfer of a document of title or of a certificated security;

    ii. the document required is forged or fraudulent;

    iii. there is fraud in the transaction;

then the issuer must still honor the draft or demand for payment if presentment is made:

    i. in the case of a draft, by a holder who has taken it under circumstances that would make her a holder in due course;

    ii. in the case of a document of title, by a holder who has taken it through negotiation. U.C.C. § 5-114(2)(a).

b. **Breach of warranty:** If there has been a breach of warranty, a forged or fraudulent document, or *fraud in the transaction*, and the draft or demand for payment is made by one other than a holder in due course or person to whom a document of title has been negotiated, the *issuer may honor the draft or demand*, but need not do so. In addition, the customer who is aware of the fraud, and who, therefore, will not want the goods, may obtain an injunction against honor of the draft or demand. U.C.C. § 5-114(2)(b).

c. **Interpretation:** There is some debate about the scope of the phrase "fraud in the transaction." Some have suggested that, in order to maintain the independence of the contracts that constitute the letter of credit transaction, the phrase refers only to fraud in the transaction between the issuer and the beneficiary. Thus, fraud in the transaction between the beneficiary and the customer would not give rise to an option to pay under U.C.C. § 5-114(2)(b). This history of the provision, however, suggests that the phrase does cover fraud in the underlying transaction for the sale of goods where the fraud is obvious and substantial. Numerous commentators have agreed with this suggestion.

Example 1: Brown enters into a contract to purchase wool coats from Smith. The terms of the contract require Brown to obtain a letter of credit from First Bank for Smith's benefit, with payment to be made against a draft bill of lading showing shipment of 50 cartons of wool coats. After the bill of lading is issued, but before the draft is presented to First Bank, Brown learns that, notwithstanding a description on the bill of lading that conforms to the contract, Smith has actually shipped 50 cartons of rags. The carrier that issued the bill of lading had no information about the misdescription of the contents of the cartons. If Smith presents the draft and bill of lading to First Bank, Brown may request that First Bank not make payment. First Bank need not make payment unless the law in the jurisdiction establishes that the "fraud in the transaction" phrase is limited to fraud in the transaction between the issuer and the beneficiary.

Example 2: Same as above, but the nonconformity is that Smith only shipped 49 of the 50 cartons of wool coats, notwithstanding the statement in the bill of lading. This nonconformity may give rise to an action by Brown against Smith, but probably does not rise to the level of fraud and, thus, First Bank must make payment.

Example 3: Same as above, but after obtaining the bill of lading and drawing a draft on Brown, Smith negotiated the draft and documents to Second Bank under circumstances that made Second Bank a holder in due course. Second Bank presented the draft and documents to First Bank for payment. First Bank must make payment and is entitled to reimbursement from Brown even though it knows of the fraud committed by Smith.

d. Warranties: The warranties that are made on negotiation or transfer of a document of title, breach of which will trigger the issuer's rights under U.C.C. § 5-114(2), include a warranty that the document is genuine, that the transferor has no knowledge of any fact that would impair the document's validity or worth, and that the negotiation or transfer confers good title to the document and the goods it represents. U.C.C. § 7-507.

2. Custom: In some situations, a custom of the trade may relax the need for strict compliance with the terms of the credit. In such a situation, a party to the custom that insists on the strict compliance rule may be liable for wrongful dishonor.

Example: In *Dixon, Irmaos & Cia. v. Chase National Bank*, 144 F.2d 759 (2d Cir. 1944), *cert. denied*, 324 U.S. 850 (1945), the letter of credit required that drafts be accompanied by a "full set of bills of lading." Only a partial set of bills of lading was presented, but it was accompanied by an indemnity agreement or guaranty against loss issued by a leading New York bank of sound financial standing. The issuer sought to dishonor the drafts. The court held that there was a long-standing custom of accepting such an agreement or guaranty in lieu of a full set of bills of lading so that the custom was incorporated into the meaning of that phrase. The issuer, therefore, had no valid reason for dishonor.

V. WRONGFUL HONOR OR WRONGFUL DISHONOR

A. **Damages:** A beneficiary who presents a draft or demand for payment that has been wrongfully dishonored may recover from the issuer the face amount of the draft or demand together with incidental damages, less any amount realized on resale of the goods. U.C.C. § 5-115. The person entitled to honor also has the right to stop delivery that is granted to a seller under U.C.C. § 2-705.

1. **Repudiation:** If an issuer wrongfully cancels or repudiates a credit before a demand for payment under it has been made, the beneficiary has the rights granted to a victim of an anticipatory repudiation. These include the right to await performance by the issuer for a commercially reasonable time, the right to resort for any remedy for breach, and the right to suspend his or her own performance.

2. **Repudiation after procurement:** If an issuer wrongfully cancels or repudiates a credit after demand for payment under it has been made, the beneficiary may bring an immediate action for wrongful dishonor.

3. **Irrevocable credits:** The right of wrongful dishonor, of course, is limited to irrevocable credits. U.C.C. § 5-115, Official Comment 3. If the credit is revocable, dishonor is one means of revocation and does not constitute a wrongful act.

B. **Reimbursement:** An issuer that duly honors a draft or demand for payment is entitled to immediate reimbursement from its customer. U.C.C. § 5-114(3). Presumably, this grant is also a limitation on the issuer's rights, so that it may not charge the customer for honor of a draft or demand that should have been dishonored.

1. **Scope:** The issuer's right to reimbursement is triggered by discretionary payments made under U.C.C. § 5-114(2)(b) as well as required payments.

VI. WARRANTIES ON TRANSFER AND PRESENTMENT

A. **Compliance with conditions:** A beneficiary who transfers or presents a documentary draft or demand for payment warrants to all interested parties that there has been compliance with the necessary conditions of the credit.

B. **Presentment and transfer warranties:** A negotiating, advising, confirming, collecting, or issuing bank that presents or transfers a draft or demand for payment under a credit makes the same warranties that are made by a collecting bank under U.C.C. § 4-207.

168

ESSAY EXAM
QUESTIONS AND ANSWERS

The following essay questions allow you to test your understanding of the materials in this text. Keep in mind that the answers do not represent the only "correct" way of responding to the questions, but do provide one appropriate analysis of the subject.

I. (60 minutes)

Early in 1985, George borrowed $100,000 from Buckingham Bank in order to open a restaurant. Unfortunately, George's tastebuds were more refined than his business acumen, and the restaurant began to falter. George fell behind in his payments and, in late 1985, the Bank requested additional security for the loan. Fortunately for George, he had earlier received a note issued to his order by Ollie's Marine Equipment ("Ollie"). The note was in the principal amount of $100,000 and was due on December 31, 1986. George indorsed the note to the order of Buckingham Bank. In addition, the Bank obtained the signature of George's wife, Martha, on the back of the Ollie note. At the time, the outstanding balance on George's loan from the bank was $75,000.

The bank subsequently sold the Ollie note to Nancy Refinance ("Nancy") for $95,000. Nancy had heard of Ollie's Marine Equipment because, in the month prior to her purchase of the note, there had been substantial reporting in the local paper relating how that company had been defrauded into signing large numbers of notes to local businessmen who had delivered substandard marine equipment. Ollie had even taken out large ads in the local newspaper naming the people who had swindled him. George was one of the persons named, but Nancy could not recall seeing his name, although she admits to having read the paper. She claims to have been unaware that the note she purchased from the Bank was one of the offending notes.

In late 1986, George's troubles mounted. First, he was divorced by Martha, who was tired of his constant financial difficulties. Then, his restaurant business collapsed and he fell further into financial distress. His only good fortune arrived on January 5, 1987, when he received a letter from Nancy saying, "I am now the owner of the note made to you by Ollie's Marine Equipment that you indorsed. Since you have informed me that you cannot currently meet your debts, I will give you an additional six months before enforcing the note against you based on your indorsement."

Nancy took no further action on the note until July 1, 1987. On that date, she requested payment of $100,000 from Ollie's. Ollie refused to pay. Nancy then sought the same amount from Martha, who also refused payment. In the meantime, George further squandered his assets and still cannot pay Nancy.

Nancy has sought your advice whether to bring an action against Ollie and Martha for payment of the $100,000. What arguments can you make on her behalf. What responses do you anticipate? Who do you believe ultimately will win? If Nancy can recover from either Ollie or Martha (regardless of whether you think she can), how much will she recover?

Answer to Question I

Nancy seeks to enforce the Ollie note against either Ollie, the drawer, or Martha. As a preliminary matter, both Ollie and Martha have contractual liability for the amount of the note because their signatures appear on the note. § 4-301. Each is liable in the capacity in which their signatures appear on the note. Nevertheless, they may be able to avoid liability on the note if they can raise valid defenses against Nancy.

Martha would seem to have the liability of an accommodation party under § 3-419. The chain of title of the note reveals that her indorsement is that of an anomalous indorser under § 3-205(d). Thus, she is presumptively an accommodation indorser under § 3-419(c). Martha satisfies the definition of an accommodation party under § 3-419(a) because she signed the instrument for the purpose of incurring liability without receiving any direct benefit from the instrument. The benefits of the instrument went to George's business, so Nancy can't claim that Martha received a "direct" benefit even if the proceeds of the note indirectly benefits her. The obligation against Martha can be enforced regardless of the fact that she received no consideration. § 3-419(b). If, however, Nancy could demonstrate that Martha was an active participant in the operation of Ollie's business, Nancy might be able to deprive Martha of the defenses available to an accommodation party.

Martha will likely claim that Nancy's extension to George on January 5 operated as a discharge of Martha's obligation under § 3-605(c). However, Martha will have the burden of proving that the extension of the due date "caused loss . . . with respect to the right of recourse." For instance, if Martha could demonstrate that George's financial condition had deteriorated during the extension period, Martha could receive a discharge in the amount of her impaired right of recourse against George. Thus, Nancy will be able to recover against Martha but the amount is uncertain and will depend upon the effectiveness of Martha's proof of loss. Nancy cannot claim that she was without knowledge or notice of Martha's accommodation status under § 3-605(h), because the existence of the anomalous indorsement on the note provides the requisite notice. § 3-419(c).

Nancy should try to enforce the note against Ollie because she will be able to recover the full amount of the note, even though she purchased it at a discount. Nancy has the rights of a holder in her efforts to enforce the instrument. Nancy took the note by negotiation from Buckingham Bank. § 3-201(a). She received possession of the note with an indorsement by the bank, which was itself a holder, having received the note in a negotiation from the original payee, George. This negotiation was also a transfer under § 3-203(a) since it was delivered by the bank for the purpose of giving Nancy the right to enforce. § 3-203(a).

Ollie will seek to avoid payment of the note on the grounds that it was given for substandard equipment. Nancy can claim that she is a holder in due course under § 3-302 who takes free from such personal defenses. However, Ollie will respond that Nancy fails to satisfy § 3-302(a)(2)(vi) because she had notice of the defense that Ollie will raise against payment of the note. Nancy admits that she knew of Ollie's fraud claims, but it is less clear that she was ever aware that George was one of the offending actors. It is more clear that she did not know of George's defalcations at the time she purchased the note from the bank, even if she was previously aware of his involvement. If the court is willing to credit Nancy's claim that she had forgotten about George's involvement at the time she bought the note, then the court would have to consider whether prior knowledge, subsequently forgotten, will suffice to deprive Nancy of holder in due course status. Given the newspaper ads, a court could find that Nancy had notice of Ollie's defenses and claims in recoupment because Nancy seems to satisfy the definition of notice under § 1-201(25)(c); she "has reason to know" of these defenses "from all the facts and circumstances known to her." Nevertheless, it is not necessarily the case that a business person will be deemed to have reason to know information simply because it appeared in a public posting that the business person admits to having seen.

Even if Nancy cannot attain the status of a holder in due course, and, thus, enforce the note free of Ollie's defenses in her own right, she may be able to obtain the same result under the shelter principle of § 3-203(b). Under that provision, a transfer vests in the transferee all rights of a transferor to enforce the instrument, including any rights as a holder in due course. In our case, Nancy took the note from Buckingham Bank. Nothing in the factual situation reveals that the bank had notice of Ollie's defenses when it received the note from George. Since Nancy was not herself involved in any fraud or illegality affecting the instrument, § 3-203(b), she is sheltered under the bank's rights and is a person entitled to enforce the instrument against Ollie under § 3-301(ii).

Ollie's defenses or claims in recoupment (assuming that the substandard equipment Ollie received for the note has some value) do not rise to the level of fraud in the factum. Thus, if Nancy is a holder in due course or has the rights of such a party, she can recover the full amount of the note. This result is similar in part to § 3-203, Comment 4, case # 1 which seems to support the result in our case.

Overall, Nancy should bring an action against Ollie rather than Martha since she can collect the full amount from Ollie and is not guaranteed that result in regard to Martha. Apparently, an action against George on his § 3-415 indorser's liability would be unavailing, as he has insufficient assets to pay a judgment.

II. (45 minutes)

This question consists of a fact situation followed by a series of statements. Please indicate whether you "Agree" or "Disagree" with each of the statements and give a brief justification for your agreement or disagreement. Your justification is more important than your conclusion. Agreement or disagreement alone will not receive any credit. If you believe that the conclusion in any of the statements is correct but that the reason given for it is incorrect, you should "Disagree" and give the proper reason for the conclusion.

*   *   *

Barclay, who lived and went to school in California, was staying in Virginia with his cousin, Hawkins, during the semester break. One day, while the two cousins were shopping at a local mall, Barclay asked Hawkins if he would mind stopping into the computer store so that Barclay could pick up a surge suppressor for his computer. They quickly found the item at the local computer store, called Norman's Computers, but when Barclay reached for his wallet, he realized that he had left all his money at Hawkins' house. Hawkins offered to pay for the item, which was only $15.00, and gave the clerk his VISA card, telling the clerk that "my cousin would forget his head if it weren't screwed on."

The next day, Hawkins slept late. Barclay, however, was up bright and early. While shopping at Norman's, he had noticed that a laptop computer he had wanted was on sale from $3,000 to $2,500. He had resolved to get the computer, even though he only had $1,200 in his checking account. Thus, while Hawkins slept, Barclay removed the VISA card from his cousin's wallet and returned to the computer store. He told the salesman who had sold the surge suppressor the day before that he and his cousin had decided to purchase the laptop that was on sale. The salesman, who remembered the two cousins from the day before, assumed that Barclay had forgotten his own wallet again, and did not ask for any identification. When he tried to get a telephonic authorization for the credit card, however, the salesman was informed that the credit card holder was within $1,500 of his limit and the card issuer would not approve a charge in a higher amount. "That's okay," said Barclay. "Just put $1,500 on the credit card and I'll write you a check for the balance." Barclay paid for the laptop with his personal check in the amount of $1,000, drawn on Second Bank, and a $1,500 charge to his cousin's credit card.

Norman's immediately deposited Barclay's check because the store was running short of cash. It simply could not compete with the large chain computer stores, and was on the verge of bankruptcy. Indeed, Barclay's check was the only one that Norman's received that day to add to the store's existing checking account balance of $2,000 in Interstate National Bank. Nevertheless, because Interstate National Bank was trying to help Norman's stay afloat, it allowed Norman's to withdraw $2,300 to meet payroll the day after the sale of the computer to Barclay, even though it had not yet collected funds from Second Bank.

Barclay returned to school with his new laptop prior to the time that Hawkins got his statement from VISA showing the $1,500 charge. When Barclay tried to use the laptop, however, he discovered that the letter "k" stuck on the keyboard and would not release until two to three lines of "k"s had been typed. He called Second Bank, which had not yet received the $1,000 check, and issued a stop payment order. Thus, when the check was presented to Second Bank, it dishonored the item and sent it back to Interstate National Bank.

Please answer the following in accordance with the instructions for this question:

1. Even if Hawkins notifies VISA that he did not make the $1,500 charge to his credit card as soon as he receives his statement from them, he is responsible for the full amount of the charge.

2. Even if otherwise responsible for the charge to the credit card, Hawkins does not have to pay for the defective laptop computer because the purchase was made more than 100 miles from the purchaser's mailing address.

3. Interstate National Bank can recover $1,000 from Barclay under his drawer's contract on the check, even if he has a valid defense against paying Norman's Computers.

4. After receiving back the dishonored check, Interstate National Bank may debit the amount of the check against Norman's account or seek a refund from Norman's in the amount of the check, even though the ban permitted earlier withdrawal of the funds.

5. If Norman's gets the dishonored check back from Interstate National Bank, it can enforce the check against Second Bank, notwithstanding the stop payment order, if Norman's can prove it is a holder in due course.

Answers to Question II

1. Agree. Hawkins is not responsible for unauthorized charges beyond $50, assuming that the requirements of 15 U.S.C. § 1643 have been satisfied, but may be responsible for any authorized use of the card. The term "unauthorized use" in § 1643(a) "means a use of a credit card by a person other than the cardholder who does not have actual, implied, or apparent authority." By charging Barclay's $15 item, and by making the statements that he did, Hawkins' statements may have misled them into believing that Barclay had apparent authority to use his card. Moreover, Hawkins' own actions appeared to cloak Barclay's with apparent authority. Hawkins, however, may respond that while Barclay could use the card when accompanied by Hawkins, nothing that Hawkins did or said granted authority to Barclay to use the card in Hawkins' absence. After all, Hawkins indicated that Barclay was forgetful, not that he was to be subsidized.

2. Disagree with rationale. Hawkins (assuming he is otherwise liable) may be able to avoid payment for the laptop. The fact that the computer was purchased more than 100 miles from the purchaser's (Barclay's) mailing address is irrelevant. The place of the purchase is only relevant to the issue of whether or not the credit card issuer takes subject to claims and defenses that would be valid against the seller of the good purchased with the credit card. The relevant mailing address, however, is that of the cardholder. The credit card issuer takes free of any such claims if the purchase is made outside the state and more than 100 miles from the cardholder's mailing address. Here, the purchase was made within 100 miles from Hawkins' mailing address. Since Hawkins, and not Barclay, is the cardholder, Hawkins may assert against the card issuer claims and defenses arising out of the transaction in which the credit card was used as a method of payment. The fact that Barclay made the purchase does not appear to affect the result. 15 U.S.C. § 1666i(a).

3. Disagree. Interstate National Bank is only a holder-in-due course to the extent of $300. It has a security interest to the extent under § 4-210(2) since it allowed a withdrawal of $300 of the credit from the check. ($2,000 was already in the account). The bank gives value to this extent for the purpose of determining its status as a holder in due course under § 3-302. Thus, the bank can enforce the instrument free of obligor's § 3-305(a)(3) defenses (against the computer company) only to the extent of $300. The other $700 is subject to those defenses.

4. Agree. Interstate Bank is a collecting bank that made a provisional settlement with its customer and failed to receive final settlement from the payor bank, Second Bank. Thus, Interstate may revoke the settlement given by it, charge bank the amount of the credit given for the item, or obtain a refund from its customer. Interstate Bank must act by its midnight deadline, or within a longer reasonable time after it learns the facts, to return the item to Norman's or to send notification of the facts. § 4-214.

5. Disagree. The bank is not liable on a check until acceptance. § 3-408. Norman's cannot enforce the draft against the drawee but must instead enforce it against the drawer since the check was dishonored. § 3-414. This is true regardless of whether the check was rightly or wrongfully dishonored and regardless of whether the holder is a holder in due course. The bank is only liable to its customer for wrongful dishonor. § 4-402.

III. (75 minutes)

Wanda and Hillard Brandywine were married for seven years. Alas, the years were not uniformly happy ones. Wanda and Hillard ultimately decided to divorce, although the decision was not an altogether amicable one. After the divorce decree was finalized, Hillard felt cheated in the division of property, even though he had been given their house, and was eager to regain what he considered his "fair share" of the marital estate. He had retained some personal stationery that had imprinted on it both his and Wanda's names and their home address, and was aware that Wanda had long maintained an account with the brokerage house of Duke & Duke from which she could write checks and direct investments. Hillard typed the following on a piece of the stationery bearing both their names.

> Dear sirs:
>
> Please withdraw $5,000 from my account #76-870-990 and send it to me at the above address. Many thanks for your prompt assistance.
>
> > Very truly yours,
> > Wanda Brandywine

Hillard then signed the letter with his best imitation of Wanda's signature.

Wanda (on advice of counsel) had already changed her address on her brokerage account. Nevertheless, the clerk at Duke & Duke issued the firm's check #13821 payable to Wanda for $5,000, drawn on Security Bank, and sent it to the address on the letter (where Hillard still resided). Hillard received the check on September 8. On that same day, he forged Wanda's signature on the back of the check and deposited it into his own account at Gulch Bank. Gulch Bank forwarded the check to Security Bank, which received the check on September 9.

Hillard, however, had a change of heart, whether from fear of detection or genuine remorse is unclear. He called Wanda on September 10 and admitted his evil deed. She immediately notified Duke & Duke. On that same day, Duke & Duke called Security Bank and placed a stop payment order on the check. In describing the check, however, Duke & Duke identified it as their check #13812 instead of #13821. They properly identified the amount of the check as $5,000 and correctly identified both the amount of the check and the check number in a letter sent to Security Bank 10 days later. At 4:00 p.m. on September 10, Security Bank debited the Duke & Duke account by $5,000 in respect of the check made payable to Wanda and credited Gulch Bank $5,000 in respect of the same check. Once Hillard realized that he had obtained the money and could be in substantial legal difficulty for his efforts, he had another change of heart and absconded with the cash.

Duke & Duke refuses to recredit brokerage Wanda's account until they receive the amount of the check back from Security Bank. Although Duke & Duke has demanded that Security Bank re-credit their account, the Bank has contended that it is not required to recredit the Duke & Duke account because the stop payment order was not effective. Wanda has demanded that Gulch Bank reimburse her $5,000 since she cannot recover from Duke & Duke. Gulch Bank insists that Hillard's signature of Wanda's name was effective, and, thus, they do not have to pay. Wanda has also threatened to bring an action against Security Bank.

Please sort all this out by indicating what claims Wanda, Duke & Duke, Gulch Bank, and Security Bank have and the responses they have to the claims of the others. Please cite chapter and verse of the Uniform Commercial Code.

Answer to Question III

Wanda's claims. Gulch Bank arguably has converted funds belonging to Wanda, the payee of the check, by taking the check bearing her forged indorsement from Hillard. Gulch Bank, a depositary bank, does not have any immunity from conversion liability under § 3-420(c). Under § 3-420(a), however, a payee who does not receive delivery of an instrument is not entitled to bring an action for conversion. Until delivery, Wanda is not considered to have any interest in the check. She was never a holder of the instrument or a person entitled to enforce it. Thus, she would appear to have a conversion action under the U.C.C. against neither Gulch Bank nor Security Bank. Instead, she must proceed against Duke & Duke. They arguably acted negligently in sending the check to an address other than the one listed on her account and would be contractually liable for making an unauthorized payment from the account.

Duke & Duke's claims. Duke & Duke has no conversion action against Gulch Bank, since the drawer of a check does not have a conversion action under § 3-420(a). Duke & Duke must seek recrediting of their account from Security Bank on the grounds that the check was not properly payable under § 4-401 because of the forged indorsement. Security Bank, however, may argue that the forged indorsement on the check is effective, and, thus, the check is properly payable, because Hillard, the signer of Wanda's name, was an impostor. Hence, under § 3-404(a), the indorsement by Hillard in the name of Wanda had the same effect as an indorsement by Wanda herself. Security Bank will assert that it paid the instrument in good faith, and, thus, has no obligation to recredit Hillard's account. In addition, Security Bank may claim that Duke & Duke acted negligently in sending the check to Hillard's address rather than to Wanda's address. Security Bank should assert that this negligence substantially contributed to the making of the forgery, and, thus, Duke & Duke cannot assert the forgery against Security Bank.

Duke & Duke may claim that Security Bank itself failed to exercise ordinary care in a manner that contributed to the loss by failing to honor the stop payment order. Hence, Security Bank would be required under the comparative negligence principle of § 3-404(c) and § 3-406(b) to share in the loss. Duke & Duke would contend that they had issued a stop payment order that described the item with reasonable certainty and that was received at a time that afforded Security Bank a reasonable opportunity to act before paying the check. § 4-403(a). Duke & Duke would argue that even though two digits on the check number were inverted, the proper check could be identified from the amount, which was correctly stated, and that, unless the misidentified check had been drawn in the same $5,000 amount, Security Bank should have noticed the discrepancy and called Duke & Duke to determine which check should be dishonored. Security Bank, of course, will claim that it did not fail to exercise ordinary care and that the improper check number on the stop payment order means that the order did not describe the item with the "reasonable certainty" necessary to make the order effective. Thus, the bank simply stopped payment on the check bearing the check number stated in the stop payment order. The bank may, for instance, claim that bank practice is to program computers to stop payment on checks identified by check number and that ordinary care consisted of following this practice. Security Bank will also contend that Duke & Duke was obviously negligent in misreporting the check number on the instrument that it did not want to be paid.

Security Bank's claims. If Security Bank is obligated to recredit (or voluntarily recredits) Duke & Duke's account, it will claim that it can recover from Gulch Bank for breach of a presentment warranty. If Wanda's indorsement was not effective (see discussion above), then Gulch Bank was not a person entitled to enforce the instrument, and, thus, breached the presentment warranty of § 4-208(a)(1). Gulch Bank will defend by attempting to prove the effectiveness of the instrument under § 3-404 or preclusion under § 3-406. See § 4-208(c).

TRUE-FALSE QUESTIONS

The following true/false questions will test your understanding of the material covered in this book. They concentrate on some of the nuances of the law of commercial paper. Enter **True** or **False** on the line provided. Answers appear on page 185 *et seq.*

1. D delivered his personal check to the order of P in return for goods sold by P. P lost the check. P can still recover the amount of the check from D.

_____

2. D delivered his personal check to the order of P in return for goods sold by P. P took the check to the drawee bank and had it certified. P can still recover the amount of the check from D.

_____

3. D delivered his personal check to the order of P in return for goods sold by P. P took the check to the drawee bank and had it certified. P can still recover the amount of the check from the drawee bank.

_____

4. M borrowed $1,000 from P and gave P in return a writing promising to pay $1,200 to P's order "when I obtain an acceptable loan." P is a holder in due course of the writing.

_____

5. M purchased construction equipment from P and gave P in return a writing promising to pay the amount due to P's order "from revenues obtained from construction of the building at 100 Main St." P is a holder in due course of the writing.

_____

6. M delivered a writing to P in which M promised to pay, on demand, to P's order, $1,000 plus 10% per annum, provided, however, that "if M shall default on payment, interest shall thereafter be calculated at 12% per annum." P is a holder in due course of the writing.

_____

7. M delivered a writing to P that was payable to P's order "30 days after demand." P is a holder in due course of the writing.

_____

8. M gave P M's note in exchange for P's promise to sell M goods that P must purchase from Z. P has already entered into an irrevocable contract with Z to purchase the goods for resale to M. P has given value for the note.

_____

9. D gave P a check for $20,000 in return for $8,000 in cash and P's promise to cancel a $12,000 debt that D owed to P. Discharge of that debt was contingent on the $20,000 check being honored. The drawee bank dishonored the check. P is a holder in due course of the check to the extent of $20,000 even though the promise to cancel the debt has not yet been completed.

_____

10. P deposited a $100 check in her bank account, which previously had a zero balance. The check was drawn on a bank located in a different city. The next day, before the check had cleared the drawee bank, P's bank allowed her to withdraw $50. P's bank has a security interest in the check and has given value for it.

_____

11. On July 1, D gave P a check in the amount of $150 in return for value. D dated the check September 1 and asked P not to deposit the check before that date. P is still a holder in due course of the check.

_____

12. P sold D some diamonds of undetermined value. D gave P a check that D had signed, but left the amount blank and told P to complete the check with the proper amount when D obtained an appraisal of the diamonds. The diamonds were subsequently appraised at $5,000. After D informed P of the amount, P completed the check with a $7,500 amount. P then negotiated the check for value to X, who knew that P had obtained an incomplete check from D, but did not know that it had been completed contrary to P's authority. X is a holder in due course.

_____

13. D drew a check in the amount of $100 to the order of P in return for goods. P negotiated the check to X. X presented the check to D and demanded immediate payment. As a check is a demand instrument, X is entitled to recover from D.

_____

14. D drew a check in the amount of $100 to the order of P in return for goods. P negotiated the check to X. X attempted to cash the check at the drawee bank. The drawee bank refused to pay the check, even though D had sufficient funds in the account. X is entitled to recover from drawee bank for wrongful dishonor.

_____

15. Bank made a loan to X Corporation and obtained the personal indorsement of Y, president of the corporation, on the note evidencing the loan. All loan proceeds were used for corporate purposes. Y is not an accommodation party because, as president of the corporation, Y received indirect benefit from the loan.

_____

16. If, in the above example, X Corporation defaults on the loan and Bank proceeds against Y, Y can avoid payment by asserting that he received no consideration for his indorsement.

_____

17. If, in the same example, Y refuses to pay on demand by Bank, X Corporation has no action against Y on his guaranty.

_____

18. If, in the same example, Y's indorsement read "I guarantee that this note will be paid, Y," and did not otherwise specify, Bank would not have to proceed against X Corporation at maturity before recovering from Y.

_____

19. If, in the same example, Y pays the note at maturity, he can recover the amount paid from X Corporation.

_____

20. D wrote a check to P in payment of an obligation. As D was taking the check to the mailbox, X stole the check from D. P has a conversion action against X.

———————

21. In the above example, P can require D to issue her another check.

———————

22. In return for P's promise to paint M's house, M delivered a note to P, promising to pay $1,000 to P's order on September 1. P delivered the note to T for value. P finished painting M's house by August 1, but the paint immediately began to peel. M has a valid defense against T's demand for payment on September 1.

———————

23. Same as above, but P gave T the note as a gift for graduation from law school. M has a valid defense against T's demand for payment on September 1.

———————

24. Same as above, but P gave T the note in return for T's promise to pay P $950, which promise T has not yet performed. M has a valid defense against T's demand for payment on September 1.

———————

25. D gave P her check in the amount of $500. P signed his name across the back of the check and transferred it to T. T deposited it in his bank for collection. The drawee bank refused to pay the check. T cannot recover the amount of the check from P until he has attempted to collect from D.

———————

26. Same as above, but P writes on the back of the check, "I will have no liability in the event this check bounces, P." T cannot recover the amount of the check from P.

———————

27. P sues D to collect under a negotiable instrument that P asserts bears D's signature. D denies that the signature on the instrument is hers and refuses to pay. P must prove that the signature is, in fact, D's.

———————

28. X, an employee of D, was authorized by D to sign her name to a company check. X signed the check "D, by X." The check bounced. X is personally liable on the check.

———————

29. D gave P D's check for $100 in return for goods of that value. The check was dishonored by the drawee bank on January 5. P did not give D notice of dishonor until January 8. P's notice of dishonor is untimely.

———————

30. On January 5, the drawee bank dishonored a check drawn by D on insufficient funds. On January 6, the drawee bank sent a notice of dishonor to D. D received the notice of dishonor on January 9. The drawee bank's notice of dishonor is timely.

———————

31. D gave P a check for $100 on January 5 in return for goods of that value. P did not attempt to cash the check until March 10. If D can prove that P's presentment of the check occurred after passage of a reasonable time, D will have no further liability on the check.

———————

32. D gave P a check for $100 on January 5 in return for goods of that value. P negotiated the check to T on January 7. T did not deposit the check until March 10. At that time, D's account had insufficient funds to pay the check. T cannot recover against P on the latter's indorsement.

_____

33. H purchased a bearer note issued by M. The note was written in blue ink, except for the amount which was written as $1,500 with the numeral "5" in black ink. H is a holder in due course of the note.

_____

34. A stranger asked X if he would cash a paycheck for $50. X thought the stranger looked well dressed and agreed to give him $50 for the check. The stranger indorsed the check in the name of the payee and gave the check to X in return for $50. The stranger had stolen the check. X is a holder in due course of the check.

_____

35. A stranger asked X if he would cash the stranger's personal check for $50. X thought the stranger looked well dressed and agreed to give him $50 for the check. The check was dishonored by the drawee bank for insufficient funds. X is a holder in due course of the check.

_____

36. F fraudulently claimed that she represented the XYZ Widget Corporation, which did not exist. D drew a check payable to the order of F in return for a promise of a shipment of goods. F indorsed the check in the name of XYZ Corporation and the drawee bank paid the check. F's indorsement is effective under the fictitious payee rule and, thus, the drawee bank can charge D's account the amount of the check.

_____

37. Same facts as question 36. F's indorsement is effective under the impostor rule and, thus, the drawee bank can charge D's account the amount of the check.

_____

38. P transferred a note payable to his order to T for value. T took the note in good faith and without any notice of claims or defenses to payment. T transferred the note to X as a gift. At maturity, M refused to pay because P, the initial payee, had failed to perform the promises for which the note was given. X can enforce the note because she has the rights of a holder in due course.

_____

39. Borrower gives Agent a check in the amount of $500 payable to the order of Lender in full payment of a debt. Agent owes Lender $1,000 and gives Lender the $500 check, telling Lender that it is in partial payment of Agent's debt. Borrower learns what Agent has done and stops payment on the check. Lender has the rights of a holder in due course and can enforce the check.

_____

40. D gives P a check in return for some goods. D subsequently stops payment on the check in the mistaken belief that the goods are defective. The drawee bank pays the check over the stop payment order. The bank is not liable to D for payment over the stop payment order.

_____

41. D gives P a check in return for goods that turn out to be defective. D phones the drawee bank and asks the bank to stop payment on the check. D takes no other action. Thirty days later, P presents the check and receives payment. The bank is not liable to D for payment over the stop payment order.

_____

42. D gave P a certified check in return for construction work that P performed at D's house. D subsequently noticed defects in P's work. D can successfully issue a stop payment order on the check.

_____

43. D issued a check to P and had her bank certify it. The certification by the drawee bank discharges D's liability on the instrument.

_____

44. P deposited a check drawn to her order into her account at First Bank. First Bank sent the check to Second Bank, which was to route it to Drawee Bank. Second Bank, however, negligently misplaced the check and did not forward it until it was uncollectible. First Bank is liable for Second Bank's negligence.

_____

45. D issued a check to P for $100. P improperly raised the amount of the check to $1,000 and negotiated the check to X. Drawee Bank paid X $1,000 for the check. Drawee Bank can only debit D's account $100.

_____

46. D issued a check to P for $100. P improperly raised the amount of the check to $1,000 and had it certified in that amount by Drawee Bank. P then negotiated the check to X. X can recover $1,000 from Drawee Bank and Drawee Bank cannot charge D more than $100.

_____

47. D issued a check to P's order. X stole the check from P, forged P's signature, and deposited it in First Bank, which forwarded it to Drawee Bank. Drawee Bank paid the check. P can recover in conversion against Drawee Bank.

_____

48. D issued a check to "Cash" and delivered it to P. X stole the check from P and delivered it to A. A indorsed the check and deposited it in her account at First Bank, which forwarded it to Drawee Bank. Drawee Bank paid the check. P can recover in conversion against Drawee Bank under the Uniform Commercial Code.

_____

49. Same as above. P can require D to issue her another check in payment of the underlying obligation.

_____

50. M issued his note in the amount of $500, payable to the order of P in return for goods. P negotiated the note to X who took it without any notice that P's sale to M had been fraudulent. X paid $250 for the note and agreed to pay an additional $250 in 30 days. Before X had paid the additional sum she learned of the fraudulent nature of the sale to M. X is not a holder in due course of the note because she has notice of M's defense.

_____

51. D drew a check payable to the order of P on February 1. On December 1, P deposited the check in his account and the drawee bank charged D's account the amount of the check. The drawee bank is liable for the amount of the check as it was deposited more than six months after its stated date.

_____

52. D drew a check payable to the order of P in the amount of $500. At the time that P presented the check to the drawee bank, D had only $400 in his account. Nevertheless, the drawee bank honored the check in its entirety. The check was properly payable and the drawee bank may recover the amount of the overdraft from D.

_____

53. W bought her husband a suit at a "final sale" price and paid by check. When her husband saw the suit he said he did not like it and W issued a stop payment order on the check. The drawee bank paid the check over the stop payment order. W is not entitled to have her account recredited the amount of the check.

_____

54. D issued a check in the amount of $500 to P, who deposited it in her account at X Bank. X Bank delivered the check to the drawee bank, Y Bank, at 10:00 that morning. Y Bank immediately credited X Bank with the amount of the check. At 2:00 that afternoon, Y Bank realized that D had only $150 in his account. Y Bank can revoke the $500 credit previously given to X Bank.

_____

55. D issued a check in the amount of $500 to P, who deposited in her account at X Bank at 10:00 that morning. X Bank was also the drawee bank. X Bank immediately credited P with the amount of the deposit. At 2:00 that afternoon, X Bank realized that D had only $150 in his account. X Bank can recover the $500 credit previously given to P.

_____

56. D issued a check in the amount of $500 to P, who cashed the check at X Bank, the drawee bank, at 10:00 that morning. At 2:00 that afternoon, X Bank realized that D had only $150 in his account. X Bank can recover the $500 previously given to P.

_____

57. D issued a demand note to P's order on July 1. P negotiated the note to X on July 5. X held the note for two months and then demanded payment from D. D was unable to pay. P is excused because X held the note for more than 30 days before presenting it for payment.

_____

58. D purchased a car from S for $8,585.96 and gave S a personal check for that amount. After 50 miles, the car died. D instructed the drawee bank not to pay a check he had just written "for $8,600." The bank paid the check. The bank can successfully contend that the stop payment order was invalid because the amount was incorrect.

_____

59. P took to her bank, First Bank, a check that she received from D drawn on Second Bank. First Bank gave her cash for the check. First Bank has finally paid the check and is accountable for it.

_____

60. X and Y have a joint checking account at First Bank. X wrote a check on the account that created an overdraft. First Bank paid the check. First Bank can obtain reimbursement from Y.

_____

61. D drew a check to the order of P on March 1, but postdated it to April 1. Any cause of action on the check against D accrues as of March 1.

_____

62. D drew a check to the order of P. X stole the check, forged P's indorsement, and transferred the check to A. A indorsed the check and transferred it to B for value. B deposited the check in his account at First Bank and received a settlement for it. B has made and breached a warranty to First Bank.

_____

63. In the same situation as above, A has made and breached a warranty to First Bank.

_____

64. X stole a blank check from D's checkbook, forged D's name as drawer, and made the check payable to the order of P, who did not know of the theft. P indorsed the check and transferred it to the drawee bank for value. P has violated a presentment warranty.

_____

65. Same as above. The drawee bank paid the check. The drawee bank may recover from P on a theory of indorser's liability.

_____

66. D drew a check to the order of P. X stole the check, forged P's indorsement, and cashed the check at the drawee bank. The drawee bank was not negligent in cashing the check. The drawee bank cannot charge D's account even though D's signature is genuine.

_____

67. Same as above. P has a conversion action against the drawee bank, notwithstanding the lack of negligence.

_____

68. C agreed to purchase goods from B and to have C's bank, First Bank, open a letter of credit in favor of B. B shipped nonconforming goods under circumstances that satisfied the criteria for "fraud in the transaction" in the governing jurisdiction. B then discounted the documents and draft called for in the letter of credit to its own bank, X Bank, for value. X Bank had no notice of B's fraud. C discovered the fraud prior to the time that X Bank presented the documents and draft to First Bank. C can enjoin payment by First Bank to X Bank.

_____

69. Same as above. X Bank had previously dealt with B in multiple transactions and is aware that B frequently fails to fulfill its obligations under its contracts. C can enjoin payment by First Bank to X Bank.

_____

70. First Bank issued a letter of credit on behalf of its customer, Smith, that called for payment against a bill of lading evidencing seller's shipment of "two containers of cashews." First Bank received a draft drawn under the credit with a bill of lading evidencing seller's shipment of "two containers of nuts." First Bank paid the draft. The containers held only walnuts. First Bank cannot charge Smith's account.

_____

71. Same as above. First Bank's payment prevents Smith from bringing a breach of contract action against the seller.

_____

72. X loaned Y his credit card so she could travel home from law school. Y agreed not to charge more than $300 on the card. In fact, she charged more than $500 on the card. X is liable for the entire amount of the charges.

_____

73. X negligently left his credit card on the counter of a store after making a purchase. Y picked up the card, went to another store, and made a purchase for $25. X is precluded from denying Y's authority to use the card because his negligence substantially contributed to its unauthorized use.

_____

74. First Bank made a loan to D after having D sign a note on which A also appeared as an accommodation maker. The note was secured by a pledge of convertible securities owned by D. First Bank received notice that the convertible feature of the securities was about to expire, but did nothing. The securities immediately thereafter lost substantial value. A is discharged to the extent of the loss in value of the securities.

_____

75. A and Z sign as accommodation indorsers on a note made by D. When D fails to pay, the holder of the note may only recover half of the note amount from A.

_____

76. In order to obtain a loan from First Bank, D asked A to serve as his surety. A agreed and signed a note to the order of First Bank in the amount of the loan. D signed a separate note, also to the order of First Bank. A is an accommodation maker.

_____

77. M issues a note to the order of C. C indorses the note in blank and it is subsequently stolen by T. C informs M of the theft. When T demands payment, M pays. M is discharged from liability to C.

_____

78. Same as above, but T transfers the note to X for value. X is unaware of the theft. When X demands payment, M pays. M is discharged from liability to C.

_____

79. D wrote a check to the order of P for $5,000 in return for some goods. D deposited the check in First Bank on June 1. On June 2, First Bank presented the check to the drawee bank, Second Bank. Second Bank immediately discovered that D only had $500 in his checking account. Second Bank telephoned First Bank the afternoon of June 3 to inform them that the check would be dishonored. Second Bank is not liable for the amount of the check.

_____

80. D draws a check to the order of P and X. P indorses the check and transfers it to Y for value. Y is a holder of the check.

_____

81. X drew her check payable to "cash" in the amount of $500 and placed it in her pocket. As she walked to the bank to cash the check, the check fell out of her pocket. Y found the check and attempted to cash it at the drawee bank. X had discovered the loss and issued a stop payment order, so the bank did not pay the check. Y may enforce the check against X because Y is the holder of a bearer instrument.

_____

82. On June 1, X Bank presented to Y Bank a check in the amount of $15,000 that purported to be drawn by A on A's account at Y Bank. The check had been deposited at X Bank on May 31. On June 2, Y Bank determined not to pay the check because it appeared that A's signature was forged. That same day, Y Bank sent the check back to X Bank in a manner that normally would have ensured that X Bank would receive it by June 3. Y Bank took no other action with respect to the check. Y Bank complied with Regulation CC with respect to returned checks.

———————

83. X drew a check to the order of Y in the amount of $500 and gave it to Y as a gift. Y cashed the check at the drawee bank, First Bank. Subsequently, First Bank realized that X closed his account the previous day. First Bank can recover the $500 from Y.

———————

84. X drew a check to Y for the sale of a television. The agreed price of the good was $500. X wrote "Five hundred dollars" in the middle of the check in words, but wrote "$50.00" on the right-hand side of the check in figures. After X had left Y's store with the television, Y noticed the discrepancy and added another "0," making the figure "$500.00." Y has altered the instrument and discharged X.

———————

85. X negligently failed to discover that his bookkeeper was stealing checks made payable to X by X's customers. The bookkeeper forged X's signature, but misspelled X's name, and deposited the checks in her account at Y Bank. Y Bank failed to notice the misspelling. The indorsement is effective as X's signature.

———————

ANSWERS

1. **True.** § 3-309 permits an owner of a lost instrument to recover from the party liable thereon on due proof of ownership and of the facts that prevent production of the instrument.

2. **False.** P is a holder of the check. § 3-414(c) provides that where a draft is accepted by a bank, as in the case of certification, the drawer of the check is discharged.

3. **True.** A drawee bank that certifies a check has accepted it and is therefore liable on it.

4. **False.** Although a payee may be a holder in due course, no one may be a holder in due course unless in possession of a negotiable instrument. The writing given by M is not payable at a definite time or on demand and is therefore not a negotiable instrument.

5. **True.** Again, a payee may be a holder in due course. This writing is a negotiable instrument under the Revision, even though payment is restricted to a particular fund. The result would have been different prior to the Revision. See PR § 3-105.

6. **True.** Although it is unclear whether and when M will default, and thus the ultimate amount due on the note cannot currently be calculated with certainty, the "fixed amount" requirement applies only to principal and the uncertainty exists with respect to the amount of interest due. Even prior to the Revision, the sum stated on an instrument remains "certain" for purposes of negotiability even if the instrument provides for different rates of interest before and after default. See PR § 3-106(l)(b).

7. **True.** A holder of this instrument can determine from the face of the instrument when it will be paid, even though no date is stated and the instrument is not payable on the day of demand. Thus, such a note should be negotiable. Some room for confusion may exist, however, as where the holder makes a demand and then transfers the note to another party, who is ignorant of that demand, prior to the expiration of the 30-day period. Presumably, that party would not know of the maturity date.

8. **True.** One gives value for an instrument by making an irrevocable commitment to a third party. See § 3-303(a)(5).

9. **False.** Under § 3-303(a)(1), an executory promise does not constitute value for purposes of making one a holder in due course. Thus, P is a holder in due course only to the extent of $8,000, the value already given.

10. **True.** Even though the withdrawal was made as a matter of the depositary bank's discretion rather than as a matter of right, the bank obtains a security interest in a check and thus gives value for it to the extent that credit given for it, final or provisional, has been withdrawn or applied. § 4-210(a)(1).

11. **True.** The fact that a check is known to be postdated does not provide notice of any irregularity that would deprive the holder of due course status.

12. **True.** Knowledge that an incomplete instrument has been completed does not give notice of a claim or defense unless the purchaser had notice that the completion was improper.

13. **False.** A check may be a demand instrument, but the drawer agrees to pay only on dishonor of the check. § 3-414(b). The drawer is a secondary party and is liable only when the party primarily liable, here, the drawee bank, fails to pay.

14. **False.** A check is not an assignment and, thus, the holder is not entitled to any funds in the drawer's account. § 3-408. Further, only a customer has an action against the bank for wrongful dishonor. § 4-402. The holder would have an action against the drawer on dishonor of the check.

15. **False.** As long as Y's benefit is indirect and Y and X Corporation are considered to be separate entities, Y will be deemed to have signed the instrument for the purpose of lending his name to another party to it.

16. **False.** The obligation of the accommodation party is supported by any consideration for which the instrument was given to Bank. § 3-419(b).

17. **True.** An accommodation party is not liable to the party accommodated. § 3-419(e).

18. **True.** Words of guaranty that do not otherwise specify, signify that the guaranty is one of payment; such a guaranty allows the holder to proceed against the guarantor without prior resort to any other party. § 3-419(d).

19. **True.** An accommodation party has a right of recourse on the instrument against the party accommodated. § 3-419(e).

20. **False.** Because the check was never delivered to P, P had no interest in it and was never the holder or owner of the check. Thus, X never converted property of P. § 3-420(a).

21. **True.** As the check was never taken by the obligee, the obligation was not discharged or suspended. § 3-310.

22. **False.** This scenario suggests only fraud in the inducement rather than a misrepresentation that prevented the maker from determining the nature of the instrument. Thus, the maker has no defense against T, a holder in due course.

23. **True.** T has not given value and, thus, is not a holder in due course. § 3-302.

24. **True.** An executory promise does not constitute value for purposes of becoming a holder in due course. § 3-303(a).

25. **False.** P's signature is presumed to be an indorsement. An indorser is liable to a subsequent holder on dishonor and receipt of notice of dishonor. § 3-415.

26. **True.** An indorser may indorse using words that indicate that no recourse is to be had against him or her.

27. **True.** Where the effectiveness of a signature is put in issue, the party claiming under the signature bears the burden of establishing it. But where the claim arises under an instrument, the signature is presumed to be genuine or authorized as long as the purported signer is not dead or incompetent. § 3-308.

28. **False.** Assuming that the "by X" language was construed to indicate representative capacity, X is not personally liable as he has indicated both that capacity and the name of the person represented.

29. **False.** Notice of dishonor is not necessary to impose liability on a drawer of an unaccepted draft.

30. **True.** Notice of dishonor must be given by a bank before midnight of the banking day following the banking day on which it received the item. But notice is deemed to be given when it is sent.

31. **False.** A drawer can escape liability on an instrument that has been presented after a reasonable time only if the drawee bank became insolvent during the period of delay and the drawer was thereby deprived of funds maintained with the drawee. § 3-414(f).

32. **True.** With respect to the liability of an indorser of an uncertified check, an indorser is discharged if the check is not presented within 30 days after the day the indorsement was made. § 3-415(e). T may attempt to demonstrate excuse under § 3-511.

33. **False.** An instrument that bears visible signs of alteration and calls into question the authenticity of the instrument precludes a holder from becoming a holder in due course. § 3-302(a)(1).

34. **False.** The paycheck was likely an order instrument and thus could be negotiated only by a holder. The forged payee's signature does not constitute an indorsement, so X cannot be a holder even if he acted in good faith.

35. **True.** X has taken a check made out to his order and, as long as X acted in good faith, can qualify as a holder in due course.

36. **True.** The person identified as the payee was a fictitious person. § 3-404(a). Prior to the Revision, the indorsement would not have been effective because no agent or employee of the drawer supplied the name of the payee intending the latter to have no interest in the check.

37. **True.** A misrepresentation of authority will constitute an imposture for purposes of the impostor rule. This is a change from pre-Revision law.

38. **True.** X is not herself a holder in due course as she gave no value for the note. But her transferor, T, was a holder in due course and his transfer to X gives her all of T's rights under the shelter principle. § 3-203.

39. **True.** Lender may qualify as a holder in due course as long as he does not have knowledge of the fiduciary status of Agent. The fact that Lender is the payee of the check does not preclude holder in due course status, and any defense that Borrower would raise is stated against Agent, not against Borrower.

40. **True.** A bank that pays over a stop payment order is subrogated to the rights of P. Since the goods were not defective, P had the right to enforce the check against D. § 4-407.

41. **True.** An oral stop payment order is only valid for 14 calendar days unless it is confirmed in writing.

42. **False.** There is no right to stop payment after certification of a check. D would have to set up a third party claim to the check or its proceeds.

43. **True.** The drawer is discharged when anyone obtains acceptance by a bank. § 3-414(d). Prior to the Revision, certification discharged the drawer where the holder obtained certification, but not where the drawer did. PR § 3-411(1).

44. **False.** A collecting bank is not liable for the negligence of subsequent collecting banks. Each bank in the collection chain serves as agent or sub-agent for the owner of the item. § 4-201.

45. **True.** Assuming that D did not draw the check so negligently as to facilitate the forgery, the check is only properly payable as originally drawn.

46. **True.** The best answer here seems to be that while one who obtains payment usually warrants that the instrument has not been altered, this warranty is not made to the acceptor of a draft, like Drawee Bank, with respect to an alteration made prior to the acceptance, if the holder, like X, took the draft after acceptance.

47. **True.** A bank that pays a check over a forged indorsement has converted it. § 3-420.

48. **False.** This is a bearer instrument on which there is no forged indorsement. Thus, § 3-420 does not apply. Can P recover in a common law conversion action? Note that § 3-420 states that the law applicable to conversion of personal property applies to instruments.

49. **False.** P is a person entitled to enforce the instrument. Nevertheless, when Drawee Bank paid the bearer instrument to A, who was also a person entitled to enforce, D was discharged on the instrument and on the underlying obligation. §§ 3-310, 3-602.

50. **False.** X is a holder in due course to the extent of $250, as that is the amount of value she gave before she had notice of the maker's defense.

51.   **False.** Although the check is stale after six months, § 4-404 allows the drawee bank to charge its customer's account for payment of such a check made in good faith.

52.   **True.** A check may be properly payable even though it creates an overdraft. § 4-401(a).

53.   **True.** W had a binding contract for the purchase of the suit with the store and no right to return the suit. The bank is subrogated to the rights of the store as payee against the drawer. This includes the right to enforce the drawer's obligation of payment.

54.   **True.** The facts reveal no conduct on the part of Y Bank that would constitute final payment. In the absence of some other act of final payment, the payor bank has a right to revoke its settlement with a presenting bank until the payor bank's midnight deadline. § 4-301(a).

55.   **True.** Where a payor bank receives an item for credit on its own books, the bank may revoke a settlement and recover the settlement if it acts before it has made final payment and before its midnight deadline. §§ 4-301(a),(b).

56.   **False.** X Bank has finally paid the item by paying it in cash and is accountable for it. § 4-215(a). As P was a holder in due course, X Bank has no right of reimbursement for a mistaken payment. § 3-418.

57.   **False.** The 30-day requirement for presentment applies only to checks. § 3-414(f). The rule does not apply here, even though this note, like a check, is a demand instrument.

58.   **Probably false.** The stop order must be received at such time and in such manner as to afford the bank a reasonable opportunity to act on it. An imprecise but close amount will be sufficient in some cases to afford the bank that opportunity. If other aspects of the check, e.g., check number or date of issuance, were misidentified, however, the bank may be correct.

59.   **False.** First Bank was a depositary bank, not a payor bank. Thus, it cannot finally pay an item.

60.   **This depends on the use of the check proceeds.** A check can be properly payable even though it creates an overdraft and First Bank can charge its customer's account for a properly payable check. But the bank will have to show that the non-signing customer benefited from the proceeds of the check. § 4-401(b).

61.   **False.** Although the Revision does not speak directly to the issue, a cause of action against a drawer should not accrue until the instrument has been dishonored.

62.   **True.** A customer who transfers an item and receives a settlement or other consideration for it warrants that he is a person entitled to enforce the instrument and that all signatures are authentic and authorized. § 4-207(a).

63.   **True.** Because A transferred by indorsement, he makes the applicable warranties to all subsequent transferees. § 3-417(a).

64.   **False.** One who presents an instrument for payment warrants only that he or she has no knowledge that the drawer's signature is unauthorized. § 4-208(a)(3).

65.   **False.** Indorser's liability is triggered by dishonor of the check. Here, no dishonor occurred. § 3-415.

66.   **True.** A check bearing a forged indorsement is not properly payable.

67.   **True.** Payment of a check over a forged indorsement constitutes conversion. Exercise of due care is irrelevant. § 3-420.

68.   **False.** X Bank is a holder in due course and no injunction against payment is permitted even where fraud in the transaction exists.

69.   **Close call.** The issue is whether X Bank, by virtue of its knowledge of past defalcations by B, is acting in bad faith or with notice in this transaction and thus fails to satisfy the requirements of being a holder in due course. Given that this is a commercial, not a consumer transaction, and that Article 3, incorporated by reference into § 5-114, defines good faith objectively, knowledge of past transactions may suffice to deprive X Bank of that status.

70.   **True.** A draft drawn under a letter of credit should be paid only when there is strict compliance with the requirements stated in the letter. A right of reimbursement exists only when a draft has been "duly" honored. § 5-114(3).

71.   **False.** The contract between the issuer and beneficiary is independent of the contract between the buyer-customer and seller-beneficiary.

72.   **True.** Certainly until X has notified the issuer that use of the card is improper, he has authorized its use by Y. After notification, he may limit his liability to $50.

73.   **False.** As long as the customer is not delinquent in notifying the card issuer of the loss, the customer's negligence is irrelevant to the limitation on the card-user's liability. Nevertheless, X must still pay for the purchase because he has liability for $50 of unauthorized use.

74.   **Probably true.** Although the securities still exist, the bank's inaction could constitute an unjustifiable impairment of their value that impedes A's ability to recover against D should A have to make good on the accommodation contract.

75.   **False.** An accommodation indorser bears any indorser's contract obligation to pay the full amount due on dishonor. But A does have a common law right of contribution against Z for one-half the amount paid by A.

76.   **False.** A is not any kind of accommodation party, because A has signed a separate instrument.

77. **Probably false.** Liability of a party is discharged to the extent of payment to a holder, and X was a holder. But an exception exists where the payor makes payment to a person whom the payor knows is in wrongful possession of a stolen instrument. § 3-602.

78. **Probably true.** X appears to be a holder in due course and a person entitled to enforce the instrument. Thus, even if X holds the instrument through one who acquired it by theft, payment to X results in discharge, apparently even if M knows of the theft, unless even a holder in due course can be considered to be in "wrongful possession" of the instrument. § 3-602.

79. **True.** Under Regulation CC, Second Bank has acted in sufficient time by acting on the day after presentment. Telephone notification of dishonor of a check in excess of $2,500 is reasonable.

80. **False.** Where an instrument is payable to two or more parties in conjunction, rather than in the alternative, both must indorse to negotiate the instrument.

81. **False.** Although Y is a holder of the bearer instrument, Y is not a holder in due course since he gave no value and had notice that it had been lost. An obligor is not obliged to pay the instrument if the person seeking enforcement does not have the rights of a holder in due course and the obligor proves that the instrument is a lost or stolen instrument. § 3-305(c).

82. **True.** Y Bank satisfied the two-day test for expeditious return under 12 C.F.R. § 229.30. In addition, since the check was for an amount in excess of $2,500, Y Bank was required to provide notice of nonpayment such that the notice is received by the depositary bank by 4:00 p.m. on the second business day following the banking day on which the check was presented to the paying bank. Although it might have been prudent to give separate notice of the nonpayment, return of the check itself should suffice as long as it arrives within the required period under 12 C.F.R. § 229.33.

83. **Possibly true.** First Bank has made final payment under § 4-215(a). But the consequence of final payment in this case may not be to impose the loss on First Bank. Y did not take the check for value. If Y also has not changed position in reliance on the payment, First Bank will be able to recover from Y to the extent permitted by the law governing mistake and restitution. § 3-418.

84. **False.** An alteration is an "unauthorized" change under § 3-407, and this change was arguably authorized. In addition, only a fraudulent alteration discharges a party, and Y's change was not fraudulent.

85. **True.** Under § 3-405, an indorsement made by a "responsible" employee is effective as that of the payee if it is made in a name substantially similar to the name of the payee. As long as the misspelling is substantially similar to the proper spelling, the signature of the bookkeeper will be effective, since she is a responsible employee with respect to the check. If the failure of the depositary bank to notice the discrepancy is deemed negligent, however, the loss will be allocated between that bank and X on the basis of comparative negligence.

TABLE OF CASES

Principal discussion of a case
is indicated by page numbers in *italics*

TABLE OF U.C.C. REFERENCES

196

TABLE OF U.S.C., C.F.R., AND RESTATEMENT REFERENCES

SUBJECT MATTER INDEX

Products for 1996-97 Academic Year

Emanuel Law Outlines

Steve Emanuel's Outlines have been the most popular in the country for years. Twenty years of graduates swear by them. In the 1995–96 school year, law students bought an average of 3.0 Emanuels each–that's 130,000 Emanuels.

Civil Procedure, *rev.* '96–97 Ed. ♦	$18.95
Constitutional Law, *rev.* '96–97 Ed.	23.95
Contracts, '93–94 Ed. ♦	17.95
Corporations, '92–93 Ed.	18.95
Criminal Law, '92–93 Ed. ♦	14.95
Criminal Procedure, *rev.* '96–97 Ed.	14.95
Evidence, '95–96 Ed.	17.95
Property, '93–94 Ed. ♦	17.95
Secured Transactions, '88–89 Ed.	12.95
Torts (General Ed.), '94–95 Ed. ♦	17.95
Torts (Casebook Ed.), '94–95 Ed.	17.95

Keyed to '94 Ed. Prosser, Wade & Schwartz

Also, Steve Emanuel's First Year Q&A's (see opposite page) $18.95

♦ *Special Offer...*First Year Set

All outlines marked ♦ *plus* Steve Emanuel's First Year Q & A's *plus* Strategies & Tactics for First Year Law. Everything you need to make it through your first year.

Complete Set	*$97.50*

Emanuel Law Tapes - Constitutional Law

Includes mnemonics, skits, a special night-before-the-exam review tape, and a printed supplement.

11 Cassette Set, '92-93 Ed.	*$32.95*

Smith's Review

All titles in this series are written by leading law professors. They follow the Emanuel style and format. They have big, easy-to-read type, extensive citations and notes, and clear, crisp writing. Most have capsule summaries and sample exam Q & A's.

Agency & Partnership, '88–89 Ed.	$12.95
Bankruptcy, *new* '96 Title	15.95
Commercial Paper, '95–96 Ed.	13.95
Family Law, '93–94 Ed.	15.95
Fed. Income Taxation, '94–95 Ed.	14.95
Intellectual Property, *rev.* '96–97 Ed.	15.95
International Law, '95 Ed.	15.95
Labor Law, '88–89 Ed.	12.95
Products Liability, *rev.* '96–97 Ed.	12.95
Torts, '91–92 Ed.	13.95
Wills & Trusts, '93–94 Ed.	15.95

Emanuel Electronic Format Software (Windows® only)

Complete Satisfaction Guaranteed or Your Money Back

Our band-new software, consisting of 10 unabridged Emanuel outlines on one CD-ROM, is based on Folio infobase technology and was developed in conjunction with LEXIS®-NEXIS®. Features: full searchability; easy insertion of your own notes and comments; complete hyperlinking; and printing of all or any part of the outline.

Pick the CD-ROM up free at your local bookstore or get it from your LEXIS®-NEXIS® representative. Or, if you wish, call 1-800-EMANUEL. Click on any Emanuel outline and review the introductory demo material. If you decide you want to utilize the full outline, just "unlock" it by means of your modem or by telephone. You will be charged $19.95 per outline via your Mastercard or Visa.

If, within 30 days after your order, you are dissatisfied with the outline FOR ANY REASON, phone us and we will arrange a full credit via your credit card...no questions asked.

Unlocking Price per Title:

Civil Procedure	$19.95
Constitutional Law	19.95
Contracts	19.95
Corporations	19.95
Criminal Law	19.95
Criminal Procedure	19.95
Evidence	19.95
Property	19.95
Secured Transactions	19.95
Torts (General Ed.)	19.95

For any titles not available at your local bookstore, call us at 1-800-EMANUEL. Mastercard and Visa accepted.

Law In A Flash Flashcards

Flashcards

Civil Procedure 1 ◆	$16.95
Civil Procedure 2 ◆	16.95
Constitutional Law, *rev.* '95-96 Ed. ▲	16.95
Contracts ◆▲	16.95
Corporations	16.95
Criminal Law ◆▲	16.95
Criminal Procedure ▲	16.95
Evidence, *rev.* '95-96 Ed. ▲	16.95
Future Interests ▲	16.95
Professional Responsibility (840 cards)	32.95
Real Property ◆▲	16.95
Sales (UCC Art.2) ▲	16.95
Torts, *rev.* '95-96 Ed. ◆▲	16.95
Wills & Trusts, *new* '96–97 Title	16.95

Flashcard Sets

First Year Law Set	95.00

(includes all sets marked ◆ *plus* the book
Strategies & Tactics for First Year Law.)

Multistate Bar Review Set	165.00

(includes all sets marked ▲ *plus* the book
Strategies & Tactics for MBE)

Professional Responsibility Set	45.00

(includes the *Professional Responsibility* flashcards
plus the book Strategies & Tactics for the MPRE Exam.)

Law In A Flash Software

Brand-new for 1996, our software (for Windows® only)
contains the following features:

- Complete text of the corresponding *Law In A Flash* title
- Side-by-side comparison of your own answer to the answer on the card
- Fully customizable sessions: pick which cards to review and in what order
- Mark cards for further review or printing
- Score your answers, to help you spot those topics in which you need further review

Individual titles	$19.95
Professional Responsibility (covers 840 cards)	34.95
First Year Law Set*	115.00
Multistate Bar Review Set*	195.00
Professional Responsibility/MPRE Set*	49.95

* These software sets contain the same text as printed card sets *plus*
corresponding Strategies & Tactics books.

Strategies & Tactics Books

◆ S & T for First Year Law	$12.95
● S & T for the MPRE	19.95
(Multistate Professional Responsibility Exam)	
▲ S & T for the MBE (Multistate Bar Exam)	34.95

Over 500 actual questions and answers from past
Multistate Bar Exams, *plus* an actual 200-question
practice MBE with correct answers and explanations.

Question & Answer Collections

Siegel's Essay & Multiple–Choice Q & A's

Each book contains 20–25 essay questions with model
answers, plus 90–110 Multistate format Q & A's. The objective is to acquaint the student with the techniques needed to
handle law school exams successfully. Titles are:

Civil Procedure, *rev.* '96 Ed.	Criminal Procedure
Constitutional Law	Evidence, *rev.* '96 Ed.
Contracts	Real Property, *rev.* '96 Ed.
Corporations, *new* '96 Title	Torts
Criminal Law	Wills & Trusts

Each title	*$15.95*

Steve Finz's Multistate Method

967 MBE (Multistate Bar Exam)–style multiple choice questions and answers for all six Multistate subjects – *Plus* a
complete 200 question practice exam modeled on the
MBE – perfect for law school and BAR EXAM review.

'92–93 edition	*$33.95*

Steve Emanuel's First Year Q&A's

1,144 Objective–style questions & answers in first year subjects. A single volume covers Contracts, Torts, Civil
Procedure, Property, Criminal Law & Criminal Procedure.

'95–96 edition	*$18.95*

Where do you find the time to...

run to the prof's office,
dash to study group,
dig through the library,
assemble quotes,
annotate class material,
search & research,
get that note to prof,
brief cases, find cites,
see if Susan knows,
outline it, write it,
print it, cut and paste,
copy, collate, assemble...

Here.

With the LEXIS-NEXIS Student Office.

The LEXIS-NEXIS services, Folio VIEWS®, The LEXIS Online Connection, Law Schools Online Global E-mail Network, the Jurisoft Legal Toolbox products & much, much more, all integrated into an easy-to-use suite that takes a lot of the work out of your work. Call 1-800-528-1891 for more information.

Get the LEXIS-NEXIS Student Office software absolutely FREE. Watch for Millennium+ Fall 1996.

LEXIS·NEXIS®
A member of the Reed Elsevier plc group

emanuel®

We'd like to know . . . .
Smith's Review on Negotiable Instruments & Payment Systems

We value your opinions on our study aids. After all, we design them for *your* use, and if you think we could do something better, we want to know about it. Please take a moment to fill out this survey and feedback form and return it to us.

We'll enter you in our monthly drawing where 5 people win the study aid of their choice! If you don't want to identify yourself, that's OK, but you'll be ineligible for the drawing.

Name: _____ Address: _____

City: _____ State: _____ Zip: _____ E-mail: _____

Law school attended: _____ Graduation year: _____

Please rate this product on a scale of 1 to 5:

General readability (style, format, etc.).......................*Poor* ① ② ③ ④ ⑤ *Excellent*

Length of outline (number of pages)..........................*Too short* ① ② ③ ④ ⑤ *Too long*

Essay questions and answers ....*Not useful* ① ② ③ ④ ⑤ *Useful*

True-False questions and answers ....*Not useful* ① ② ③ ④ ⑤ *Useful*

Tables and Subject-Matter Index ....*Not useful* ① ② ③ ④ ⑤ *Useful*

Outline's coverage of material presented in class ......*Incomplete* ① ② ③ ④ ⑤ *Complete*

OVERALL RATING..*Poor* ① ② ③ ④ ⑤ ***Excellent***

Suggestions for improvement: _____
_____
_____
_____

☞ **What other study aids did you use in this course?** _____
_____

☞ **If you liked any features of these other study aids, describe them:** _____
_____
_____

☞ **What casebook(s) did you use in this course?** _____

☞ **For other subjects, what study aids other than Emanuel do you use, and what features do you like about them?** ____
_____
_____

☞ **Please list the items you would like us to add to our product line:**

   Outline subjects: _____

   Flashcard subjects: _____

   Other products (e.g., software, multimedia, etc.): _____

☞ **If you win our drawing, what one study aid would you like?** _____

Send to: *Emanuel Law* **Survey**   OR   Fax to: *(914) 834-5186*
           1865 Palmer Avenue, Suite 202
           Larchmont, NY 10538

Cut here

Please
complete & return
the Survey Form
on the other side